# Democracy, Education and Research

Considering how practices and processes of research and education can create fundamental, radical social change, *Democracy, Education and Research* assesses the meaning of 'public impact' by rethinking what is meant by 'public' and how it is essential to the methodologies of education and research.

Focusing on empirical illustrations of the use of research and educational processes in contemporary and emergent forms of social organisation, this book:

- Covers the traditional forms to be found in education, health systems, community, business and public institutions, as well as emergent forms arising from innnovation in technologies
- Explores the forms of learning and knowledge creation that take place across the everyday interactions in places of learning, communities or workplaces
- Discusses how learning and knowledge can be intentionally shaped by individuals and groups to effect social and political change
- Considers the research strategies required to forge new practices, new ways of working and living for a more socially just world

Including practical examples of research that has created real change, *Democracy, Education and Research* will be a vital resource to professional researchers in their roles as teachers, educators and activists as well as students of education, sociology, politics, cultural studies.

**John Schostak** is Emeritus Professor at the Education and Social Research Institute, Manchester Metropolitan University, UK.

**Ivor Goodson** is a Professor of Learning Theory in the Education Research Centre, Brighton University, UK, an International Research Professor at the University of Tallinn, Estonia and a Senior Fellow at the Guerrand Hermes Foundation.

# Democracy, Education and Research

## The Struggle for Public Life

John Schostak and Ivor Goodson

LONDON AND NEW YORK

First published 2020
by Routledge
2 Park Square, Milton Park, Abingdon, Oxon OX14 4RN

and by Routledge
52 Vanderbilt Avenue, New York, NY 10017

*Routledge is an imprint of the Taylor & Francis Group, an informa business*

© 2020 John Schostak and Ivor Goodson

The right of John Schostak and Ivor Goodson to be identified as authors of this work has been asserted by them in accordance with sections 77 and 78 of the Copyright, Designs and Patents Act 1988.

All rights reserved. No part of this book may be reprinted or reproduced or utilised in any form or by any electronic, mechanical, or other means, now known or hereafter invented, including photocopying and recording, or in any information storage or retrieval system, without permission in writing from the publishers.

*Trademark notice*: Product or corporate names may be trademarks or registered trademarks, and are used only for identification and explanation without intent to infringe.

*British Library Cataloguing in Publication Data*
A catalogue record for this book is available from the British Library

ISBN: 978-0-415-60513-7 (hbk)
ISBN: 978-0-415-60512-0 (pbk)
ISBN: 978-0-203-81809-1 (ebk)

Typeset in Galliard
by Taylor & Francis Books

 Printed in the United Kingdom by Henry Ling Limited

# Contents

Introduction                                                                 1

1  What's wrong with democracy at the moment and why it matters for
   research and education                                                    5

**PART I**
**What Went Wrong?**                                                        21

2  The challenge for researchers and educators                              23

3  What is wrong with contemporary practices of social/collective
   learning?                                                                37

4  The organisation and disorganisation of power                            50

5  Engaging with power through *radical* research methodologies             63

6  Radical educational strategies                                           76

End of part one: Reflections on the research and educational implications
of chapters 1–6: Realising the challenges to become a public                89

**PART II**
**What Can Be Done?**                                                       97

7  What might turn social learning into social movements?                   99

8  What is happening today in terms of social learning becoming social
   movements?                                                              112

9  How do you get from social movements to public space?                   125

10 Towards the creation of public spaces                                   137

11 New rules for research, social learning and creating a socially just
world 150

End of Part Two: Discussion on the implications for research education:
The critical role of publics in realising futures for a better present 163

12 Making it happen 169

Conclusion: No end 185

*References* 188
*Index* 212

# Introduction

Democracy reimagined – that's the challenge for education and research. As the politics of hope, what sort of hope is democracy when poverty, climate change denial, and perpetual wars are killing on a grand scale? What sort of politics is it that ignores, discounts, dismisses the consequences of decisions and actions for those who do not count as citizens? And what sort of public is it whose 'consent' sustains inequalities and hostilities towards others and celebrates displays of military power? The sort of politics, perhaps, that Steve Bannon, ex-advisor to Donald Trump's presidential campaign and, until sacked, during his presidency, described?

> "Darkness is good," says Bannon, who amid the suits surrounding him at Trump Tower, looks like a graduate student in his T-shirt, open button-down and tatty blue blazer—albeit a 62-year-old graduate student. "Dick Cheney. Darth Vader. Satan. That's power. It only helps us when they"—I believe by "they" he means liberals and the media, already promoting calls for his ouster—"get it wrong. When they're blind to who we are and what we're doing."
>
> (Wolff, 2016)

For Bannon when he was executive chair of Brietbart:

> "Our big belief, one of our central organising principles at the site, is that we're at war," he said.
> "It's war. It's war. Every day, we put up: America's at war, America's at war. We're at war," he said in December 2015. "Note to self, beloved commander in chief: We're at war."
>
> (Reilly and Heath, 2017)

Through war power is mobilised – but, with who and in whose interests? Bannon's answer is: "We think of ourselves as virulently anti-establishment, particularly 'anti-' the permanent political class" (Farhi, 2016). The establishment is the liberal establishment, particularly those in education, the arts, research, politics and social movements who fight for rights for all, social justice, are anti-capitalist, anti-climate change, want to save the environment from pollution and are anti-war. It is not, however, the billionaire Mercer family who were backing him, nor of course the billionaire Donald Trump, his 'commander in chief'.

Are research and education blind to what is going on? Or just dismissed? Research and education in 'dark times', as many have called it, faces a great challenge as it confronts the onslaught of a war that is effectively waged against 'truth' by the hard right-wing billionaires and media such as Brietbart in the US and in the UK the right-wing media campaigns led by billionaires to leave the European Union. With this book we want to contribute what we think is an approach to resist, reimagine and renew what was started in the Enlightenment revolutions in philosophy, science, education and politics during the eighteenth and nineteenth centuries. Their aim was to bring about a new society, one built upon freedom and equality. It involved, essentially, we argue, the struggle for a 'public' composed of free and equal people able to constrain the arrogance of the elites. We ask, where did it go wrong? And how can it be fixed?

Recognised for his role in both the French and American revolutions Thomas Paine had this to say about the ambitions of the elites to mould the future to their desires:

> There never did, there never will, and there never can, exist a Parliament, or any description of men, or any generation of men, in any country, possessed of the right or the power of binding and controlling posterity to the "end of time," or of commanding for ever how the world shall be governed, or who shall govern it; and therefore all such clauses, acts or declarations by which the makers of them attempt to do what they have neither the right nor the power to do, nor the power to execute, are in themselves null and void. Every age and generation must be as free to act for itself in all cases as the age and generations which preceded it. The vanity and presumption of governing beyond the grave is the most ridiculous and insolent of all tyrannies.
>
> (Paine, 1791)

In the following chapters we will explore how research and education can create these conditions where each generation is 'free to act for itself in all cases'. That means education and research being freed from strategies of domination by elites of all kinds as a foundation for people to make their own futures.

Each chapter addresses the question of what can be done by exploring the recent histories, describing the current state of affairs, undoing the knots of discourses, deconstructing the apparently fixed and natural forms of social life as it is. The closing chapters in particular turn to the practical strategies by which people can create anew. Throughout, we argue for education and research to be grounded in democratic debate, argument, research, evidence and reason. There is, we argue, an intimate relationship between a democratic public and the forms of research and education that support and maintain critical public discourses.

The chapters are grouped into two parts. Part one explores the themes of 'what went wrong' in the development of democracy from chapters one through to seven. Part two, from chapters seven to eleven, undertakes the processes of reconceptualising and renewal in education and research necessary to accomplish an effective public. Each part ends with a discussion of the implications for research and education.

Chapter 1 then begins the critical step of remembrance required to understanding how debates and the democratic idea of 'the public' and the 'will of the public' have become manipulated and undermined through deception, lies and a disregard for 'truth' or 'validity' in the production of 'facts' and 'evidence'. It is a process of remembering that enables us to understand that the Trump and Brexit campaigns were not the first to deploy the arts of deception, nor will they be the last. The task is to prepare the ground against them recurring. To do this, we need to identify what has historically been established as a preparation for how their legacies can be undone.

Research and education demand the freedom to think, to critique, to evaluate, to produce forms of reasoning that result in knowledge; methodology creates the conditions under which this can be done. The great challenge of enlightenment methodology was to all forms of 'knowledge', 'belief', ways of 'thinking' and 'acting' that were dictated by authorities who claimed special insight, special right, ultimate power. As such it was a process of renewal involving the struggle for a critical, effectively engaged public. Neoliberalism and in particular neoconservatism represent reactionary moves against the enlightenment values of a democratic public based upon equality of voice and the freedom of the individual. Chapter 2 explores the implications for 'truth', 'validity' and 'objectivity' when neoliberal and neoconservative philosophies treat the values of a liberal, enlightenment democracy as the enemy that leads to chapter 3, exploring the neoconservatives' attempts to take knowledge away from the masses to replace it by beliefs that would build character and good conduct. That is, the sort of character required to work and do their duty without challenging the elites and able willingly to create tools to mathematise democracy in the interests of traders.

Chapter 4 tackles the question of power, how it is organised and how, crucially, it may be disorganised. That is, how the power of the rich and privileged can itself be tamed. This exploration is continued in chapters 5 and 6 by exploring how radical research approaches can put 'power out of joint' and how education can create the conditions for people to organise their powers through a logic of freedom and equality. Part one ends with reflections upon the research and educational conditions necessary to realise the development of a 'public' appropriate for democracy.

Part two begins with chapter 7. Social learning, we argue, can promote the conditions for social movements to reimagine democracy as the only road to freedom. The extent to which current social movements are able to prefigure democratic futures is explored in chapter 8. We say at this point: protest is not enough. Research and education have to be engaged in the struggle to develop the conditions for genuine public space; that is, space where people are free to engage with each other in the real decision-making that affects their lives must be created if democratic futures are to be created. Both education and research, we argue in chapters 10 and 11, are essential in setting the ground conditions that pre-figure new ways of living together. Part two ends with reflections on the role of education and research in creating a 'public' to realise futures for a better present.

And the final chapter 12 turns to the question of actually making it happen. We are essentially at a critical crossroads: we either choose a direction which leads to a democratic way out or we get further lost within the heavily walled and policed pathways leading to an authoritarian nowhere. This book is written in the belief that there is a way of creating, as Harvey (2014) nicely put it, the poetry of our own futures. Or, more prosaically: how through research and education can we create political systems that bring about an effective public, empowering the spirit of universal democracy?

# Chapter 1

# What's wrong with democracy at the moment and why it matters for research and education

What is wrong with democracy is mirrored in the policies, practices and forms of organisation that have reduced education to schooling and research to an instrument of social manipulation, exploitation and control. How were these established? And how can they be undone? We argue here that both research and education have been critically deployed in the taming of democracy. There is a key principle at stake here: the active participation of all voices in the debates and decisions that impact upon people's lives. Both education and research depend upon the principle of freedom and equality for all voices in determining what is 'real', 'good', 'desirable', 'do-able'. It is precisely this principle that comes under attack by elites.

Following the extension of franchise after the 1868 Reform Act in the UK, Robert Lowe, realising its threat for the privileges of the wealthy classes, supposedly said: "we must now educate our masters". What this meant was reinforcing the split between an 'education' for the masses as supposed 'masters' and the upper classes that has been well documented in historical and sociological research. What Simon (1960) called the 'two nations' between 1780 and 1870 had its continuation in the post-1870 education system that was created around elite schools where the wealthy were to be 'educated' for leadership, the middle classes for the professions and management and the working classes 'schooled' for labour. The pattern was largely reproduced even in the reforms of education following the Second World War designed to increase social mobility and opportunity for working class children. Indeed, as Schostak (1983) argued, schools were largely maladjusted to people, that is, to their needs, interests, hopes and demands and in particular to democratic processes and practices (Roberts and Schostak, 2012). Although there have been democratically organised schools, they have been largely at the margins (see for example Fielding and Moss, 2011). It has been argued that mainstream schools prefigure the model of organisation, social division of labour, class, gender and cultural inequalities necessary to reproduce the status quo throughout society. Countervailing research, curriculum and pedagogical practices emerged during the post-war period, drawing upon democratic and critical legacies. For example there were curriculum innovations such as the

Humanities Curriculum Project (Stenhouse, 1975) and Man a Course of Studies (Bruner, 1965). In 1967 the Plowden Report (Plowden (Lady) and Committee, 1967) had seemed to give such innovations its blessing. There were, as it were, a flowering of approaches stimulated by the writings and practices of people like Postman and Weingarten (1969), Kohl (1967), Kozol (1967) and the publication of the Letter to a Teacher (School of Barbiana, 1969). There was a critical *zeitgeist* revealed by works such as Freire (1972), Shor (1980), Giroux (1989). More than just creating the conditions for child-centred discovery learning and problem-solving methods, critical pedagogy had as its goal social justice (see its range in: Sandlin et al., 2011). Perhaps, for a time, such views seemed to be winning the battle of ideas if not the mainstream practice to such an extent, indeed, that it led to a right-wing backlash stimulated in part by the Black Papers (Cox and Dyson, 1975; Bloom, 1987). The attacks picked up speed with a media campaign following the election of the Thatcher government in 1979 (see for example Schostak, 1986; 1993). There was a clear attempt to manage the engagement of adults in the education of their children through the management of 'public opinion'. In this sense public opinion replaces actual engagement. How this is done is vital to understanding the contemporary relations between democracy, education and research under 'austerity' following the financial crisis of 2008.

## The management of opinion

The management of opinion is key to the production of pseudo-democracies for the government of people in the interests of elites. The subversive use of 'education' and 'research' are critical to that management. This line of thinking was well developed by the early pioneers of the public relations industry. It was Lippmann (1927) who coined the phrase the 'manufacture of consent' that was later picked up by Herman and Chomsky (1988) in their study of the influence of the media on the formation of opinions and the shaping of behaviour in the interests of the powerful. In Lippmann's view the fundamental means to manage opinions was to paint pictures in the mind. The role of the picture was to simplify the complexity of modern life into a believable whole. As a journalist, Lippmann saw controlling the story as the role of the media. Working at the same time, Bernays (1928) drew upon the power of the media to generate the kinds of stories he wanted in the interests of his clients, whether these were Roosevelt in 'selling' the New Deal, or American Tobacco in 'selling' the cigarette as a symbol of women's emancipation (Tye, 1998). For both Lippmann and Bernays:

> The conscious and intelligent manipulation of the organised habits and opinions of the masses is an important element in democratic society. Those who manipulate this unseen mechanism of society constitute an invisible government which is the true ruling power of our country.
>
> (Bernays, 1928: 27)

The significance of public relations was not lost on President Hoover who in his speech to an audience of public relations men in 1928, said: "You have taken over the job of creating desire and have transformed people into constantly moving happiness machines, machines which have become the key to economic progress." (Curtis, 2002)

It was the recognition both of the potential power of people and of the significance of the market in the management of people that led to strategies for managing, or taming, democracy. Paul Mazur of Lehman Brothers, who worked with Bernays, commented, "We must shift America from a needs to a desires culture. People must be trained to desire, to want things, even before the old have been entirely consumed." (Gore, 2007: 94). Desire, of course, has to be translated into effective demand, that is, a willingness to purchase in the market place that is backed by money. Hence, the role of the new public relations professionals was to free action from the determination of particular needs by replacing them with the fluidity of desire and also to fix those desires with the firmness of demand for a particular object marked as 'desirable'. But of course, not too firm, the desire must soon evaporate from the recently purchased object and coalesce around another, motivating further opportunities for purchase. In short, two kinds of 'demand' were being managed through effectively the same system, the market place. There was the political demand of an effective democratic public and the economic demand of a consumer public. By reducing the first to the second, the public as 'constantly moving happiness machines', it was believed, could be managed through public relations strategies directing the public's desire and constructing their picture of 'happiness'. In doing this Bernays drew upon the psychological and sociological theories along with evidence drawn from the research of the day, in particular, those of his uncle, Sigmund Freud (Tye, 1998). Propaganda, in his view, was critical to the management of opinion in complex societies which he saw as a form of educational process:

> But education, in the academic sense of the word, is not sufficient. It must be enlightened expert propaganda through the creation of circumstances, through the high-spotting of significant events, and the dramatisation of important issues. The statesman of the future will thus be enabled to focus the public mind on crucial points of policy, and regiment a vast, heterogeneous mass of voters to clear understanding and intelligent action.
> (Bernays, 1928: 114)

It may be called a public relations pedagogical practice where: "Social progress is simply the progressive education and enlightenment of the public mind in regard to its immediate and distant social problems." Essentially, modern society is the propaganda society dependent upon a largely acquiescent public who are to be 'educated' to the current social problems and the elite's desired solution to them. Research provided the theoretical and evidential underpinnings to that process of 'education' or engineering (Bernays, 1947), which may also be called the pedagogy of public relations. Combining this with the traditional social functions of schools to reproduce society creates the conditions for a life-long management of the minds and behaviours of people by those whose policies direct schools and whose business interests fund public relations. It was, essentially, a way of managing the radical freedom implicit in the concept of democracy. In this view, democracy was, then, to be increasingly aligned with business culture rather than business being subjected to democratic culture and practice. This latter view was implicit in Dewey's (1938) own more optimistic views as to the capacities of individuals to engage democratically and the role of education in developing those capacities. Essentially, in so far as possible, business was to be seen as part of a private domain of decision-making and action rather than public. The public was deemed to be the realm of government and government was to be as minimal as possible so as not to interrupt the free play of private interests. Nevertheless, such private interests are dependent upon political freedoms and democracy opens the way for all people to make demands in their own interests. Democracy implies both freedom and equality for all.

## Equality, greed and the exceptional

The only legitimate equality, for Hayek, is equality before the law. All other sorts are "bound to produce inequality" because "if the result of individual liberty did not demonstrate that some manners of living are more successful than others, much of the case for it would vanish" (Hayek, 1944). In short, in his influential book – *The Road to Serfdom* – he opposed socialism and capitalism and equated equality with serfdom and capitalism with freedom. Along with Milton Friedman, this liberal economic credo has come to equate freedom, democracy and market capitalism. It has merged with and become the 'American Dream', a dream that universalises its values globally so that America is promoted as the leading democracy (Roberts and Schostak, 2012). In effect, to be against American interests is to be against freedom and democracy (Friedman, 1962; Fukuyama, 1992). It is what might be called, in Billig's (1995) terms, a flagging of democracy, essentially a public pedagogy where nationalism, capitalism and politics become written together (Schostak and Schostak, 2013; Roberts and Schostak, 2012) in the symbol of a flag. This was symbolised perfectly by Trump, following an anti-immigrant speech, hugging an American flag (Pleasance, 2018).

It is in such a context, for example, that the Wikileaks founder Julian Assange can be accused of engaging in Anti-American activities with demands that he – an Australian – be extradited via Sweden where he was accused of sexual offences and brought to trial in America for the publishing of leaked material (or, in the words of Senator Huckabee, executed (Wing, 2010). Crudely, therefore, if there is a global 'law' then it is pedagogically flagged as American in so far as American interests are market interests and in populist terms by definition these are 'free' and 'democratic'. It is the political rationale of what has been called American exceptionalism, a view that there is something special about American history and destiny (Tyrrell, 1991: Walt, 2011), that gives it the right to intervene on the world stage and undertake regime change. This something is its insistence on individual freedom, the right to pursue self-interested happiness and the equation of these with 'free' market democracy. Furthermore, the notion of exceptionalism can be merged with a concept of 'the exception' employed by Schmitt (1996) as the foundation of 'the political' and with his notion of sovereignty (1985), both further developed by Agamben (1998; 2005). In short, their combination authorises, as it were, the sovereign decision of the state to suspend laws as in extraordinary rendition and the setting up of Abu Ghraib as a prison camp that is outside the law for prisoners deemed to be of exceptional danger (Comaroff, 2007).

Generalising, these terms can now be applied to any form of organisation that has the power to suspend the law in its own 'sovereign' interests. In particular, they may be applied to the 'too big to fail' financial institutions that were able to operate in de-regulated markets where the borderlines between criminal and lawful were pushed to and beyond the limits, creating the conditions for the financial crisis to explode in 2008. Expanding Eisenhower's (1961) phrase, the financial banks became an underpinning dimension of the military industrial complex he feared, where "The potential for the disastrous rise of misplaced power exists and will persist." More than this, with revelations of money laundering, interest rate manipulation (Treanor, 2012), hiding trillions of pounds/dollars in off-shore tax havens (Stewart, 2012) and media corruption (Levenson inquiry – undated), there are the grounds to argue that the hidden/criminal economy and the official economy are co-dependent.

In Bernays' terms a complex of economic, military, media and political power is essentially the *dispositif* for an 'invisible government' that pulls the strings of States and manipulates the consent of the 'public'. As a key feature of the invisible government there is what has been called a 'revolving doors' strategy. In an empirical study Etzion and Davis (2008) concluded there was "evidence that government service can serve as a conduit for joining the ranks of the corporate elite." However, the financial crisis made clear the extent to which key directors, executives and consultants of such institutions as Goldman Sachs and J. P. Morgan constitute a revolving door with government positions internationally (Reid, 2010; Foley, 2011). Add to this the scale of party political funding by corporations and wealthy individuals where the top financial 1% of the 1% according to Drutman (2011) provided 24.3% of all political donations to American political campaigns with 'super PACs' (Political Action Parties) being formed that can finance political parties without limit (Berman, 2012). Indeed, it was all too well illustrated in accusations of vote influence and interference arising from the web of connections between the Billionaire Mercer family, Aaron Banks, Cambridge Analytics, Russian individuals and groups and the Trump and Brexit campaigns (Cadwalladr, 2017; 2017b). Whether this, as Scott (1996) and Ahmed (2012) argue, is deep politics constituting a kind of 'state-crime symbiosis', it can at least be argued the transnational elite prefigures an emergent global invisible government that has considerable influence on what constitutes democracy and the 'law' of given nations through its influence on political parties and the manufacture of public consent through funded campaigns.

A popular fictional metaphor of the world managed by global elites was *Atlas Shrugged* written by Ayn Rand (1957). As a form of curricular material, intended to be a way of introducing readers to her philosophy, it described and justified a world dependent upon the decisions of Atlas-like figures symbolised on the book jacket as shouldering the world. However, it is not that such Atlas figures care about others; their decisions are entirely governed by an honest self-interest. Such a 'utopia of greed' inspired Alan Greenspan, one of Rand's inner circle, who was chair of the American Federal Reserve from1987 to 2006. The fictional world portrayed an extreme version of the economic philosophies of Hayek, Friedman and what has come to be known as the Austrian School of Economics. In each case the view is that the complexity of economic processes is beyond anyone's ability to grasp them. However, through the unfettered market there is a spontaneous organisation that will bring order and the optimal allocation of resources to demand. The resulting ideology draws upon Adam Smith's (1776) proposition of the 'invisible hand' of the market through which prices that bring supply and demand into equilibrium will be 'discovered'. For this to happen, there must be no, or at least minimal, government interference. Although for many years Hayek's and Friedman's views made little mainstream headway against the prevailing post-Great Depression Keynesianism of the Western market democracies, their plan was to create the philosophical direction and theory and wait for their time. The right time, for them, was a time of crisis as in an economic depression or a natural disaster. In such a period, populations would be frightened, vulnerable and thus more submissive. There was, in Friedman's view, in a crisis, a brief period of six to nine months when change can be implemented without effective opposition:

> Only a crisis—actual or perceived—produces real change. When that crisis occurs, the actions that are taken depend on the ideas that are lying around. That, I believe, is our basic function: to develop alternatives to existing policies, to keep them alive and available until the politically impossible becomes politically inevitable.
>
> (Friedman, 1962: xiv)

Of course, ideas that are taken up in periods of crisis are not just 'lying around'; they have been carefully set into place, as key elements in a curriculum – both informal via the media, and formal via university law, politics and economics courses – available for action when the time allows. Norton (2004) provides an account of students of Strauss joining positions of power in the US State Department and the Whitehouse; similarly, Klein (2007) describes students steeped in the monetarist economics of Friedman taking up critical positions of power in government and key financial institutions around the world. Neo-liberal principles embedded by these changes include the equation of competitive individualism with freedom, the valorisation of the self over the other, the privileging of the private over the public sectors, the belief that the market works best when left alone (hence a demand for no, or at least minimal, State), the rejection of equality, and the equation of politics with the focus on naming friends and enemies. Certainly, monetarist or neoliberal forms of economics came to dominate university teaching (Earl et al., 2017). Only when such theoretical and philosophical principles are articulated with the legal, governmental, business, educational and social organisations through which material and symbolic resources are allocated and people managed is there the real power to make change.

Given that equality is repressed in contemporary individualist views of representative market democracies, it is only to be expected that wealth and power should accumulate in the hands of the few. Indeed, there is a strong historical heritage arguing that the good society depends upon the expertise of the most talented making the key decisions. These are to be found in Plato's 'philosopher kings' ruling over the baser elements of society. The good Republic, according to Plato, is to be founded upon a 'noble lie', which, in people's best interests, creates specialist classes ranged hierarchically with the best at the top. What people must believe is that this order is natural if, in Bernays' terms, there is to be rule by the propaganda of an 'invisible government'. More formally, it is a matter of schooling.

The contemporary 'noble lie' is well exemplified not so much as Rand's trope of Atlas as in the current trope of the elite financiers – or bankers – being 'the masters of the universe' (e.g. Das, 2011). The noble lie can be usefully mapped against Hilgers' (2011) three approaches to analysing neoliberalism: as culture, as system, as governmentality. A feature of the cultural analysis is the focus on the speculative nature of neoliberalism, often called casino capitalism. It appeals to a sense of the 'magical' or what Comaroff and Comaroff (1999) call 'occult economies' where "New forms of enchantment are produced by a casino relationship to the world" (Hilgers, 2011: 353).

The noble lie is inscribed under the name of enchantment. The casino 'players' are those like the 'London Whale', a J. P. Morgan trader called Bruno Iksil who made a bet so large it caused losses of $5.8 billion (*The Observer*, Business Leader, July 15, 2012) and could have threatened destabilisation of the market itself. Such players are Rand's Atlas' reborn as elite magicians who when they fail can be scapegoated to save the system itself. They are beings much greater than the normal mass of humanity who stand in awe and incomprehension of their powers. This trope is pedagogically played out in the press and political speeches that seek to prevent 'banker bashing'. For example, mass newspaper *The Sun* reported John Cridland of the CBI (Confederation of British Industry) proclaiming his fears that continued banker bashing would threaten the economic recovery (Hawkes, 2012). It is a theme reiterated in the policies and action of politicians, business leaders and commentators around the world. This dependence of the economy on the giants of finance and industry signals a move towards a system approach where inequality of all kinds is necessary to maintaining the system. For Harvey (2005) neoliberalism is essentially about elite accumulation of wealth through dispossession that involves for example privatising the public sector, rent seeking and using public money when the 'too big to fail' enterprises threaten failure. For Stiglitz (2012) inequality is endemic to the system due to 'asymmetric information' where the rich and powerful are able to make decisions based on information the rest cannot access. It aligns with an asymmetric education system in recreating the 'two nations' described by Simon (1960). As Roberts comments, reviewing Stiglitz's book, under the influence of the neoliberals:

> nationalisation was reversed, public assets privatised, natural resources opened up to unregulated exploitation (anyone like to buy one of our forests?), the unions and social organisations were torn apart and foreign direct investment and "freer" trade were facilitated. Rather than wealth trickling down, it rapidly found its way to the pinnacle of the pyramid. As Stiglitz explains, these policies were – and are – protected by myths, not least that the highest paid "deserve" their excess of riches.
> 
> (Roberts, 2012)

Myth and system work together pedagogically to reinforce an inevitability, a sense of 'there is no alternative' as Margaret Thatcher famously phrased it. It continued to be a phrase repeated to justify austerity measures. It reinforces an erosion of democracy in all matters, since democracy is the politics of differences, of alternatives. Indeed, if the market is the definition of the private sector then a vast proportion of everyday life is controlled by non-democratic practices, forms of organisation and interests. Corporate employees are schooled into the culture, the knowledge, the skills required by the corporation (Giroux, 2004). It is an arena where the promise of equality of opportunity has all but vanished. However, the illusion of rugged individualists able to make their way equally with others is hard to erase. Through it governance can be better achieved through a more subtle use of public pedagogy that places responsibility on individuals rather than through overt forms of militarised coercion that might generate resistance, protest and the legitimisation of alternative forms of social organisation. The imbrication of self, justice and the logic of the market has been discussed by Boltanski and Thévenot (2006) in their analysis of changes in management discourses and forms of justification, an approach inspired by Walzer's (1985) view that there are multiple domains of value each with their own specific forms of justification. Developing this, Boltanski and Chiapello (2002) identify a 'new spirit of capitalism' focused on individual capital derived from the knowledge and experience of undertaking projects. It creates an 'expertise' located in the individual, and thus a kind of rent value where individuals can demand their 'worth' as in the case of the 'indispensability' of bankers, like Bob Diamond, CEO of Barclays, before he resigned after the LIBOR (London Interbank Offered Rate) rate-fixing scandal. This was the key interest rate upon which all other interest rates are based, pedagogically instilling in the minds of the populace the noble lie that sustains the myth that towering worth is, as Plato (Waterfield, 1994) argued, essential to a State's governability. So too is the myth that with talent and hard work anyone can make it in the open market. It is a myth at the heart of the pioneer narrative routinely exploited – à la Bernays – by American presidential hopefuls (Roberts and Schostak, 2012) and in the Trump and Brexit campaigns where 'talent' would be released by freeing up markets. Of course, the reality is different:

> Ariely and Norton found that Americans think they live in a far more equal country than they in fact do. On average, those surveyed estimated that the wealthiest 20 percent of Americans own 59 percent of the nation's wealth; in reality the top quintile owns around 84 percent. The respondents further estimated that the poorest 20 percent own 3.7 percent, when in reality they own 0.1percent.
>
> (Bennett, 2010)

The world's third richest man is, of course, under no illusion: "There's class warfare, all right," Mr Buffett said, "but it's my class, the rich class, that's making war, and we're winning" (Stein, 2006). More specifically, on a world scale, the gap between rich and poor within nations and between nations is increasing and the WHO Report 2008 has stated: "Social injustice is killing people on a grand scale". The extent to which his class continues to win is demonstrated in the 2017 Global Wealth Report: just 0.7% of households have 45.9% of global household wealth (Credit Suisse Report, 2017). How have they been able to get away with it?

The workings of the major corporations are largely 'invisible' to public scrutiny except for glimpses in periods of crisis or when there are 'leaks' from 'whistleblowers'. The voices of ordinary 'citizens' have no place in the boardrooms. In order to attain this state of affairs, there has been a powerful schooling of the public, a pedagogy of engineering consent:

> Throughout the 20th Century business associations and coalitions coordinated mass propaganda campaigns that combined sophisticated public relations techniques developed in 20th Century America with revitalised free market ideology originating in 18th Century Europe. The purpose of this propaganda onslaught has been to persuade a majority of people that it is in their interests to eschew their own power as workers and citizens, and forego their democratic right to restrain and regulate business activity. As a result the political agenda is now largely confined to policies aimed at furthering business interests.
>
> (Beder, 2008: 1)

In short, there has been an inversion of democracy and in the next section we begin to address the historical emergence of this inversion and how it impinges on the public space of educational provision.

## Historical periods and the inversion of democracy

It is important to get a sense of the different historical periods and contexts because they constitute conflicting 'windows of opportunity' or spaces for the delineation of educational and democratic activities. By furthering our understanding of historical periods we can begin to explore how different social projects and movements can achieve different purpose and purchase at different times. Not only does the role of the State, and particularly the nation state, vary according to the historical period in question but also financial and corporate activity vary especially if there are major shifts in regimes of capital accumulation. With varying degrees of refraction and time lag public and private practices, social projects, personal projects and democratic modalities are reformulated and reconstituted within the context of the main historical periods discerned.

It is a recurrent mystery to those with historical training that so many of our social studies, particularly one might argue our educational studies, take time for granted. We might seek to explain this by the current obsession with contemporary change, by the 'velocity of change' itself, or by the progressive erosion of foundational disciplines, such as 'history of education'. But such assertions would themselves be a-historical, ignoring time, for in fact the taken-for-grantedness of time is one of the great continuities.

Yet we live our lives by the clock, we are in fact regulated by time everyday. This is the paradox – that which is all-pervasive becomes invisible to us. As Young and Schuller (1988) noted in their pioneering study *The Rhythms of Society*: "if we are not only obsessed with clock-time but getting more so, it is all the more strange that social scientists should have done so little to make time one of their special apprehensions" (p. 2). This is a common omission in studies of education and schooling that reflects the consciousness of the teachers, administrators and students who take time for granted. Indeed, "The everyday authority of time is, even in a permissive society, so complete that it rarely appears as problematic, and if it is not problematic to the people who are the subjects, it will not be all that problematic to the other people ..." (p. 3). There is, however, a particular and peculiar irony when studies of social 'change', and in particular educational and school 'change', ignore time. There is a wide-range school change research, including cross-site studies, that only use snapshots of social context and time (e.g. Lieberman, 1995; Fullan, 1999; 2000). This approach does not allow the change and reform efforts to be 'grounded' in trajectories of influence and causation linked to the past, or indeed pursued longitudinally from the past to the present and on into the future. This a-historicity is pervasive and endemic, indeed, it enters the very rhetoric of 'change' which is somehow seen as uniquely powerful at this time of global restructuring. However, there are continuities:

> Once time is recognised as a continuous flow — with the essential continuity being the flow itself — what is being observed cannot be anything other than change, continuous change. This is not to say there is no pattern, no structure

in the welter. But whatever has pattern, structure, an appearance of the static, is made up of change, change wrapped within change.

(Young and Schuller, 1988: 5)

Where continuities have been systematically observed by some historians of education, the focus has tended to be on broad patterns of organisational persistence and evolution (e.g. Cuban, 1984), on the "persistence of the recitation" (Westbury, 1973); on the fate of specific reform policies (Tyack and Tobin, 1994; Tyack and Hansot, 1992) or on reforms in particular areas — such as curriculum (e.g. Goodson, 1994). Again, what is missing in the broad longitudinal sweep of educational change, is a concentration on the 'long waves' of change and reform. This longitudinal sweep needs to search beyond internal patterns of organisational persistence and evolution to study the interaction between these and external movements. External movements, that is, within economic and social structures and in the "external consistencies" (Meyer and Rowan, 1978), which condition the possibilities for educational change and reform.

Historians and social scientists following the Annaliste School see change operating at three levels of time – long, medium and short – which interpenetrate in a complex manner. Here, theorists provide an allegory of the ocean to capture the main characteristics of these three categories or levels and their interdependent mode of operation. In England, this approach was developed by the late Philip Abrahams and Peter Burke (Burke, 1993). The Journal of Historical Sociology (1988) has pursued the same themes of enquiry since it was founded.

Looking at the ocean, at the bottom, representing long-term time, are deep currents which, although apparently quite stable, are moving all the time. Such long-term time covers major structural factors: world views, forms of the state, etc. The movement from pre-modern to modern, or modern to postmodern forms can be understood in terms of these broad epochal shifts (Mills, 1959; Bell, 1973; Lyotard, 1984; Denzin, 1991). The effects of the emerging social, economic and political conditions of the postmodern era upon the organisation and practices of schooling might be understood in these terms (e.g. Hargreaves, 1994; Giroux, 1989).

Above this level are the swells and tides of particular cycles representing medium time. Such medium-term time has been conceived in boom–bust-like spans of 50 years or so – although with the compression of time and space in the postmodern age, these cycles may themselves undergo compression (Giddens, 1991). It is within these medium-term cycles that one might explain the establishment of the current 'grammar of schooling' for example, as classroom-based, graded and subject-specialised schooling in the latter years of the nineteenth and early years of the twentieth centuries. As Tyack and Tobin (1994) admonish, unless reformers begin to talk the historical 'grammar of schooling', their attempts to initiate educational change will be forever thwarted.

At the top of the ocean, representing the waves and froth, is short-term, everyday time: the everyday events and human actions of ordinary daily life.

Proponents of this view of history often celebrate its empirical specifics against the grander theoretical claims of epochal shifts between different historical periods (e.g. McCulloch, 1995). These theorisations of history should not be treated as competitive, though. Fine-grained empirical detail and broad-based theoretical sensibility are complementary forces in history and complementary resources for interpreting such history.

The most interesting points for inquiry and investigation are when the different layers of historical time coincide; for it is at such points that inclinations towards, and capacity for, change and reform are strongest. Such co-incidences or conjunctures can be seen in key moments of educational history and change.

Why then should these historical perspectives be of such commanding interest in our analysis of the prospects for democratic education? The answer is that the different regimes of capital accumulation accompanying different historical periods have substantial implications for forms of economic and social organisation. Hence the prospects for social democratic forms of governance and welfare states are crucially linked to the historical periods in which they are contextualised.

Social democratic governance and emerging welfare states essentially grew in the years that Eric Hobsbawm called "The Golden Years", and the French called "Les Trente Glorieuses". Hobsbawm says that it was only at the end of the period of "The Golden Years" at the end of the 1970s that observers "began to realise that the world, particularly the world of developed capitalism, had passed through an altogether exceptional phase of its history: perhaps a unique one" (Hobsbawm, 1994: 258).

The important point about "The Golden Years" was that for a time regimes of accumulation and social democratic governance and the building of a welfare state could exist in a reasonably benign alliance. David Harvey called this the period of "expanded reproduction":

> Investments in education, the interstate highway system, sprawling suburbanisation, and the development of the South and West, absorbed vast quantities of capital and product in the 1950s and 1960s. The US state, to the chagrin of neo-liberals and conservatives, became a development state during these years
>
> (Harvey, 2003: 56).

In this historical period we have an example then of national social-democratic governments, growing welfare systems and a capitalist system working, to some degree harmoniously, for the overall good. The watershed in terms of this period of economic organisation was the oil crisis of 1973. This reversed the expansionary momentum of the golden years and posed new problems for capital accumulation. In pedagogical terms, then, there was a 'new' agenda to address; or perhaps, an old agenda that had lain benignly latent in the golden years for capital accumulation. As Harvey has argued, the new mode of accumulation became 'accumulation by dispossession' which he says "became increasingly more salient after 1973. In part as compensation for the chronic problems of over-accumulation arising within expanded reproduction" (Harvey, 2003: 156). The election of Margaret Thatcher in 1979 and Reagan in 1981 solidified this new mode of economic organisation, the "IMF capitals and the World Bank changed their policy frameworks almost overnight", public assets were privatised leading to an "incredible pressure to find more and more arenas, either at home or abroad, where privatisation might be achieved" (Harvey, 2003: 157–158).

In Britain one of the first assets to be privatised was the large stock of council housing which had been such a feature of the social democratic settlement in post-war Britain. The sale of council houses became a trademark of the Thatcher government and their pioneering model for privatisation and accumulation by dispossession. But the privatisation went much further to include water, energy, transport, the Royal Mail, with inroads into the health service (Meek, 2014). These changes in the pattern of economic organisation from 'expanded reproduction' to 'accumulation by dispossession' have profound and continuing consequences for those interested in broader conceptions of democracy and democratic education. Leading up to and following the election of the Thatcher government in 1979 there were media campaigns against 'progressive education', comprehensive schools and 'trendy leftie' teaching (Schostak, 1986; 1993), and for a return to 'basics' and the kinds of skills presumed to be required by employers. Indeed, since what the above commentaries make clear is how the governing parties in the state are all drawn into a similar process of privatisation, then it is to be expected that 'right' and 'left' become increasingly indistinguishable in their policies. What the commentaries also show is how this favours particular groups and completely discriminates against other groups. So the notion that there can be a representative democracy representing all people – with an education system to match – is undercut by the economic order in which governance is taking place. By whole-heartedly operating under the 'accumulation by dispossession' mantra, governments forgo their previous duty of 'representativeness'. Instead of democracy being a process of representing 'the people' against powerful interests, democracy is inverted so as to represent powerful interest groups against 'the people'. This inversion of democracy goes hand in hand with the new economic order. Donald Savoie in his study 'Power: Where is it?' makes this point about political institutions 'having come off their moorings'. He says:

> Representative democracy is slowly being replaced by opinion surveys, focus groups, pressure groups, lobbyists and powerful individuals pursuing their own economic interests. Citizens are left on the outside watching a game called politics on TV screens and seeing an over-mighty executive restrained only by unelected judges, and journalists.
>
> (Savoie, 2010)

Perhaps he is being over-optimistic in seeing unelected judges and journalists as countervailing forces to the overbearing power of the current regime. In fact, unelected judges in the US and the UK and indeed unelected Lords in Britain were accused of being 'enemies of the people' by the right-wing media for supporting democratic oversight during the Brexit period (Phipps, 2016) and for the challenges made to Trump's policies driven by far-right campaigns and discourses (Neiwert, 2017; Stocker, 2017). Journalism has long been seen as a way of holding power to account; however, apart from such examples as *The Guardian* in the UK and *Mediapart* in France, media outlets not owned by billionaires and corporations are becoming rare. This impacts their independence and compounds the 'inversion of democracy' at the level of formal politics and in turn on education and research.

In schools, universities and research, restrictions on the freedom to teach and research have been made through targeted research funding, privileging some subjects and topics over others and, in particular, general funding being dependent on inspections and assessment of performance according to managerialist criteria of measurable outputs. Yet, despite all the managerialist effort, social mobility seems broadly an illusion (Marsh, 2011) with even, it may be argued, a falling rate of learning (Blacker, 2013). Indeed, a disproportionate number of the privately educated dominate the top professions, politics and business (Kirby, 2016). Alongside this, politics has largely favoured the interests of elites as wealth has been systematically drawn from the many while the poor have been increasingly made destitute (c.f. Piketty, 2014; Haymes et al., 2015). In short it can be said, accumulation for the few accompanied by dispossession for the many is being compounded through elite schooling and higher tuition fees for the 'best' universities. We should expect such strategies to be the norm during this period of 'accumulation by dispossession'. The object of these global and pervasive patterns of privatisation accompanied by the inversion of democracy has been to bring about a 'hollowing out' of democratic space.

## Conclusion

Knowing what went wrong is not enough. The challenge for the later chapters is how to reverse the 'inversion of democracy', and how to expose the pervasiveness of strategies of dispossession is an urgent task for research and education to re-engage with the democratic project, a reclaimed and rethought Enlightenment project perhaps, where people develop the courage 'to use reason publicly in all matters'. It needs to be done, we think, not only because we share an enduring belief in fairness and social justice, but also because generally we think people believe 'social cruelty' of the sort epitomised by the new political strategies is bad for all in the long run. As Judt so elegantly shows in his last polemic (Judt, 2010), there is strength in the Goldsmith quote that, "ill fares the land, to hastening ills a prey where wealth accumulates and man decay."

As Wilkinson and Pickett show, equality is 'better for everyone'. The fact that the right-wing think-tanks have targeted their work shows that they recognise the dangerous force of this empirically -confirmed argument for social justice. (Wilkinson and Pickett, 2009). Democracy, we argue, must be rebuilt in the places that it has been so successfully attacked: the workplace, the public sphere, education and, indeed, in politics itself. We have personally argued that pre-figurative politics (see Goodson, 1997; Schostak and Schostak, 2013) is vitally important as a strategy for regeneration. Reclaiming democracy in education in dark times (Giroux, 2005) means re-appropriating the democratic educational heritage for present purposes (Moss and Fielding, 2011). Rather than schools modelling the world of public- and private-sector organisations maladjusted to democracy, the grounds can be developed for organisations where the voices, needs, demands and interests of all are drawn into debate, decision-making and action (Schostak, 1983; Schostak and Schostak, 2013). Certainly there are important existing examples of democratic practices which prefigure the world that we want to create and sustain. An example would be the cooperative movement but there is a range of other enduring pre-figurative forms that research may discover. These have now to be allied to a new strategy for recovering democratic life, otherwise they will fall within specious narratives like the 'Big Society'. The audacity of this narrative, pursuing dispossession for the many and privilege for the few whilst arguing we are all in this together 'in a mystical big society', is a warning of the scale and scope of the emerging political project. It makes the challenge of re-imaging and prefiguring new democratic forms all the more urgent. What has gone wrong with democracy is that people have, whether wittingly or unwittingly, allowed it to be crowded out by the interests of the few as they create their private, poorly regulated spheres of self-interested wealth accumulation. A new wave of radically inspired educational research (Schostak and Schostak, 2008; 2013), that focuses on making a democratic difference, is urgently required. Without it the 'geological plates' of history as discussed above may well shift our lives into more autocratic unjust configurations of crisis, austerity and exploitation.

# Part I

# What Went Wrong?

Part 1

What Went W.ong?

# Chapter 2

# The challenge for researchers and educators

If research is to impact on public decision-making, the research and educational challenge is to create the conditions for free and equal access to knowledge and the conditions of further discovery. This is essential to the kind of democracy we envisage, where *all* people participate. By all, we mean a democracy that is in no way restricted merely to age groups, 'citizens' or any other categories of individuals. As to the definition of 'the people', we mean all who live regardless of birthplace. In this sense, there are no frontiers to manage apart from the ever-expanding horizon of actively inclusive democracy – as Hannah Arendt put it, each birth adds a new perspective to be taken into account. For such a global dynamic multitude, the conditions framing the contemporary political challenge focus attention on how to control, or at least constrain, the leaders, their territorial ambitions and the management systems put into place by elites. How? By creating the conditions for an effective public (Schostak and Schostak, 2013) that is co-extensive with the work of research and education involved in establishing truth, facts, objectivity, reliability, validity, subjectivity, representation, generalisation and universalisation. This is the challenge.

We say it is false to argue that because no given individual is capable of having all the skills and knowledge necessary to tackle the complex problems of contemporary life, that publics are therefore necessarily phantoms and so are to become the objects of manipulation by 'experts'. Rather, we think of a public as the dynamic combination of the powers of all individuals capable of thinking, critiquing, imagining, and experiencing the world about. Such a public organised on the principle of freedom as coextensive with equality – what Balibar (1994) calls *égaliberté* (equaliberty) – threatens the privileged positions of elites to control agendas, frame what counts as knowledge, and undertake decisions and courses of action that address their interests. Critical to the working of the public as the organisation of democratic debate is 'truth'. However, 'truth' as a concept is problematic, left to experts and thus taken out of the hands – and minds – of the public. The challenge for researchers and educationists is how to get it back where it belongs, with the public.

In exploring this, both schooling and education are here being employed in their widest possible senses as forms of social learning where either the process is guided by success in winning privilege, power and wealth over others (schooling) or by critically reflecting on the challenges posed by multiple perspectives, experiences, values, insights and truths in order to bring about creative resolutions that contribute equally to the cultural enrichment and the mental and physical wellbeing of all (education). Both draw upon material that seems so obvious that they are 'just lying around' ready to be picked up and used. This is the material of collective learning piled up over the ages in libraries and in the common sense of peoples. These are the paradigmatic texts and discourses through which perceptions about what is real are shaped (Kuhn, 1970). The challenge for education and for research begins with unpicking these ideas lying around to see how their 'truths' have been constructed and for what purposes they have been used. The fundamental purpose we explore here is to create the conditions for freedom: the freedom to think, critique and use research-informed reason as a basis for making decisions.

## The ideas lying around

In the context of early twentieth-century debates on freedom and the challenge of totalitarianism – whether communist or fascist – the paradigm texts for the management of western liberal democracies emerged. Rather like a symptom that draws attention to underlying stresses, so a conference called by philosopher Louis Rougier in Paris in August 1938 focused upon Lippmann's recently published book (Audier, 2012). The Lippmann colloquium drew together a number of participants such as Friedrich Hayek, Ludwig von Mises and Karl Polanyi (2001) who in their own writings added to the growing library of paradigmatic texts. It was here that Alexander Rüstow coined the term 'neoliberalism'. After the Second World War, following the publication of his book *The Road To Serfdom*, Hayek founded the Mont Pelerin Society in Switzerland along with Karl Popper. The book, according to Hayek, was inspired by Lippmann to whom he wrote in the hope he would recommend it to a publisher (Jackson, 2012). In short, the book picked up on the key themes of individual freedom threatened by dictatorial states discussed during the Colloquium in Paris. For Hayek it was socialism that destroys freedom, turning individuals into 'serfs'. As such it easily aligned with the East–West Cold War between Russia and the USA as summed up in the rhetorical imagery of the 'Evil Empire' (Reagan, 1983) and continued after the fall of the soviet Russian Empire. This later flexibly transformed under friend–enemy discourses into the 'axis of evil' following the September 11, 2001 World Trade Centre and Pentagon attacks (Bush, 2002) and the war on terror. It continued into the rhetorics and policies of Trump as a reason to ban Muslim refugees and immigrants (Siddiqui, 2017). The friend–enemy rhetoric was inflected more widely to blame the liberal elites and their policies of globalisation for making the white communities in the 'rust belts' vulnerable to unfair competition by immigrants and imports produced by cheap labour abroad leaving them to rot (Longworth, 2016). Similarly, the Brexit referendum result has been attributed by many to a rejection of globalisation and the liberal elites who ignored the plight of the 'left behinds' particularly in the white, economically depressed areas where the once centres of mining and heavy industry have closed down (Elliott, 2016). In an ironic reversal, rather than the miners as symbolic of being the enemy within as Thatcher had called them, it had by the third decade of the neoliberal experiment become the elites as symbolised by bankers. Both the Brexit campaigners and Trump, steered by Bannon and supported by Breitbart and other extreme right-wing media, knew this. The further irony, of course, 'the peasants revolt', as Liam Fox (Johnson, 2016) and Delingpole (2016) writing for *Breitbart* called it, on both sides of the Atlantic was led and financed by those who had most benefited from the liberalised and globalised financial regimes and digital social media (Cadwalladr 2017, 2017a, 2017b).

The power of the irony is that its structure is never clearly seen by those who are duped. It operates doubly: asserting as true/real something that is known not to be true/real in order to state a hidden, an implicit or 'deeper' truth/reality (see for example Booth, 1974). At its surface, the statement made has a plausibility, perhaps keying into prejudices or beliefs about the nature of the world. However, within the structure of the irony something jars. It is this grating or perhaps a little itch that points to an alternative reading and its truth. When the millionaire ex-banker Nigel Farage, a long-time and leading campaigner for the UK to leave the European Union, spoke of the 'peasants revolt' and was accepted by 'ordinary people' as 'speaking for us' he presented his words as a truth for the 'peasantry', not his as a member of a wealthy elite funded and supported by multi-millionaires (Monbiot, 2016), hoping to make money. When Trump was accepted as speaking for those in the rustbelts, the truth he co-opted was theirs, not his. Key to his campaign were far-right media, particularly Breitbart and data analysis companies and the family that funded them, the Mercers (Cadwalladr, 2017a, 2017c).

Irony has the power both to cover and to reveal. But only if processes of critical interpretation are either suspended in order to engage in a narrative fantasy, or operated so as to break from delusion to what in the eighteenth century became known as 'enlightenment', that is, as Kant put it, "the freedom to use reason publicly in all matters" where "by the public use of one's own reason I mean that use which anyone may make of it as a man of learning addressing the entire reading public" (Kant, 1784). Kant, of course, was bound by the ways of talking, conventions and prejudices of his time. Just as we are caught within our own. In his view, although we have not achieved full enlightenment, and perhaps never will, by the use of reason in public matters we may at least take some steps. Such use of reason in public is an active power that is distinct from, in Kant's view, the 'teachings' of a priest, that he calls a private power. The priest's reasoning in relationship to teaching is the private use of reason for use in a 'domestic gathering' where: "In view of this, he is not and cannot be free as a priest, since he is acting on a commission imposed from outside." This split between the conditioned private and free public use of reason resumes the double play of irony where truth is not immediately evident, but is hidden in its expression. In both irony and the play of private and public there are alternative truths that must be decided upon. There are many contexts in everyday life that are typically, even legally, constructed as private as distinct from public. Business organisations are part of the 'private domain' where the reasoning of employees is unfree to the extent that it is directed by management under the rules, values and purposes of the owners or chief executives and directors. Mainstream schools may be thought of as undertaking public education, but they do so within an adult–child *in loco parentis* relationship where the free use of reason to organise their days for both child and adult is restricted. The vast majority of business and school organisation, just like the private domain of family life, is hierarchical. Those at the top limit and shape the use of reason to choose and guide the activities of those under their authority. These forms of organisational practices are essential to a range of social orders. Indeed, so pervasive and persistent are they, whether in 'democracies' or totalitarian states, their character of being natural and/or all powerful gives the impression of being for ever – until, like the Soviet Union, they are over: when due to the coming of "perestroika and *glasnost*" (openness, public discussion) in 1985, most people did not anticipate that any radical changes would follow (Yurchak, 2005: 2). They were experienced as a "break of consciousness" and "stunning shock" and resulted in the tearing down of the Berlin wall in 1989. The changes were expressed initially in terms of new publications, publications that had been suppressed (Yurchak, 2005: 2). There is a change in terms of 'intelligence'. By this we do not mean that mechanical, calculating, machinelike process done at speed as in the IQ tests beloved of the puzzle solvers, not the puzzle challengers. Intelligence here is employed to convey a way of making sense of the world as open to possibilities for human expression and action. For a while at least, in the fall of the old order possibilities for a new form of social order were glimpsed and believed to be possible. Until, that is, there was a fall back to the apparent securities of a 'strong leader' in a society where neoliberalism saw its chance to write its demands for capital accumulation instead of poetry. Such a chance for Friedman and his followers was to be found under conditions of crisis, because:

> Only a crisis – actual or perceived – produces real change. When that crisis occurs, the actions that are taken depend on the ideas that are lying around. That, I believe, is our basic function: to develop alternatives to existing policies, to keep them alive and available until the politically impossible becomes the politically inevitable.
>
> (Friedman, 1982: xiv)

His ideas were 'lying around' in the form of 'shock therapy', a term used to express applying 'laissez-faire' – or free market – ideas advocated by Hayek, Friedman and others. Jeffrey Sachs was one of the economists associated with the term, one that he did not like. According to Sachs the ideas forming 'shock therapy' may have begun with Ludwig Erhard's "very bold moves in 1947, '48 to get Germany on a market economy track, and to end monetary chaos in the country, and had acted quite decisively" (Sachs, 2000). They had been applied fully fledged by the Freidman-influenced Chicago Boys (Letelier, 1976) undertaking their experiments on Chile where "*laissez-faire* dreams and political greed of the old Land-owning oligarchy and upper bourgeoisie of monopolists and financial speculators, the military has applied the brutal force required to achieve those goals." This, of course, should have been a warning. Nevertheless, these laissez-faire ideas in their neoliberal form became what John Williamson in 1989 called the Washington consensus. This consisted of "a list of policies that I claimed were widely held in Washington to be widely desirable in Latin America as of the date the list was compiled, namely the second half of 1989" (Williamson, 2004) That list included: 1) fiscal discipline; 2) redirecting public expenditure towards "neglected fields with high economic returns and the potential to improve income distribution, like primary health and education, and infrastructure"; 3) tax reform to "sharpen incentives"; 4) financial liberalisation to achieve "market-determined interest rates"; 5) competitive exchange rates; 6) trade liberalisation; 7) reducing barriers that impede foreign direct investment; 8) privatisation of state enterprises; 9) deregulation to abolish rules restricting the entry of new firms or that restrict competition "and ensure that all regulations are justified by such criteria as safety, environmental protection, or prudential supervision of financial institutions"; and 10) a legal system ensuring secure property rights (Williamson, 1993: 1332-3). They became essentially a policy paradigm, a consensus view that was seen to be necessary to underpin democracy.

The elements described above of the Washington consensus had formed a major part of the Thatcher 'monetarist' revolution. Friedman, interviewed in October 1979, commented:

> The Thatcher government is a kind of an experiment in whether it will be possible in a democratic society that has gone as far as Britain has gone to change course in an orderly, effective way, to set Britain on a new road. If the Thatcher government succeeds it will be an example that will not be lost on the United States or the rest of the world.
> (Curtis, 1992, Ep. 3, 29.00)

Curtis' (1992) response in his documentary was to show unemployment quickly doubling as traditional industries cut back on investment, factories closed, and inflation rose. As the Chief Economic Advisor on Monetary Policy at the Bank of England (1980–1985) put it "it was all a bit embarrassing" because after implementing the policy to squeeze monetary growth gently, it "took an enormous jump and it was very difficult to know why" (Curtis, 1992, Ep. 3, 32.00). This might suggest that the theory was not adequate for the complex realities of practice. Thatcher and her followers believed differently; despite any evidence that might give pause for critical reassessment, she said of monetarism and monetary control, that "you all know full well that if you produce too much of something its value will fall. That's elementary. It isn't a new-fangled theory it is as essential as the law of gravity and you can't avoid it." It was this kind of certitude that there was a simple, universal relationship between economic theory concerning the market place and actual behaviour that suffused policy. There could be no mistake. There was, as Thatcher would say, no alternative. Indeed, for Sir Keith Joseph who had introduced Thatcher to monetarist ideas,

> People used to say you're destroying my job and I was absolutely secure in my conscience that their negotiators and employers were destroying their jobs by not following rational expectations and seeing that if they didn't accommodate [their demands to enable products to be internationally competitive], jobs would go.
>
> (Curtis, 1992, Ep. 3, 33.04)

However, while he was clear in his conscience, they were, he said, convinced in "their invincible ignorance" that he was the enemy (Curtis, 1992, Ep. 3, 33.40). Such certitude has continued.

The prevailing certainty in economics, Earl et al., (2017) argue, has reduced the teaching of economics in universities to a form of indoctrination which reinforces the practice of economists and policy makers. There is, they say, an 'econocracy', meaning there are "increasingly diverse areas of life" which have to "justify their existence in terms of their contribution to the economy" (Earl et al., 2017: 8) such as: literacy programmes, mental health care, disabilities welfare support. Since everything is measurable and has a price under an econocracy, then it is not surprising that economic theory took a mathematical turn which has the advantage of making it seem like a science, having laws as essential as the law of gravity if, as Keith Joseph put it, people act according to rational choice theory. The problem is: "To satisfy the fixation on maths and equations, economic models may have to leave important details behind, sometimes oversimplifying to the point of uselessness compared to the complexities that can be detailed by written argument" (Earl et al., 2017: 174). In a sense, then, there has been a performative shift, as Yurchak (2005) called it, in the context of his study of the fall of the Soviet Union. Yet such simplified models form the basis of policy. Underlying this acceptance is a process of normalisation where:

> A model of authoritative discourse in which the literal precision of statements and representations was evaluated against an external canon (described in the opinion of an external editor) was gradually displaced by a model in which the external canon was no longer available. As a result of this shift of conditions, the authoritative discourse underwent a major internal normalisation at the structural level. The normalised and fixed structures of this discourse became increasingly frozen and were replicated from one context to the next practically intact.
>
> (Yurchak, 2005: 25–6)

The external canon for Western democracies since the Enlightenment has produced discourses underpinned by the success of engineering, technological advance and science to formulate theories that are testable and work in the material world. However, for such models to be produced and to work in the social and psychological worlds of everyday life, there has to be a performative shift. People have to be engineered in such a way that they conform to the models. If they do not conform to the models, then the people are wrong, not the models. That is the upshot of Sir Keith Joseph's judgement on people's 'invincible ignorance' when they do not behave as rational choice theory requires.

There is then a disengagement between the world as it is and the world as it is modelled and institutionalised. In the context of the Soviet Union the language that produced this engagement became what Yurchak called *hypernormalisation*,

> that is, the process of its normalisation did not simply affect all levels of linguistic, textual, and narrative structure but also became an end in itself, resulting fixed and cumbersome forms of language that were neither interpreted nor easily interpretable at the level of constative meaning. This shift to the hypernormalised language in which the constative dimension was increasingly being unanchored is key for our understanding of late socialism.
> (Yurchak, 2005)

For Curtis (2016) in his BBC documentary *HyperNormalisation*, it was also key to understanding the contemporary impact of Western practices, forms of institutionalisation, ideologies and discourses globally. The econocracy perfectly symbolises this self-referential process of hypernormalisation where mathematised economic models are produced and implemented as an end in themselves, regardless of the wider real-world impacts on lives. Perhaps the perfect example is to be found in the financial instruments that led to the financial crash beginning in 2007 that Warren Buffet called "financial weapons of mass destruction". While many thought that this latest capitalist crisis would change matters, it was quickly realised that the moment of change could not be realised. The econocracy knew no alternatives – bluntly, the alternatives had not been part of their professional development and there was no institutionalised alternative to take its place. Thus, drawing upon imagery from popular culture, Quiggin (2010) called the contemporary inertia 'zombie economics' and Giroux (2014) judged it as zombie politics. In each case, it was argued 'dead ideas' were stalking the corridors of power sustaining their quasi-life through their exploitation of the population. Effectively, these are ideas producing simplified models of how the social worlds of people should work divorced from the real complexities of the workings of everyday life.

It is a state of affairs where openness and critical public discussion are cast adrift, leaving actors with an increasingly slippery hold on what is 'true', 'ethical', 'real', 'valid', 'reliable' and 'objective'. It may well be the case that as many have stated, particularly taking a postmodern line of argument, that 'the truth' cannot be known. However, people can at least know when they have been hit hard and crushed.

## Answering the crisis of thinking 'truth'

When there is a disconnect between criteria for establishing the truth of statements through forms of argumentation and the world as lived and experienced, then thinking itself is in crisis. If there is a disconnect between the hurt people feel and the cultural, social, political and economic descriptions, explanations and narratives presented by experts then the split raises the question: what is the truth? What then are the other kinds of ideas 'lying around' offering explanations more readily credible as to the causes of hurt?

For Irving Kristol, if liberalism had failed then the answer was a return to the common sense of traditional values and truths – but not just any. He distinguished what he called the democratic dogma from Republican philosophy. The dogma, in his view, consisted of the assumption that people could be shaped in particular ways. In his view this was: "Presumptuous, because there is no superior knowledge available as to how people should be shaped. Superfluous, because the people will, if left alone, shape themselves better than anyone or anything can shape them" (Kristol, 2011: 64). For him the Republican philosophy of self-government is based on 'self improvement' guided by social authorities, whereas the democratic idea of self-government is based on the premise that one's natural self is the best of all possible selves, and that it is the institutions of society which are inevitably corrupting of goodness (p. 75). This distinction is critical for research about society, the 'nature' of the person and the education of individuals. Rather than individuals either being reduced to being like atoms in a mass whose 'natural' laws can be determined through observation, measurement and experiment as in the 'positive' sciences, or left in a natural state as in some child-centred utopia, there is here the offer of 'the common man' who can be 'improved'. Improved in what way? Kristol, for example, extols the pre-Civil War businessmen thought to be 'honest' and an "honourable class of men engaged in an honourable activity – i.e., an activity from which they emerged better men than when they first entered it, as a result of the discipline which this activity exercised upon their characters" (p. 71). Kristol agrees with the founding fathers who "believed that people, if they lived carelessly and unreflectively, could corrupt themselves" (p. 70). In that sense, then, good institutions are required to ensure that people receive the discipline necessary to be improved. What makes for good institutions? For example:

> When our schools were 'republican' institutions, instructing young citizens in the three R's, in elementary civics, and in the rudiments of good manners, they had both self-confidence and universal respect. Today, when they are 'democratic' institutions, when they are making few demands on their

students but feverishly trying to satisfy all the demands which students make on them, they are in a condition of perpetual crisis.

(p. 74)

So, a good institution is one that makes demands on the individual such as self-discipline, honesty and a work ethic (cf. p. 91). And these are best undertaken under the "spiritual mother" of American Republicanism, "the Protestant religion" (p. 91).

Of course, there are other 'ideas lying around' that also refer to the development of character, or self-improvement such as to be found in the work and practice of Robert Owen (1816). Such ideas were developed and modified through the pioneering work in Rochdale of 28 people who set up the shop that became the model for the worldwide co-operative movement. Here 'self improvement' was accomplished as a democratic and co-operative practice, a form of entrepreneurial socialism – a co-operative ethic as distinct from a Protestant ethic. The self-discipline involved was to do with keeping the principles of co-operation together. As Holyoake (1858) in his history of the movement put it: "The moral miracle performed by our co-operatives of Rochdale is, that they have had the good sense to differ without disagreeing; to dissent from each other without separating; to hate at times, and yet always hold together." These, however, were not the ideas 'lying around' that either neoconservativism nor neoliberalism wanted to take up. Rather the contemporary neoliberals drew inspiration from the anti-socialist free market ideas of Hayek and Friedman and the neoconservatives from the political theories of Carl Schmitt and Leo Strauss who espoused friend–enemy strategies, nationalism, the state as the sovereign decision maker and the 'noble lie' of Plato's Republic. Essentially, the lie consisted in claiming that the distinct classes of his Utopian Republic were 'natural'; that indeed, the philosopher kings were naturally superior to the guardians who were themselves superior to the working masses who in turn were superior to slaves. It was called a noble lie because it was a fiction that contained wisdom – a truth – about how to maintain social order and shape the character of people to obtain the best form of society for all: the Republic. Thus the lie teaches that there is a natural hierarchy and a natural right of rule. Strauss calls it a tyranny since there is no alternative but to maintain the lie in the interests of order. In short, as a tyrannical teaching it follows that secrecy and lies are necessary in order "to spare the peoples' feelings and to protect the elite from possible reprisals" (Postel, 2003). How then can a philosopher, a political theorist or indeed anyone who seeks to go beyond the lie to speak the truth that is concealed by the lie, go about telling it if, in telling, the speaker will be persecuted and punished by the powerful and, indeed, the people whose world views are grounded in the lie? According to Strauss (1952: 25), one has to write between the lines which of course means learning how to read between the lines. Secrets are everywhere: governments, the military, police, health and welfare services, the education system, political parties, corporations, trades unions – and, of course, the family. The rationale given for such secrecy is typically to protect the nation, competitive advantage, privacy. To give away such secrets is treason, betrayal and disloyalty. It is thus not hard to draw comparisons with contemporary circumstances. In Drury's (Postel, 2003) view, Strauss intended to "convince his acolytes that they are the natural ruling elite and the persecuted few" so that they would accept that "dissembling and deception – in effect, a culture of lies – is the peculiar justice of the wise".

Strauss had a profound impact on his students, of which one was Kristol (1995: 7–9) who with others founded a journal *The Public Interest* which became a platform for neoconservatism (p. 29–31). In particular, Kristol was impressed by Strauss' form of reading and writing developed from his studies of pre-French Revolution 'Great Books' because "They have to be studied, and in a special way; for if they are truly great, it is probably their intention to conceal as well as to reveal, and they do not yield their secrets easily" (Kristol, 2011: 26). To read, then, is effectively a search for hints that resolve confusions or paradoxes in the "art of writing" that Strauss employs (p. 31–32). This art of writing which is also an art of reading can then be applied to reading the contemporary public. He saw in the public confusions, paradoxes and contractions, a yearning for the values and principles of a pre-Enlightenment, pre-French revolution, pre-American Civil War past. Indeed, he saw in the idea of the democratic public the potential for a tyranny of the majority (p. 326–327) which could lead them astray from their true yearnings. Through a double reading what he saw emerging was "The Coming 'Conservative Century'" (p. 364–368) which would undermine democratic liberals with a return to the "three pillars of modern conservatism": "religion, nationalism and economic growth"; and "Of these, religion is easily the most important because it is the only power that, in the longer term, can shape people's characters and regulate their motivation" (p. 365). However, this conservatism defined not a political party as such, but a popular movement that was specifically "America's 'Exceptional' Conservatism" (p. 373). This exceptionalism he distinguishes from that of Oakeshot's secular conservatism because it does not sufficiently bind people to a past and a future as does religion. Nor does it evoke the sense of a 'creed' whereby he says Americans are ideological bound to the past as exhibited by the fact that children in schools "in all fifty states begin their day with a recitation of the Pledge of Allegiance to the flag and the Constitution of the United States of America". Indeed, "at the opening of every high school, college, and professional sporting event … players and spectators rise to their feet and sing the national anthem". Not to do so, he says would bring about "hostile encounters". Something of the continuing significance of this 'creed' can be seen when kneeling instead of standing became a potent symbol of protest against Trump's policies by National Football League (NFL) players causing outrage from Trump who had said "Wouldn't you love to see one of these NFL owners, when someone disrespects our flag say, 'Get that son of a bitch off the field right now'" (Siddiqui, 2017). And the symbolism of the flag was further employed by Trump when he hugged it following a speech defending his anti-immigration policy that separated children from their families. To read Trump's act is not to see its 'bizarreness' but its evocation of a past to which recent immigrants could not belong. For the separation of children from their families Trump blamed the democrats whose liberal policies had caused the problem. For Kristol the rise of American conservatism "differed in one crucial respect from its conservative predecessors: Its chosen enemy was contemporary liberalism, not socialism or statism in the abstract" (Kristol, 1995: 378–379). Neoconservativism offered the chance, then, to create the conditions not for better democracy but better conservatism. For him the public's improvement was not to come from their own imaginations, intelligence and experience in critical dialogue with others but by the improving demands of religion and work as a disciplining activity.

In summary, as McCormack put it,

> Kristol believed that the American people were not as liberal as their ruling overlords, and that the right leader could use the democratic process to overthrow them. This new leader, in keeping with the views of Schmitt and Strauss, would then impose a national religion on America, thus unifying the country and saving it from the moral disintegration of liberalism.
> (McCormack, 2017)

Trump, however, is not an example of Kristol's neoconservatism steeped in the best of the past in relation to producing a better future grounded in what he claimed was the wisdom of the 'Great Books' of the past. Trumpism by that standard is but a cynical deployment.

## Popularism, truth, facts and values

In "The New Popularism: Not to Worry" published in 1985, Kristol (1995: 359–363) anticipated the rise of populism and in particular its use as a way of constraining the 'elites', that is, the liberal elites whose ideas of thinking, reasoning and truth are, in his view, embedded in enlightenment thinking. Based on his reading of the views of the founders, he argued that although ultimately the will of the people cannot be denied, it could be delayed, "refracted in their expression, revised in their enactment, so that more deliberate public opinion could prevail over transient popular opinion" (p. 359). Alongside this he noted that many politicians claimed to be populist, and the issues of crime and education "clearly illustrate why this new populism exists and flourishes" (p. 362). What it showed, for him, was an anger raised "to bring our governing elites to their senses" (p. 363). Of course, by elites he meant the 'liberal elites' of the left not the right-wing Republican rich. How, then, to mobilise this anger in a neoliberal and neoconservative direction?

Each story of immigrant crime, violence, rape or faith-related terror attacks builds a narrative of dangerous others who must be kept out of the country. Each story builds as common sense drawn from common observation of contemporary events. Such common sense based on 'what everyone knows through everyday experience' is where people who call themselves 'ordinary' can feel secure. More than that in Kristol's view: "political wisdom" is "itself distilled from popular common sense" (Kristol, 2011: 305). And that common sense, he wrote in 1985, "had become outraged" (Kristol, 1995: 360) due to the "unwisdom of their elected and appointed officials" (p. 361). This unwisdom had led to "since the 1960s ... a veritable revolution in social policy in this country, a revolution-from-above, a revolution imposed on the people" (p. 361). What constitutes common sense and wisdom, however, is founded upon accepted norms guided by tradition that had developed over time, that people, even those in the minority, could broadly live with. These distinctions between common sense, wisdom as distilled common sense, and opinions that have to be firmed up by leadership (p. 361), are useful tools in what Lippmann (1922) called the manufacture of consent. In this sense, then, it is not evidence that is critical but the degree to which politicians achieve the confidence of the common people. All this, for example, was at stake in the Brexit and Trump campaigns. The issue was not the 'truth', not the 'evidence', not the 'facts' of experts but 'speaking for the common people'. As Michael Gove put it during a Sky News interview in response to a challenge to name an economic authority in support of Brexit: "I'm glad these organisations aren't on my side," he said. "I think people in this country have had enough of experts." (Deacon, 2016). Two thirds of those who wanted to leave the European Union, according to a YouGov poll, did not "believe the opinions of academics, economists and experienced businesspeople" (Kirk and Dunford, 2016).

The strategy then became to focus on the key fears of those target groups who were inclined to vote to leave. This was accomplished by exaggerating the benefits of leaving and the threats posed by staying. The exaggerations were amplified both in the broadcast media sympathetic to the leave campaign and through targeted social media outlets. Indeed, there are investigations into the links between Brexit and Trump campaign groups as well as far-right internet media, and possible Russian election interference (Cadwalladr, 2017; Cadwalladr, 2017b; Cohen, 2017). Despite this, once the votes were counted, the winners argued that political wisdom as the distillation of common sense had been transformed to become 'the will of the people'. Thus, for example, the right-wing press following the referendum to leave the EU presented themselves as the "Champions of the People" (Daily Mail Comment, 2016) against those who are "THWARTING the will of the people" (Millar, 2017). That 48.1% voted against is irrelevant in calling on the 'will of the people', a will that is made to exist regardless of the complexity of the issues, debates, fears, hopes of the population. The truth – that is the truth of the will of the people – is made-to-be, regardless of evidence. In this sense, the 'will of the people' acted as the noble lie underpinning the legitimacy for a neo-conservative/neoliberal remake of British, American and European futures.

This made-to-be truth resembles what Stephen Colbert, in his American TV show *The Colbert Report*, called 'truthiness' to refer to evidence claims or statements that feel right regardless of evidence (Zimmer, 2010). During the presidential campaign of Trump, Colbert revisited truthiness and moved it a stage further in terms of Trumpiness: "Truthiness has to feel true, but Trumpiness doesn't even have to do that," so that "In fact, many Trump supporters don't believe his wildest promises, and they don't care" (Weber, 2016). Trump – or rather his ghost writer – called it "truthful hyperbole" where "I play to people's fantasies. People may not always think big themselves, but they can still get very excited by those who do. That's why a little hyperbole never hurts" (Trump, 1987: 58). The campaign and the early days of the presidency have been characterised by what has more prosaically been called post-truth, a condition where truth no longer matters and conspiracy theories and 'alternative facts' are deployed to support a desired fantasy or policy (Swaine, 2017). Even when what had been said, was on record, no longer mattered. It was denied.

The more earthy term, for such Trumpiness or truthful hyperbole, is bullshit. Frankfurt (2005) distinguishes truth, lying and bullshit. Honest people have their eyes on the facts. The lier cannot lie without assuming there is a truth. The bullshitter is not interested in facts nor in truth: "He does not care whether the things he says describe reality correctly. He just picks them out, or makes them up, to suit his purpose" (p. 56). As to Trump:

> Precise words, like facts, mean little to Trump, as interpreters, who struggle to translate his grammatical anarchy, can attest. Chuck Todd, the anchor of NBC's *Meet the Press*, observed that after several of his appearances as a candidate Trump would lean back in his chair and ask the control booth to replay his segment on a monitor – without sound: "He wants to see what it all looked like. He will watch the whole thing on mute."
>
> Kakutani (2018)

Why watch? If the words do not matter, then what remains is the visual performance, how it plays to the eye, the emotions. This suggests a return to Strauss' "reading between the lines" to present a covert message in plain sight to the faithful who viscerally respond to the visual clues.

## Next steps towards research and educational freedom

The challenge for research and education begins with what counts as common sense and how it is constructed and used as a basis for decision-making and action – whether to reduce or to increase freedoms. Next, the challenge is to address the friend–enemy oppositions which follow from setting so called 'traditional', common sense moralities and forms of political and social order against enlightenment philosophies of critical rationality and democratic organisation. Then there is the challenge to undertake critical explorations of 'the ideas lying around' during times of natural, unexpected or engineered crisis that if adopted have consequences for all; and then to know what counts as 'true', 'valid', 'objective', 'real', 'moral' under multiple readings of discourses along with their visual, emotional, tactile presentations in public. From such analysis the challenge is to establish criteria for validity, truth and objectivity that can be publicly scrutinised and accepted as a basis for decision-making and action. This is only possible if each individual has an effective voice in public to express their views in the knowledge that they will be counted in any public decision-making.

In the context of threats to freedom, threats to equality and threats to safety, the democratic challenge for research and education then is how to structure voice in public as a precondition for creating new forms of social organisation for individuals to engage freely and equally in the projects that realise their visions for the 'good society', 'happiness' and justice. The critical issue for each voice is how to handle and include the voices of others in the organisation of life projects, the framing of one's own history and identity for self and for others. If it is only through critical public debate that decisions and actions can be determined that are acceptable to all, then the *dispositifs* required for creating the conditions for the emergence of an effective critical public become urgent, so that what has gone wrong with twentieth-century democracy can be addressed in the twenty-first century. For this, the social, political, economic and cultural conditions under which collective learning takes place must come under scrutiny.

# Chapter 3

# What is wrong with contemporary practices of social/collective learning?

The Enlightenment revolution submitted, what is known and believed collectively, to doubt, dethroning traditional authority as the privileged arbiter of knowledge. For Bloom (1987), as a student inspired by Strauss, this entailed the loss of traditional bearings, and the erosion of religious faith and of the political authority of the 'superior' classes along with the individualism that this entailed culturally, politically, socially and psychologically. For him, it was in the pre-Enlightenment 'Great Books' where the insights addressing the universal and eternal problems facing the people of the world were to be found. And as a key text, Plato's Republic was "the book on education, because it really explains to me what I experience as a man and a teacher, and I have almost always used it to point out what we should not hope for, as a teaching of moderation and resignation" (Bloom, 1987: 381). The Enlightenment went wrong, so he and fellow neoconservatives thought, in believing everyone should have access to "Knowledge of the nature of all things" (p. 256). In short, Bloom argued, echoing Kristol, the enlightenment elites imposed their views on the as yet unenlightened masses. This entailed a conflict between belief and expert knowledge which set the knowledge of the enlightenment elites against the laws constructed by the beliefs that continued to guide the 'unenlightened' mass. Thus to progress the enlightenment project, on the one hand it "entailed freedom for the rare theoretical men to engage in rational inquiry in the small number of disciplines that treat the first principles of all things" (p. 261). On the other, it entailed overruling firmly held opinion however erroneous, and strongly committed belief however delusional. The neoconservatives concluded only "the rare theoretical men" should pursue enlightenment while providing the common people with something to believe in as a basis for self-improvement. This 'something' entails proclaiming a Plato-like noble lie: access to knowledge and governance for the few is *natural* because they have greater talent, expertise, virtue, merit and so on than the 'ordinary' person. Of course, the lie benefits the capitalist who, in a freely operating market, employs his or her *natural* business expertise in the pursuit of profits that are simply the result of giving people what they freely demand.

Neoconservatism, then, has the effect of maintaining the broad hierarchies of the social order benefitting those who already have wealth and privilege; while neoliberalism provides an economic argument justifying the accumulation of wealth as proof of being naturally talented, hard-working risk takers. So, between them the hierarchies are sustained. For the wealthy this double writing produces a 'heads I win (get wealthier), tails you lose (become poorer)' argument. For the rest of the population – faced with, for example, the power of wealth to influence laws, law enforcement, political parties, economic organisation and media discourses about what is real and true – what are their options? One can perhaps accept the prevailing order as 'natural', or cynically exploit it, or be resigned and apathetic to it, or challenge it.

## Collectively learning what is natural and what is not

Elite learning, as C. Wright Mills (2000) pointed out in his 1956 book *The Power Elite*, takes place quite separately to that of the common people. It is not just that elites go to the same schools, universities, clubs, churches and holiday locations but that their experience of what they have collectively in common is not challenged by coming into face-to-face contact with those who have no access to their wealth and privilege. For example, the *Johnson & Johnson* pharmaceutical heir Jamie Johnson, in his films *Born Rich* (Johnson, 2003) and *The One Percent* (Johnson, 2006) interviewed friends and parents from similarly wealthy families focusing on their experiences, their ways of life, their worries and what they wanted to do with their lives since none of them actually needed to work. In one telling early episode, *The One Percent* showed Johnson caught trying to film a game of croquet and being told that he should not do that. There was a sense of 'giving the game away' about this privileged world, a game that should be kept secret. However, it is in this secret world that decisions are made in privacy that impact upon ordinary lives in a world outside of it. Ideological discourses stand between the two worlds that have the purpose of naturalising their separation and, from this, justifying inequalities of wealth, power and privilege.

Key neoliberal tropes naturalising inequality include the self-made individual, the Atlas figure, and 'the invisible hand' of the market where 'true' values are created that arise spontaneously due to aggregate choices made by large numbers of buyers and suppliers so long as there are no distorting rules and regulations imposed by governments. In the market place, the private individual survives and thrives through hard work, natural talent and competitive risk taking. For Ayn Rand (1957), the best of such individuals are the self-made Atlas figures upon whose shoulders rests the world. Her circle of acolytes included Alan Greenspan who became the chair of the American Federal Reserve along with Treasury Secretary Robert Rubin and Larry Summers who held several economic posts including Chief Economist of the World Bank and Treasury Secretary. *Atlas Shrugged* and Rand's book *The Fountainhead* became the must-read books of the Silicon Valley generation of billionaires, Trump and many of his team as well as ministers in the Theresa May government (Freedland, 2017).

The Atlas trope is a figure capable of being refracted through the narratives of popular culture. There are the heroes and pioneers of the old west and, of course, the American Dream, the myth of 'self-made man' – and in contemporary times 'the self-made woman'. It was a phrase attributed to Henry Clay (1832: 20) during a speech in the Senate defending his idea of the 'American System' to unify and develop the nation arguing for protective tariffs – a focus given a contemporary flavour by Trump's 'America First' policy on tariffs in order to protect American business. Clay's American System was to be constructed through the self-made man in association with others working together under a 'superintending head'. The accumulation of wealth by individuals was then justified in terms of 'patient and diligent labour'. It is a myth, as Miller and Lapham (2012) point out, that underplays the collective actions of associations between people each contributing their knowledge, skills and imaginations. Thus this mythical idea of individuality and the 'self made' is in contrast with the 'built-together reality' of everyday life. It is precisely this 'built-together reality' that was deliberately undermined in Thatcher's (1987) interview with *Woman's Own* magazine when she sought to justify reducing the role of government in helping vulnerable people who cast "their problems on society and who is society? There is no such thing! There are individual men and women and there are families and no government can do anything except through people and people look to themselves first."

This fantasy world of individuals independently looking after themselves first as the basis of a self-sustaining moral economic order has been ratcheted up as a 'consensual hallucination' in the form of cyberspace. It was a term taken by Davidson and Rees-Mogg (1997) from William Gibson and used in their book *The Sovereign Individual* to explain that, as they saw it, the internet threatens big systems like the Welfare State and Nation States and thus investors had better be prepared for the world to come. In this new world of cyberspace – the fourth revolution – "The most obvious benefits will flow to the 'cognitive elite,' who will increasingly operate outside political boundaries" (p. 2). The image is not the Atlas figure of Rand shouldering the world but of Prometheus Unbound released from it, where:

> those who can educate and motivate themselves will be almost entirely free to invent their own work and realise the full benefits of their own productivity. Genius will be unleashed, freed from both the oppression of government and the drags of racial and ethnic prejudice.
>
> (p. 17–18)

It is a world where "the ideas you have in your head rather than physical capital alone, anyone who thinks clearly will potentially be rich" (p. 18). Such sovereignty will at first be achieved only by a few since it will, of course, depend upon 'full financial sovereignty' and there are not many who have or can get that kind of wealth. Those who achieve such sovereignty "will compete and interact on terms that echo the relations among the gods in Greek myth" (p. 50). The book has been a hit with the Silicon billionaires (O'Connell, 2018) who, of course, may be considered pioneer Sovereign Individuals. One such is Peter Thiel, founder of PayPal, investor in Facebook, an early supporter of Trump's campaign for the Presidency, who saw in democracy an enemy of capitalism (Thiel, 2009) because: "Since 1920, the vast increase in welfare beneficiaries and the extension of the franchise to women—two constituencies that are notoriously tough for libertarians—have rendered the notion of 'capitalist democracy' into an oxymoron." Thus the more people who are included in democratic decision-making, the less capitalists can continue to exist. Basically, someone has to be exploited, manipulated, deluded, otherwise who could stand apart as a Greek god? Essentially Thiel and his like want to escape the public and create a new space for their freedom to be gods in cyberspace, outer space or through 'seasteading' – that is colonising the irreal, the off-world and the sea; or, more practically, New Zealand where Thiel has bought property in the event of an apocalypse.

These new frontiers echo in part the old frontier myths of the west, of freedom, of being outside the political system, being a survivor and being self-made. To achieve it work has to be done politically, judicially, institutionally and educationally. It is largely a work of un-doing. What must be unmade, if the future is to be owned by the Sovereign Individuals, are the twentieth century's advances in democratic institutions, welfare and health. This was very much the programme put forward by a group of British politicians in their book *Britannia Unchained*. It presents a narrative of decline in the 1970s with a return to a revitalised business culture in the 1980s under Thatcherism then a return to decline from the crash of 2007 along with the growth of a 'dependency culture' supported by an inefficient welfare state, a state bureaucracy where "initiative and individual enterprise have been stifled by an obsession with rules, regulations and 'health and safety'" (Kwarteng et al., 2012). It contrasts this – along with the laziness of British workers – with a vision for a regenerated buccaneer risk-taking business culture. A call that was taken up by, amongst others, Jacob Rees-Mogg (2018), a conservative MP and leader of the anti-European factions in his party who was the son of the co-author of *The Sovereign Individual*. The call was for a return to the Thatcher policies that in their view had returned competitiveness to the economy not so much by "taking on the unions or liberalising the economy, but making Britain believe in itself again." Each of the authors helped bring about and consolidate a free market political ideology. They saw Brexit as the "opportunity finally to complete Margaret Thatcher's economic reforms three decades after they began" (Lawson, 2016). Their problem as capitalists, as neoconservatives and as neoliberals, was: how to ensure the mass continues to make them rich since it is so obviously against their interests to do so? The answer is a Straussian double writing, one for the masses and the other for the elite initiates. Thus, the collective learning of the masses – the un-sovereign individuals, the bounded – must be filtered, shaped, manufactured in ways that nationalistic undemocratic ideas seem inevitable, obvious, good while the demands for more competitiveness and risk are to be read as being in the interests of those masses who are hard working and

British. The elites can read the counter message in the light of the paradigm texts of the free marketeers.

## Rational risk, choice and the manufacture of false reality

The BBC documentaries of Adam Curtis (1992, 2011, 2016) illustrate the question of how corporations and politicians learnt to predict and shape public behaviour to make the 'right' choices. They are to be found, he said, in the methods developed to counter the fears aroused by the Soviet Union's early lead in the space race. It motivated the air force to fund scientists at the Rand corporation to solve the question of American security in the nuclear age by applying scientific method to the complexities of the world. In particular, they drew upon Von Neumann's developments in game theory to model choice making. As in a poker game, numerical values could be given according to what each player should rationally do in given circumstances. In Cold War logic this translated to sides composed of friends and enemies where each side had at least some information about the capacities of the other side to attack or defend. A scenario was then created that Albert Wohlstetter (1958) called the "delicate balance of terror" where it made no rational sense for either side to strike first. However, such rational calculation did not stand up well to the messiness of real life as shown by the Cuban Missile Crisis where threats of real war, real annihilation, placed fear above reason (Curtis, 1992, Ep. 2, 22.55).

That the strategists' theories were of little practical use in a real-time confrontation did not stop future presidents, such as President Johnson, continuing to draw on scientific studies to solve highly complex social and political problems. Indeed, even in the Vietnam War, as Adam Curtis put it, "their methods had been used to create a fiction. The scientific approach had been corrupted to preserve the politicians' power." It was done by rigging the figures that were entered as data to fit was was supposed to happen according to the model (Curtis, 1992, Ep. 2, 33.24). The construction of the fiction – which is perhaps the modern version of the noble lie – was conceived to reassure the American public. It continued through Reagan's 'Star Wars' programme where science fiction writers were a part of the team employed to make the ideas understandable. The technology did not work but the results were presented as if they did.

In the everyday world of economics, the same methods were then applied to construct a science of money. As Friedman said of his approach:

> It was scientific. Inflation was not a Communist phenomenon. It's not a Capitalist phenomenon. It's a printing press phenomenon. That's a scientific statement. And you will only have inflation if the quantity of money increases more rapidly than output. You can only stop inflation by slowing down the rate of monetary growth.
>
> (Curtis, 1992, Ep. 3, 15.43)

The key influence under Thatcher and Reagan in these developments was Buchanan's (Buchanan and Tullock, 1962) contribution to public choice theory for which he received the Nobel Prize in 1986. Essentially, for it to work, people would need to be placed into conditions where they had something of importance to them that was at stake. That something was property. For this he drew on Friedrich Hayek and John C. Calhoun, slave owner and vice president of the USA (1825–1832) for whom having freedom meant having property. Thus as Buchanan and Tullock argue, democracy is best supported by a property-owning public because having property interests means their political interests in terms of what is economically at stake in making one choice rather than another can be given a measurable value and thus calculated. Hence it makes sense for rational expectation theory to argue for a property-owning democracy. There were good precedents in enabling it to be acceptable. Jackson (2012a), for example, points out that conservative politicians began to use this phrase from the 1920s. In 1975, Thatcher indeed employed it in her first speech as leader of the conservative party:

> Let me give you my vision: a man's right to work as he will, to spend what he earns, to own property, to have the State as servant and not as master – these are the British inheritance. They are the essence of a free country and on that freedom all our other freedoms depend.

This was an anti-egalitarian vision having the purpose of driving privatisation and undermining the welfare state. However, it could also be sold as social justice. Rawls, for example, called upon a property-owning democracy but as a way of moving towards a more politically egalitarian society. Nevertheless, it was Buchanan's game theoretic approach that provided a quasi-scientific justification. His ideas

> had a huge impact, especially in America and in Britain, where it inspired the public sector reforms undertaken by Margaret Thatcher, John Major and Tony Blair, all of whom were committed to the concept of challenging the old public sector elites.
>
> (Telegraph Obituary, 2013)

The idea was attractive to politicians because "One of the great advantages of an essentially economic approach to collective action lies in the implicit recognition that 'political exchange,' at all levels, is basically equivalent to economic exchange" (Buchanan and Tullock, 1962: 182). His model thus opened the possibility of controlling the public through economic manipulation. But not just any old public. Hence, Buchanan and Tullock (1962: 247) approvingly quoted Lippmann from the 1961 *Washington Post*, who wrote that in a democracy "The crux of the question is not whether the majority should rule but what kind of majority should rule". That majority should be property owning since they would make rational choices according to the impacts of policies and party political programmes on the value of their property.

Friedman saw Thatcher's turn to monetarism as a brave experiment (Curtis, 1992, Ep. 3). However, within 13 months there were factory closures, unemployment had risen substantially, so had inflation (Ep. 3, 29.20) – and so had the money supply, a result, according to Friedman's monetary theory, that was supposed to be impossible. Nevertheless, despite what was happening in the real economy, Thatcher confirmed her belief in monetary theory in her speech at the Press Association Annual Lunch, June 11, 1980, because it was scientific and so "it is as fundamental as the law of gravity, and you cannot avoid it". None of the problems were due to the theory. This was emphasised by Sir Keith Joseph, one of the architects of the Thatcher policy, who was clear in his conscience that rises in unemployment were not his fault because "negotiators and employers were destroying their jobs by not following rational expectations" (Ep. 3, 33.08). Even though it was increasingly obvious that monetarism did not work the government's response to the problems was to "take an enormous amount of money out of economy" (Sir John Hoskyns, Chief Policy advisor to Margaret Thatcher 1979–82 – see Ep. 3, 34.35). The only way they could do this was by cutting public expenditure. The impact on unemployment was to push it above 3 million in 1982 and:

> The number of people out of work reached a peak of officially 3.4 million in January 1986. However, considering that in the 1980s numerous changes had been made in the way the official unemployment statistics were calculated, the real picture was bleaker still.
>
> (Barlow, 2008: 78)

The UK 'experiment' in monetarism, as Friedman called it, had failed. Thatcher expressly denied ever having employed monetarist theory during an interview with Peter Jay on Channel 4's *A Week In Politics*, February 1, 1985, saying "It's not a doctrine to which I've ever subscribed" (Thatcher, 1985).

If efforts at planning and control through the manipulation of the money supply did not work, then there was little else to do but as in neoliberal theory let the market itself decide. In short, monetarism slipped into neoliberalism, by hiding just below the name change. The key 'rational' step was to de-regulate in order to free up the City of London finance houses to play on the stock exchange. Thatcher lauded the young dealers:

> The City's growing confidence and drive owe a good deal to young people. Its vast new dealing rooms are run by the young. People who made it not because of who they know or what school tie they wear, but on sheer merit. That is the kind of society I want to see. Gone are the controls which hampered success.
>
> (Thatcher, 1986)

These were the 'new' self-made people pioneers leading the way in the 'financial experiment' as it might be called. Its focus on youth, merit and risk-taking dynamism, however, did not prevent youth unemployment passing one million in 1986 – a level not achieved again until 2011 (Bowater, 2011) under David Cameron's conservative-led coalition government that came into power following the lingering impacts of the financial crisis in 2008. Rather than reform the money markets, and end the experiment, the government employed a policy of austerity focusing on reducing the public sector by privatising it. The policy of – or indeed 'experiment' in – austerity remained a central feature until the political impasse of the populist 'experiments' of Brexit and the market unpredictabilities of Trumpism stole the attention of media commentators.

Overall, the period from Healey's acceptance of the International Monetary Fund's demands in December 1976 to Trump's presidency in January 20, 2017 saw over 40 years of various flavours of market, corporate, monetarist and neo-liberal driven experimentation where exploitation by the very rich brought about an ever-increasing gap between the global rich and the rest of the world's populations (Haseler, 2000; West, 2014). They created a world whose corporate power is highly networked (Coghlan and MacKenzie, 2011), is capable of setting political agendas (Cronin, 2013; Drutman, 2015) and uses 'dark money' – that is, money the source of which is kept hidden – to influence elections and political decision-making (Mayer, 2016).

Too often the counter hope, as Zizek (2013) put it, is for a Thatcher of the Left. But when it happens, the global networks, the corporate-friendly laws and economic grip on national and local economies turn those hopes to frustration, disappointment and resentment. Indeed, the hope that had been placed in Obama to break the neoliberal grip on society was, as could be predicted (Roberts and Schostak, 2012), ended with a triumphant Trump, where "We are witnessing the postmodern version of the full-scale gangsterization of the world" (West, 2017).

It seems as if nothing had been learnt in those 40 years. But of course, that is not true. It could be argued that the kind of learning Robert Lowe had in mind in campaigning for mass education that led to the 1870 Education Act, has worked very well. Rather than free collective learning, the masses had to be taught to recognise their superiors and defer to their knowledge. Even if this is now long recoded in the language of self-made wealth from 'merit', 'hard work' and 'talent' rather than inherited wealth and privilege it is still the case that formal state education does not lead to significant social mobility (Marsh, 2011; Blacker, 2013), nor does it break down the inherently hierarchical system of elites, their managers, their police and their workers. Nor does it, in its neoconservative and neoliberal colours, intend to, where choice continues to be gamed in the favour of the rich and powerful.

## What other choice is there?

The whole effort of the billionaire class has long been to replace free democratic choice with the choiceless choice of: no other choice. Robert Morris, who was a financier of the American Revolution, saw the dangers of democracy and sought to tame it by "taking control of the government"; he argued that gentlemen should use it "to enrich themselves", and then scale it back "so it did not threaten their interests". He did not give his plan a name, but with his belief that it would bring "Salvation", it is fitting to call Morris's programme the "gospel of moneyed men" (Bouton, 2007: 70). This gospel of the moneyed men can be seen in operation through Jane Mayer's (2010; 2016) investigation into billionaires', notably the Koch brothers, covert funding of a 'war against Obama'. More damningly it can be seen in MacLean's (2017) discoveries of papers revealing the deep connection between Buchanan's work on choice theory and the billionaire Koch family's funding of his work.

In the post-politics, post-democracy consensus that grew following the fall of the Soviet menace, the focus turned increasingly to policy delivery (Barber, 2007). In short, how can they remove choice? That effectively was the upshot of Sunstein and Thaler's nudge theory:

> A nudge, as we will use the term, is any aspect of the choice architecture that alters people's behaviour in a predictable way without forbidding any options or significantly changing their economic incentives. To count as a mere nudge, the intervention must be easy and cheap to avoid. Nudges are not mandates. Putting the fruit at eye level counts as a nudge. Banning junk food does not.
> 
> (Sunstein and Thaler, 2009: 6)

A "choice architecture" involves the design of a multiplicity of small steps that increase the chances of making the 'right' decision by breaking up complex decisions into simplified parts or by providing default options that effectively do the thinking for them. The architecture of nudges is constructed to provide feedback about consequences and, in particular, error is to be expected so options for correction are built in. It sounds simple. At its heart they are 'incentives'. Indeed, Obama, who knew Cass Sunstein the co-author of *Nudge* from his student days, appointed him as "'regulatory tsar' in his government in 2008" (Halpern, 2015).

The ideas expressed in the book were persuasive enough for David Cameron in 2010 to set up the Behavioural Insight Team of the UK Cabinet Office, otherwise known as the 'nudge unit' (Halpern, 2015). It was to be an experiment in government – an experiment that essentially did not have any need for a critically reflective public, just one suggestible enough to be 'nudged'. It was an approach that concentrated on policy issues such as how to get people to pay their tax, put insulation in their houses, pay motoring fines. They demonstrated "how small changes in processes, or even just the wording of letters, led to significant shifts in outcomes. More tax collected; more homes insulated; and more fines paid. And the cost? Almost nothing" (Halpern, 2015: 4). The trick to accomplish this was simple, as in the case of collecting more tax they put in a sentence that was true: "most people pay their tax on time" (p. 4). It led to an increase in the payment of millions in tax. But what if a sentence is delivered that stretches the truth, or is not true, or is even pure fantasy?

While the nudge unit might plausibly claim success in delivering policy impact, outside of the nudge-fuelled fantasy, unemployment and cuts in welfare continued to increase the sense of precarity. A weakened Trade Union movement since the Thatcher governments, along with weakened employment rights, meant that employers could increasingly offer 'zero hour contracts' to a rising 'self-employed' workforce – the 'precariat' as Standing (2011) called them. His book was subtitled "The new dangerous class" – a reference that harks back to the nineteenth-century fears of the masses picked up in the title of Frégier's (1840) book on the cities of France and later the American Brace's (1872) book on his work in New York. This neatly sets up the contrast between a nudge world where all was working well and that of a precarious world where nothing worked well and people were made anxious and resentful by constant austerity measures. There was then a 'hidden' constituency who could with legitimacy feel aggrieved at being let down by politicians in favour of their fancy whizz kids in the city. In what did their 'choice architecture' consist? What if the statements pushed to this constituency were not a 'truth' designed by Cameron's and Obama's nudgers but more like Trump's (1987: 58) truthful hyperbole? Or indeed, downright lies, or bullshit? Through such strategies Kristol's (1995: 359–363) 'new populism' could quite easily become a 'ploy', an experiment, as it were, in populism (McCormack, 2017).

The constant grooming of opinion, or what Lippmann called the manufacture of consent, could easily be turned against the liberal elites who Kristol (1995: 378–379) defined as the enemy. Yet, the neoconservatives were themselves elites. Thus the anger of the poor could quite as easily be directed at them. To deal with this required a Straussian stealth-like strategy of double writing. It was precisely this, that the billionaire Koch brothers employed in their adoption of Buchanan's choice theory:

> In his first big gift to Buchanan's program, Charles Koch signalled his desire for the work he funded to be conducted behind the backs of the majority. "Since we are greatly outnumbered," Koch conceded to the assembled team, the movement could not win simply by persuasion. Instead, the cause's insiders had to use their knowledge of "the rules of the game"—that game being how modern democratic governance works—"to create winning strategies."
> (MacLean, 2017: xxii)

Collective learning as an enterprise managed by stealth has a long history in the mainstream popular media promoting right-wing views on trade unions, social class, gender, immigration, enemies of the state, and the traditional values underpinning national identity that excludes the languages, faiths, beliefs and practices of newcomers. The campaigns of Bernays (1928; Tye, 1998) in particular became the model for corporations, political parties, networks and pressure groups in what the BBC documentary by Adam Curtis called *The Century of the Self* (Curtis, 2002).

Broadly speaking, technologies have been produced that are capable of providing the material support – effectively the curriculum materials for the masses – designed to present 'choice architectures' that influence behaviour. It is schooling by grooming values, opinions and behaviours – a form of taming, or dressage of the masses. The architecture to shape collective learning works simultaneously at individual, family, community, national and global levels to present a world where individuals are alone, competing to maximise their interests in rigged markets and can do nothing to change these 'realities'. These are stealth architectures (Schostak, 1999; 2002; 2006) that reveal only a very minimal surface presenting an apparent set of choices for the masses, but like a stealth bomber, conceal the power within to accumulate wealth for elites. A contemporary example would be the algorithms in computer programs that enable high-frequency trading in the stock market (Lewis, 2015). These are essentially instructions – that is, automated choice architectures – about when to buy and sell that can be undertaken faster than human capacities. Indeed, they can be used to make markets when there are none, forcing up prices in order to skim profits even before any actual money has been transferred. However, computer advances have a siren-like lure attracting speculators with the promise of great benefits that come from great computing power "that out-computes everyone else on the network, and seems to grant its owners a guaranteed path to unbounded success at first. But the benefits are illusory, and lead to a grand failure before too long" (Lanier, 2013: xiii). Similarly, the advent of social media had a stealth architecture that both provided opportunities for friendships as well as exploitation of the data associated with those friendships whether for the marketing of products and services or for politically motivated campaigns. In all forms of networked stealth architecture, their power resides in computational power across networks, the consequences of which exceed the more limited purposes for which they were apparently constructed. In short, whether constructed to serve neoliberal market or neoconservative nationalist interests it uses an architecture formed of rational control and processing technologies, rigged to shape collective learning and action against working towards the free and equal interests of all; and in doing so, it potentially risks a meltdown of unintended consequences.

Both the Brexit and Trump campaigns, for example, were able to draw upon the decades of anti-immigrant discourses conditioned by leading right-wing media. Racism, as Van Dijk (1992, 2008) showed, was re-positioned by learning the discourse of 'I'm not racist but ...' and 'it's not racist to be concerned about immigration ... it's common sense'. As leader of the Conservative party, Michael Howard brought the immigration as common sense rhetoric back into the mainstream (Howard, 2005) that Cameron continued (Cameron, 2011), and May turned this into the policy of the 'hostile environment' (Travis, 2013), destroying the lives of many families in the process who had the right to live in the UK but did not have the papers to prove it. In his Presidential campaign Trump demanded the building of a wall (Trump, 2016) as a common-sense strategy and temporarily banned people from seven Muslim-majority countries and all refugees entering the USA (Diamond and Almasy, 2017). Any objection to such policies on the grounds of infringements of human rights or charges of racism could be developed as an 'us' versus 'them' politics. On the side of 'us' would be common sense, and on the side of 'them' would be liberals with their multicultural, politically correct (PC) discourses, values and laws that in the view of 'us' led to an immigration crisis that took away jobs and 'threatened our way of life'.

Political correctness was a term invented by the conservative right wing, it can be argued (Weigel, 2016), to cover all liberalising attempts from attacks on sexist and racist language to laws on health and safety and human rights. The 'us' in this discourse referred to the 'ordinary person' or more precisely 'the common man' since to use 'person' in that context would be an example of being PC and to use 'man' would, in its common sense meaning as a general term, include 'woman'. Such re-positionings enable a silent Straussian-style reading, privileging traditional gender, racial, social hierarchies. Thus a strong and pervasive choice architecture formed around the binary axes of 'friend–enemy', 'us–them', 'common sense–PC' and 'common man–liberal elite' was over a long time persistently, discursively constructed for the shaping of collective learning. This could be operationalised both openly and stealthily where the key question – whether asked explicitly or implicitly – framing immediate choices concerning any issue impacting on daily life is: whose side are you on? Learning whose side you are on is critical – for jobs, standard of living, quality of life and health.

It was a discursive architecture that the online right-wing media site Breitbart was central in articulating:

> Our own study of over 1.25 million stories published online between April 1, 2015 and Election Day shows that a right-wing media network anchored around Breitbart developed as a distinct and insulated media system, using social media as a backbone to transmit a hyper-partisan perspective to the world. This pro-Trump media sphere appears to have not only successfully set the agenda for the conservative media sphere, but also strongly influenced the broader media agenda, in particular coverage of Hillary Clinton.
> (Benkler et al., 2017)

Providing the funding behind Breitbart and the Trump and Brexit media campaigns were a few billionaires, one of whom was Robert Mercer. The Guardian journalist Carole Cadwalladr began investigations into the complex networks of relationship that focused around Mercer, Breitbart, Bannon, the Trump campaign, the Leave campaign, social media and data analytics companies (Cadwalldr, 2017; 2017a; 2017b; 2017c). Although presented as a sophisticated use of data processing to precisely target audiences, it was not the sophistication that mattered because "The underbelly of it is sowing doubt in people's minds and reinforcing their prejudices. The method was messaging, constant iteration and the testing of it" (Tucker, 2018). The neoliberal stealth strategies for the management of collective learning appeared to have paid off at least in the success of Trump, Brexit and the rise of extreme right-wing parties across Europe.

What would it take to change this and create a real choice to achieve social justice for all? Even if the left employs the media to subvert the right's use of it, it still reinforces the architectures of consent, choice, and belief deployed by the right wing; only in the opposite direction. It is thus in this game of whose side are you on, down to who has the better campaign strategy targeting the underbelly of prejudices. Surely there are better options than this?

## What is missing?

For a liberalism that seeks freedom through a radical inclusivity, everything must be 'transparent', 'in the open' that is, on the surface of all public debates. The more open the systems of decision-making, the more democratic the forms of organisation. That is what is missing from the rational choice and the stealth architectures designed to deliver targeted messages to manufacture consent and nudge behaviours. Democratic organisation is what is missing in the vast majority of organisations whether in the private or the public domains that impact upon everyday lives. Rather than, whose side are you on, the choice structure is shifted to the issue of: how do I get my voice heard and counted in decision-making?

The question then, for those whose freedom has been circumscribed, whose thoughts and behaviours have been the subject of manipulation, coercion and discipline is: are there alternative forms of organisation whether at home, in the community, at work or in the open public that provide the freedoms to participate in the decisions that impact on my life?

# Chapter 4

# The organisation and disorganisation of power

There is a crisis of power, whether for those who do not have any or those who have too much and fear losing it. There is something fragile about great power, particularly in a world of wars, protests, revolutions and likely environmental breakdowns, where the global rich are outnumbered by many millions to one. Rushkoff tells of the fears that became apparent during a meeting called by several billionaires:

> Finally, the CEO of a brokerage house explained that he had nearly completed building his own underground bunker system and asked: "How do I maintain authority over my security force after the Event?"
>
> The Event. That was their euphemism for the environmental collapse, social unrest, nuclear explosion, unstoppable virus, or Mr Robot hack that takes everything down.
>
> This single question occupied us for the rest of the hour. They knew armed guards would be required to protect their compounds from the angry mobs. But how would they pay the guards once money was worthless? What would stop the guards from choosing their own leader? The billionaires considered using special combination locks on the food supply that only they knew. Or making guards wear disciplinary collars of some kind in return for their survival. Or maybe building robots to serve as guards and workers – if that technology could be developed in time.
>
> (Rushkoff, 2018)

This is an extreme expression consistent with Ayn Rand's philosophy of individual survival and greed – the paradigm of the silicon billionaires, the financiers who see themselves as the masters of the world, or the media moguls who want mastery over public perception and opinion (Das, 2011) or, like Lloyd Blankfein when CEO of Goldman Sachs, believe they are doing God's work (Arlidge, 2009). Rushcroft, however, in his face-to-face with the masters of the universe sees a world where "Technology development became less a story of collective flourishing than personal survival" (Rushkoff, 2018). There are then two stories here to unpack: the first is of what has been called the Californian ideology, a collective flourishing; and the second, its collapse into cynicism and self-preservation. These two stories were arguably first outlined by Barbrook and Cameron (1995).

The first is a story of 1960s radicals in California and the emergence of a hybridised ideology composed of a medley of sources. These were essentially utopian dreams that included the psychedelic culture of drugs, particularly the perception-altering LSD. Gregory Bateson was an early devotee who in his writings on ecology drew on the idea of feedback circuits whereby the natural world would, if not interfered with, create its own balance (edmundberger, 2013). The drug seemed to offer the possibility of opening the mind to deconstructing old patterns of behaviour and ways of seeing and stimulating innovation. The old ways of seeing were no longer the only reality. This he thought could be applied to a rethinking of schizophrenia. It led him to the idea of the double bind to explain how schizophrenia is socially constructed from two opposing instructions given at the same time. Birdwhistel (1973) illustrated this through a detailed analysis of the videoed behaviour of a schizophrenic mother changing the nappy of her baby. To put the nappy on the baby he had to part his legs. However, every time he did so, following the instruction to open them, the mother gave a slight slap which made the baby close his legs thus preventing the nappy from being placed. Within a few seconds the baby was in an impasse, unable to satisfy either instruction but having to do both. This was interpreted as a process of learning to become schizophrenic. The task was to unlearn. More generally, it was about unlearning or ridding oneself of the authorities whose inconsistencies and demands push individuals into untenable positions, personified by members of a family as much as by the traditional authorities represented by police, teachers and as Rhodes-Boyson, a paternalistic conservative UK politician in Thatcher's government, put it, park keepers. In Rhodes-Boyson's view, the old representatives of authority were under threat and if nothing was done, then society would 'reap the whirlwind'. The battle was internalised in the popular psychologies. As advocated by David Cooper (1971), for example, to be free of the past one has to get one's family out of one's head. That is to say, in his view we carry around dramatic personae of family members each having a view about us, each having their expectations of us. These may be positive or negative but they all influence behaviour, whether inhibiting or encouraging. However, to gain full agency of oneself required their radical removal from the inner world. Thus the popularised psychologies of the New Age which along with counter cultural drugs, particularly LSD, could be used to shape ways of thinking, behaving and perceiving according to one's own agency. Popular youth culture mixed psychotherapy, anti-psychiatry, fun, sex, drugs and mysticism to produce a hybridised culture of individuality and self-help and creativity. Whether drawing on Eastern meditation or shamanism, as popularised by the drugs and mysticism narratives of Carlos Castaneda in his inner journeys, or the Transcendental Meditation of Maharishi Mahesh Yogi made famous by The Beatles pop group, or the Zen of Alan Watts at the Esalen Institute, the revolution was essentially a process of recreating one's self and making one's own world free from the repressive regimes of authorities at home, at work and in politics.

In Mouffe's (2018) agonistic political theory, it can be said that a frontier was to be drawn between the old and the new age of possibilities. The forms of organisation on either side were fundamentally different. On the one side, these differences in organisation were articulated along lines of conformity to the traditional and corporate forms of authority and discipline; on the other, it was both an inner and outer struggle against subordination to these forms. Where the inner struggle was manifest in trying to free oneself from the authorities as inner demons as it were, the outer struggle was manifest in sexual freedom, feminism, anti-racism and black power movements as well as the 'drop-out' egalitarian lifestyles of communes and the search for gurus who could lead people into a freer, more fulfilling way of life. To some extent this accords with Mouffe's approach to political analysis:

> The struggle against forms of subordination cannot be the direct result of the situation of subordination itself. For relations of subordination to be transformed into sites of an antagonism, one needs the presence of a discursive 'exterior' from which the discourse of subordination can be interrupted. This is precisely what the democratic discourse has made possible.

Thus in this logic, the New Age philosophies and movements found their 'discursive exterior' in the promises of freedom through self-creation and new multicultural worlds of greater equality between all persons could be created. However, since for Mouffe liberty and equality are always in tension with each other, there is always the possibility of creating a political frontier between the two as in the case of Hayek's disdain for the egalitarian aspirations of socialism or Rand's glorification of freedom founded upon individual greed. And the emergence of new technologies seemed to open up the space where all was possible.

The model of cybernetic feedback, where systems could be constructed that learnt through positive and negative feedback, could be applied to the world's ecology as a complex feedback system that, if there was no outside interference, would keep itself in balance as say between predators and prey. James Lovelock's Gaia principle, for example, viewed the earth as a single organism which, left alone, would keep itself in harmony. In short, through a principle of laissez-faire, ecotopia could be achieved. As Curtis (2011) comments, this was simply untrue. Later research showed the natural world to be dynamic with no homeostatic point of equilibrium. Moreover, with the turn to the radical neoliberal and neoconservative politics of Thatcher and Reagan, the dreams of a self-regulating market turned sour creating the conditions for economic crises and increasing inequalities. But all was not lost. At least not for the pioneers of Silicon Valley. They could transplant the dreams into the digital realm creating a new realm of self-organising networks outside of political interference. For them, as Rhode (2018) put it: "It was a religious creed. Its central tenet was uncomplicated: the machines would fix everything." In particular, the World Wide Web provided an infrastructure for self-organising networks where there is no centre, no leader thus disrupting mainstream discourses of hierarchy. Illustrating this, Curtis (2011) gave an anecdote of Emily Maitlis interviewing Lucy Annson, a member of the UK Uncut movement:

> Annson swiftly opened the door that leads to the nightmare interview, saying: "We are a network of people who self-organise. We don't have a position on things. It's about empowering the individual to go out there and be creative."
> "But is it wrong for individuals to attack buildings?" asked Maitlis.
> "You'd have to ask that particular individual," replied Annson.
> "But you are a spokesperson for UK UnCut," insisted Maitlis. And Annson came out with a wonderful line: "No. I'm a spokesperson for myself."

Curtis saw in this interview exchange the implicit if not explicit erosion of the political, that is, in his terms the problem of assuming the chosen form of organisation presumes there is no issue of power in relationships since the system itself will bring about a natural resolution. His BBC documentary, *All Watched Over by Machines of Loving Grace*, described the fate of experimental communities that were founded on egalitarian principles, that excluded leadership roles and assumed the system self regulates. They did not, many ending in recriminations. More significant than odd experiments in counter culture which may simply signify simplistic acceptance of poorly thought out beliefs, has been the persistence of free market assumptions that an unregulated market self-regulates not despite but because it is driven by the greed of individuals. In Ayn Rand's highly influential first novel, *The Fountainhead*, the lead character portrayed an individual whose life was guided only by his own selfish desires. It expressed her philosophy that she called 'objectivism' in which she created what she proclaimed was a new code of morality,

> a morality not based on some arbitrary edict, mythical or social. I hold that if men want to live on earth his highest moral purpose is the achievement of his own happiness. And that he must not force other people nor accept their right to force him, that each man must live as an end in himself and follow his own rational self interests.
> (Curtis, 2011, Ep. 1, 2.57)

As one of the members of her circle, Barbara Branden, enthused:

> We are heroic, we can know the world, we can tame nature, we can achieve our goals, we can do what we, what we want. What does it matter that we're alone? Who do we need? Why do we need anyone? We have ourselves.
> (Curtis, 2011, Ep. 1, 4.20)

This was a narrative that seemed to accord with the aspirations of the young entrepreneurs who did not share the egalitarian ground up dreams of early internet innovators:

> The original mission of the Internet was hijacked by a small group of right-wing radicals to whom the ideas of democracy and decentralization were anathema. By the late 1980s, starting with eventual PayPal founder Peter Thiel's class at Stanford University, the dominant philosophy of Silicon Valley would be based far more heavily on the radical libertarian ideology of Ayn Rand than the commune-based principles of Ken Kesey and Stewart Brand.
>
> (Taplin, 2017: 19–20)

Where the early discourse of the internet innovators was of decentralisation, that of the readers of Ayn Rand was of monopolisation through the creation of platforms through which content and communications was to be mediated and revenues created through advertising and the selling of personal data. And in that way they built the digital empires of Silicon Valley creating the conditions for a global technological dominance while promoting the belief that in doing this they were benefitting all. In the writings of Rand were a readymade narrative of the entrepreneur as god and a philosophy where one could be a greedy individual in a self-organising network and all would be well because the system would find its own equilibrium. In short, you could have your cake and eat it. It justified them in making a grab for wealth in the new opened-up digital machine frontiers without having to worry about issues of equality. Davidson and Rees-Mogg (1997) argue that we are now at the beginnings of the fourth industrial revolution, the Information Age, and that in order to be prepared the rich must become 'sovereign individuals'. In short, the sovereign individual is dependent upon nobody and independent of the State. Only great wealth would enable this to come about. Their book became essential reading for the Silicon Valley billionaires fearful of a coming apocalypse (O'Connell, 2018) and looking to create their own self-sufficient world. One could at least be sovereign and hold the promise that all could become sovereign. If individuals failed it was due to a lack of merit, talent or hard work. After all, the argument went, everyone had the opportunity in the new fields to make a mark if they wanted. Meritocracy, the self-made man or woman, individual sovereignty of the Davidson and Rees-Mogg kind and social mobility are, however, myths (Dorling, 2015; Miller and Lapham, 2012). What is covered over and ignored are the background historical legacies of resources, infrastructures, knowledge and skills that create the conditions for present and future action, dependency upon knowledgeable workers, and the sharing of ideas that are involved in any community where ideas and practices are developing.

This background of legacies is repressed by the narrative of the sovereign individual who moreover wants nothing, particularly the politics of democracy, to stand in the way:

> The 1920s were the last decade in American history during which one could be genuinely optimistic about politics. Since 1920, the vast increase in welfare beneficiaries and the extension of the franchise to women – two constituencies

that are notoriously tough for libertarians – have rendered the notion of "capitalist democracy" into an oxymoron.

In the face of these realities, one would despair if one limited one's horizon to the world of politics. I do not despair because I no longer believe that politics encompasses all possible futures of our world. In our time, the great task for libertarians is to find an escape from politics in all its forms – from the totalitarian and fundamentalist catastrophes to the unthinking demos that guides so-called "social democracy".

(Thiel, 2009)

Clearly, Thiel is not writing for the "unthinking demos" – or for women! His audience is the billionaires who will have the wealth to follow him into his vision of libertarian domains built on artificial islands or in near-earth orbits outside of the jurisdiction of the politics of any nation state. However, Thiel and other billionaires saw in the Trump and the Brexit campaigns a chance to escape from democratic politics. In particular, Thiel saw in Trump

> a disruptor-in-chief who will destroy a dying system and build a better one in its place. Trump isn't just a flamethrower for torching a rotten establishment, however – he's the fulfilment of Thiel's desire to build a successful political movement for less democracy.
>
> (Tarnoff, 2016)

In this logic, the authoritarian Trump disciplines the "unthinking demos" through his populist racism and his anti-liberal elite rhetoric while the state

> bankrolls scientific research at midcentury cold war levels – without the comparatively high tax rates and social spending that accompanied it. Corporations would mine this research for profitable inventions. The public would foot the bill and ask for nothing in return.
>
> (Tarnoff, 2016)

In the works of Rand, Thiel sees himself as the Atlas, or as in the book that Thiel admired by Davidson and Rees-Mogg (1997), sees himself as a 'sovereign individual' preparing for the fourth industrial revolution. In an echo of his father the leading Brexiteer Jacob Rees-Mogg (2018) sees Brexit as a strategy to embed the 'fourth industrial revolution': Big Data. His call for sovereignty is essentially a call for the sovereignty of the very rich able to exploit and navigate the new political and economic frontiers opened up by the 'fourth revolution' where there is the free flow of data, but of course, not of people. Thus, for example, Rees-Mogg has opened an outlet for his hedge fund in the European base of Ireland and advises clients to take their money out of the UK due to Brexit uncertainty while demanding 'sovereignty' to control immigration and close borders to unwanted people.

The accumulation of wealth by these potentially 'sovereign individuals' straddling sovereign domains has been aided in other domains by neoliberal demands for the privatisation of public sector organisations under the name of 'efficiency'. Hence both Thiel and Rees-Mogg have accused the 'socialism' of the public sector of being a burden on entrepreneurs, inhibiting the efficiency of the market. Such views impact upon politics and thus democracy not just nationally, but globally. According to a report by Oxfam (2017) just eight people currently have as much wealth as half the world. What happens if half the world decides to object? More importantly, why

In Rushkoff's (2018) encounter with the fearful global rich there is thus another story: if there is such potential for a crisis and such a fear of the masses – that is, the little people - why has there been no, or at least so little, effective mass action to overthrow the tiny numbers of extraordinarily rich families who have control over so much when so many have so little? Part of the answer has already been discussed in terms of what went wrong with democracy, education and wider forms of collective learning. However, it is still a puzzle. It can only happen if the mass of 'little people' let the much fewer 'big people' win. Why do they do this?

## The power of the master and the organisation of voluntary servitude

It is equality that is the truly radical edge of democracy, as de Tocqueville (1863: 67) recognised:

> It is impossible to believe that equality will not finally penetrate as much into the political world as into other domains. It is not possible to conceive of men as eternally unequal among themselves on one point, and equal on others; at a certain moment, they will come to be equal on all points.

Yet, inequality is everywhere driven by obedience to masters. What went wrong?

The question of mass obedience to the few exercised the mind of de la Boétie (1552). As he showed, although it can be analysed in terms of hierarchical control whether by reward or by coercion, there is also the puzzling question of freely given subjection to a 'lord', 'master', 'leader', 'hero', 'deity', or a 'celebrity'; as well as subjection to more abstract ideals defined as 'duty', 'righteousness' and 'love' in relation to 'tradition', 'culture', 'the people', or more recently the 'country' or the 'state'. The exercise of brutal power, La Boetie recognised, is in itself insufficient to ensure the maintenance of a social order. Voluntary servitude however, he argued, is fundamental to the organisation of Power in all its forms. Without it, the few could not rule the multitude. And no one would become a billionaire.

Underlying voluntary servitude is the fatal love – or awe, or jouissance in Lacan's terms – of leadership in all its modalities: celebrity, hero, role model, captain of industry, boss, monarch, tyrant, demagogue – and their translation into saints, idols, gods. The love and awe of each modality is a tack, a securing point – *le point de capiton*, in Lacan's terms – holding down the always potentially drifting components or fabrics of a social order so that it forms a sensuous way of seeing that counts as real and excludes the possibility of challenging that perceived reality. This sensuous way of seeing, Rancière (2004) called 'the police':

> The police is not a social function but a symbolic constitution of the social. The essence of the police lies neither in repression nor even in control over the living. Its essence lies in a certain way of dividing up the sensible. I call 'distribution of the sensible' a generally implicit law that defines the forms of partaking by first defining the modes of perception in which they are inscribed.
>
> (Rancière, 2001)

In a quite literal sense, those who have high levels of wealth see a different world than those who have insufficient to pay for food. Unless deliberate decisions are made by the rich, those who have wealth do not have contact with the worlds of the poor. Protected from sorry sights inside gated communities the world looks good. The aesthetics, as it were, of the rich and the poor are different but also depend on each other. The trick then is to maintain that this distribution of the sensible is inevitable.

Combining the 'police' in its symbolic role in terms of dividing up the ways in which society is seen, heard, felt, sensed with the organisation of the police in its narrower form as law enforcement, voluntary servitude is put to work in the interests of elites where there is also the pleasure, the thrill, the taste of being on the side of organised power, the side, as Warren Buffet (Stein, 2006) put it, that is winning the war of the classes; or, indeed, the war of cultures (Huntington, 1996), the war of faiths, the war of skin colour – or more abstractly, the war of ideas (Kristol, 1995; 2011). It is when politics is divided perceptually in terms of distinguishing 'friends' (who sound, look and act like 'me') and enemies (who are foreign to my ways of being in the world) that people can best be bound and – according to their circumstances, interests and excitements – their sides chosen, however freely or imposed is the case. Once 'chosen', each side demands a collective enthusiasm in procuring the ends of that side, as well as the sense of personal propriety involved in minding your own business, not getting actively involved in the personal affairs of others, particularly when it involves criticism of the powerful. Without voluntary servitude and personal propriety, governance by masters at the top of great hierarchies is impossible. As such it must be seen to be the only possible reality, that is, in the Thatcher-Reagan-Bush formula: there is no alternative. If this is true, then there is no longer a need for democracy. There is only a need for the management of society through the principles of technocratic reason. Its fullest expression is in 'corporatism'.

Historically, corporatism referred to Mussolini's fascist integration of the state with corporate power. Schmitter (1974), in a review of the term, attempted to provide an account of corporatism that would purge it of its pejorative connotations and render it a useful academic tool for political analysis. He defines it as "a system of interest and/or attitude representation, a particular modal or ideal-typical institutional arrangement for linking the associationally organised interests of civil society with the decisional structures of the state" (p. 86). This has the use of liberating corporatism "from its employment in any particular ideology or system of ideas" (p. 87). It is then, he argues, a useful way of thinking of the practices of private and public sector corporations and other interest groups that engage with government to create dialogue as a means of influence over regional, national and international decision-making in the realm of politics, economics, law and the institutions of internal and external forms of coercion. Through it, experts operating via specialist organisations influence, or indeed as agencies of government, undertake policy formation and implement policy. This, of course, was the very reason why Lippman, Bernays and others adopting a conservative liberal viewpoint, argued that consent needed to be 'manufactured' or 'engineered' in order to ensure that the 'public' at least imagined they were part of a decision-making process and that their leaders were indeed representing the will of the people. That, of course, is the more positive spin on the rationale for government by elites acting through government agencies and corporates. Less positively, it is important to keep in mind that historically corporatism is about consolidating elite powers and interests. In its fascist extreme, it is a union of state and private corporate interests. As such, corporatism, far from extending democratically the voices of interests to be included, defines what is to count as a genuine interest and interest group that represents that interest. In its weakened versions, it maintains the key motive of harmonising government with the interest groups that compose actually existing market capitalism (Vitali et al., 2011).

In a more utopian notion of capitalism, Phelps (2010) makes an opposition with corporatism echoing Hayek's polemic against socialism as being the path to serfdom. If utopian capitalism is a form of governance where all are free to pursue their interests, then certain organisational conditions must obtain. To be free to exercise one's powers of reasoning, decision and action requires that no one will suppress that power. That is to say, it requires an equality of condition – as in the perfect competition of classical market economics where no one individual, no one firm, has sufficient power to influence the market mechanism. This utopian focus on a capitalism formed of competition between small to medium enterprises is often taken up in the right-wing media which like Phelps (2010; 2013) sees capitalism as good and the new corporatism as the problem. Capitalism is good because it aids 'mass flourishing'. Phelps argues that American capitalism – or free enterprise – is more dynamic and thus more able to exploit the profitability opportunities of inventions and innovations than the corporatist European model. Adopting this kind of approach, a liberal, market centric, capitalist political economic framework would be the antidote to servitude in its various forms. That is to say, it claims to underpin a form of social interaction and organisation that facilitates the free development and expression of the powers of individuals whether singly or together. However, flourishing in Phelps' sense seems to be viewed only from an agenda framed by economic exploitation of the results of 'flourishing' in the pursuit of prosperity (Phelps, 2013: xi).

There is then within capitalist discourse a clash between a utopian capitalist flourishing of individual powers and a corporatist capitalist concentration of market power over individual powers involving a capture of democratic forms of governance. These two contrasting forms of perceiving capitalist organisation as between a bustling, thriving market of relatively small players enabling participants to 'flourish' as self-empowered individuals and a contrasting vision of a disciplined hierarchically organised system dominating both the market and forms of political, cultural and social governance represent two versions of the capitalist police in Rancière's terms. There are, of course, variants either side of these two forms. In any case, however, it can also be argued that the idea of the market under contemporary global circumstances is rather a chimera hiding the reality of the corporatist version. It is here, in the latter case, that lurk the 'sovereign individuals' of Davidson and Rees-Mogg who are, as they say, preparing for the disruptive event of the fourth industrial revolution: Big Data. The argument of the sovereign individual is to become so rich that one is independent of States in the event of crises.

Touré (2018) in reviewing the satirical film *Sorry to bother you*, which imagines a world of corporate elites running a world of perfectly obedient workers, wrote:

> A wealthy man once told me that you can't get really rich unless you have other people working for you. To achieve the American dream of boundless wealth, you need to stand on many other people's backs. That's capitalism. But how do you entice them to let you stand on their backs so you can make more money than them, and what do you owe them for that privilege?

Nothing is owed, it would seem. Indeed, to the contrary, the British MP and lead Brexit campaigner Boris Johnson (2013) considers that ordinary people should 'humbly' thank the rich, not bash them. Essentially, the film asks, what will people do for money and what will elites do for obedient employees? In the film, the lead character, "Cassius 'Cash' Green, a low-level telemarketer, learns that, in order to succeed at work, he has to put on a white voice. This does not mean a nasal affectation, along the lines of that corny old nerdy-voice stereotype that mid-level black comedians do. It means putting into your voice an embrace of the ease that white privilege brings. It means sounding as if you're entitled to the good life. It means feeling calm way down in your soul. It means never having to be afraid someone will call the police on you just because you're breathing." In effect, Cassius 'Cash' Green learns to fit in and become accepted perceptually and is rewarded until bit by bit he reaches the point of marketing virtual slaves. As Touré concludes:

> the film is a devastating takedown of capitalism, portraying people giving up their freedom so they don't have to worry about money. Owners and

management are shown as depraved, vacuous, corrupt and downright evil, scheming to create workers who are ever cheaper, more compliant and more profitable.

Eventually, as technology radically progresses, how to get people to work for you becomes, how to get people to work for nothing – as in uploading personal data freely that can be processed for corporate ends – or better, how do you get everything you want without the irksome 'unthinking demos'? For Capitalists, that is the dream not just of Big Data through which people can be manipulated and made profitable but the fourth industrial revolution involving artificial intelligence on a grand scale where the mass are no longer part of the production equation for producing elites as 'sovereign individuals'. There is a chance in the disruptions of Big Data and the widespread spread of fourth revolution technologies in all aspects of daily life for elites to complete what Robert Morris – whose "image adorns the inside of the rotunda of the US Capital building" (Bouton, 2007) – had started at the time of the War of Independence. In his view democracy was the enemy because the ordinary people – the "lower sort" – could out-vote the wealthy due to their preponderance as citizens. His tactics – like the billionaires of today – to do this included using 'government positions to make a killing from the war' and his wealth and position to recruit other rich people for the purpose of "combining together the Interests of moneyed Men" into "one general Money Connection".

It is a capitalist hegemonic strategy that remains in practice amongst the 'moneyed Men' and Women. In the US one can find for example the Koch brothers funding political campaigns in the US along with their fellow billionaires in the US and around the world (West, 2014). Wolin (2008) calls it managed democracy. The results of the management of democracy through the strategy of the contemporary 'money connection' can be seen in Piketty's remarks about "the considerable transfer of US national income – on the order to 15 points – from the poorest 90 per cent to the richest 10 per cent since 1980" ((Piketty, 2014: 300). As a consequence: "The bulk of the growth of inequality came from 'the 1 per cent,' whose share of national income rose from 9 per cent in the 1970s to about 20 per cent in 2000–2010 (with substantial year-to-year variation due to capital gains)" (p. 296).

As Morris and his friends knew, the increase in the wealth of the 1% – the 'Moneyed Men' – can only occur if there are effective machineries built specifically to sustain and augment it. As in Morris's early strategy, those machineries have been systematically structured into the mechanisms of governance of the Western democracies, whether by the wealthy like Morris taking up important political positions or through funding political parties or funding 'think tanks' and pressure groups that influence politicians. The strategic machineries include the legislative structure, the laws and law enforcement agencies that underpin social order – in particular, the desired inequalities of the social order to the benefit of the richest. Similarly, Cronin writes, with specific reference to the 'European Project', democracy is strangled in secret:

When presidents and prime ministers gather for summits in Brussels, they meet entirely behind closed doors. No recordings or transcripts of their deliberations are published. In September 2012, a report in *Le Monde Diplomatique* provided a glimpse into how the leaders of France and Germany have been pursuing an anti-democratic offensive at these events. Both Angela Merkel and Nicolas Sarkozy recommended in October 2010 that governments should have their voting rights as EU member states suspended if they do not comply with the Union's rules on budgetary rigour, according to notes taken by diplomats attending the summit that month. This means that the duo wished to install a new system, whereby entire nations could be punished as if they were errant teenagers for spending more on healthcare than the deficit hawks in the Brussel's bureaucracy would allow.

(Cronin, 2013: 5)

In his book Cronin goes on to describe the large numbers of lobbyists working to further the interests of corporations, as well as the 'revolving doors' between business and government where political appointments, when leaving their jobs, enter key positions in the industries relevant to their recent political employment (Sculthorpe, 2016).

When democracy is absent from the day-to-day organisation of people's lives, decision-making becomes the prerogative of ever smaller elites, and as digital technologies increase in sophistication so the surveillance of the masses by elites is amplified to enable the management of decision-making in every aspect of everyday life. Such views appeal to discourses of an 'invisible government' (Bernays, 1928) which, of course, acts in its own interests to ensure legislation that protects the machineries of wealth appropriation which are played out on a global scale. The notion of an 'invisible government' at a national, international and indeed on a global scale becomes increasingly plausible when, as the Oxfam (2014) report indicates clearly, the 85 richest people in the world have as much wealth as the poorest half of the world. However, by 2017, Oxfam reported that the richest eight in the world held assets equivalent to half the world. In 2018, Oxfam reported that 82% of wealth generated in 2017 went to 1% of the richest in the world and the poorest half received nothing. Little wonder, then, there is an increasing view that the world's super rich constitute a global plutocracy (Freeland, 2013) or that they, in Stedman Jones' (2012) terms, have become in effect the "Masters of the Universe".

## Taming the masters – what hope? What next?

Following that moment of the Enlightenment and the revolutionary drive to make a world anew, what went missing? In Mack's (2010) view there is a hidden enlightenment beginning with Spinoza whose politics, Del Lucchese (2009) argues, was influenced by Machiavelli. Perhaps here, in rethinking the richness of such enlightenment debates, some new steps can be made. The key to this reimagining the Enlightenment is in Spinoza's rethinking of Descartes split between reason and the body in terms of the mind being an idea of the *powers* of the body. That is to say, there is no split; there is only the powers of the body itself. The project then is to organise those powers in ways that bring to full fruition the creativity of all. In brief, Spinoza argued for an equality of powers, that is, a democracy. However, regarding the practical realities, the political question is: how do we address the prevailing inequalities?

In McCormick's (2011) reading, Machiavelli's first step was to point out to the 'princes' – or in contemporary terms masters of the universe – that there is a danger that in struggling to be The Leader – or The Sovereign Individual – one may not be sufficiently strong or lucky and thus be removed, killed, and one's wealth appropriated either by the sole winner or the much greater weight of the mob. The better strategy is to work as an oligarchy or some structure of 'equals' – where making some compromises may at least maximise the chances of holding onto wealth, privilege and power over the masses. Critical to such compromises was to ensure that no one oligarch could move the masses to their benefit. Hence, the powers of the oligarchs had to be constrained. How, when the sentiment of hero worship of the rich and powerful is so pervasive? It was a problem that Adman Smith raised, perhaps ironically:

> This disposition to admire, and almost to worship, the rich and the powerful, and to despise, or, at least, to neglect persons of poor and mean condition, though necessary both to establish and to maintain the distinction of ranks and the order of society, is, at the same time, the great and most universal cause of the corruption of our moral sentiments. That wealth and greatness are often regarded with the respect and admiration which are due only to wisdom and virtue; and that the contempt, of which vice and folly are the only proper objects, is often most unjustly bestowed upon poverty and weakness, has been the complaint of moralists in all ages.
>
> (Smith, 1759: 45)

It is to the undoing of such heroic leadership, the celebration of the rich, and the management by experts inherent in contemporary expressions of corporatism, the corruption of democratic voice and all the forms of organisation under the discourses of mastery that is the central focus of the Spinozan and Machiavellian turn in the following chapters.

Chapter 5

# Engaging with power through *radical* research methodologies

Research methodology is drawn into the ambit of the agendas constructed by power elites as soon as it is limited to the puzzle-solving techniques deployed to bring about answers to elite defined problems. Radical research methodologies begin by critiquing the claimed legitimacy and dominance of elite forms of organisation and their agendas. That is to say, they begin in what Mouffe calls a critical discursive exterior. For her that exterior involves equality and freedom as key elements. In her view the relation between these two is contingent; they can become dissociated from each other. For the developing arguments in this chapter, however, we adopt Balibar's neologism *égaliberté* to express that freedom and equality are necessarily co-extensive, which we consider offers a more radical discursive exterior. Nevertheless, Mouffe's formulation provides a practical perspective on the constant hegemonic play that is necessary in the unending aspiration towards *égaliberté*. Thus, for example, reading disobedience alongside *égaliberté* and disciplinary hierarchies occupied by leaders who define directions aligns both a methodological and a political practice. *Égaliberté* stands as a form of refusal, a "refusal to accept as final the limitations imposed upon freedom and happiness by the reality principle, its refusal to forget what can be" (Marcuse, 1964: 149). Égaliberté is a constant reminder. As a methodological principle it identifies the fields of conflict where freedoms and equalities are out of joint in a given 'social reality'.

## Putting power out of joint

Power, whether as an already aggregated, organised, reified presence or as the emergent creative and dynamic powers of people realising their potential, creates the key forms of realised power, prefigurative power and figurative power. Where prefigurative power acts *as if* its desired state has been realised whether or not change has occurred, figurative power undoes, displaces and replaces power. It is the latter that is the greater threat to realised power, since it creates a new aesthetic form of power where what was seen, heard, tasted, felt as natural, real, and without the possibility of alternatives is no longer experienced as such at all, unless as a delusion of a previous age. The power of research is to 'see' potential realities and to explore the conditions of possibility for their realisation. This, like democracy itself, becomes an object for taming by entrenched powers.

Since all research methodologies that focus upon the world of affairs of people are the work of an applied politics, they align either with the practices that tame or with those that release the powers of activism in the pursuit of a desired vision of the 'good society'. Potentially, all individuals are capable of associating in a vision of mutual benefit.

> For Spinoza, humans must collaborate with one another to enhance their *potentia*, their power to act. In the maximization of this objective, a collectivity that would form for the purpose of exploiting another would lose the possibility of a still greater collective power. Rather, to maximize potentia "nothing is more useful to man than man ... all [humans] should look simultaneously to the common advantage of all" and "seek for themselves nothing that they would not desire for the rest of human beings" [...] This, for Spinoza, is not a moral imperative handed down from above by a transcendent God, but an immanent reality – the logical outcome of the relational nature of our being in the world, although this course of action is by no means guaranteed.
>
> (Ruddick, 2010: 24–25)

It is this potential of association where individuals combine to create organised actions, directed towards achieving their mutual benefit, that is most feared by those who seek to control the multitude. The multitude "necessarily thought of as a disorganized, differential, and powerful multiplicity" (Negri, 2008: 11) is dangerous precisely in its power of suspending organisation, that is, in particular, elite organisation. Disorganised and differential, the multitude creates a sense of subjectivity where each is equal, more or less, in power in the midst of that multitude to the other. This resembles Rancière's condition for the emergence of 'the political': that glimpse by members of the crowd that mainstream organised power has fallen and no one has a greater power than another and that, in that moment of equality and openness, anything is possible. In this context of openness and possibility, in Lucchese's (2009) reading of Spinoza it is precisely here in the multiple associations of free and equal individuals who converse, debate and share experiences that knowledge is produced. This has key implications for both research methodology and education. The masses independently producing knowledge was precisely the fear of the elites expressed by Robert Lowe following the extension of voting for certain of the skilled working classes in 1867. The more the unpredictability of associations, the more multiple readings disrupt elite dictation and facilitate inscribing knowledge in the discourses that frame interpretation and action for individuals who compose the masses.

There are overlaps, family resemblances or consistency between Spinoza and contemporary radical democratic theorists (Rogers-Cooper, 2011) where for example:

> Laclau's own conception of populism and "populist reason," with its emphasis on collective bodies excited to "excessive" positions on the left and the right, can be productively situated next to Spinoza's descriptions of multitudes. Stripped of its universal and spontaneous character, "the" multitude Hardt and Negri describe might still usefully describe smaller-scale qualities of revolutionary collectives – or singular multitudes – that Laclau conceives as "short-term" and "autonomous." The temporality of these multitudes, which act in "short-term" bursts of affective passion, is also consistent with other influential positions within contemporary Marxist thought – notably, in interpretations of Spinoza's multitudes as crowds, such as in Warren Montag's *Bodies, Masses, Power* and Étienne Balibar's *Masses, Classes, Ideas*.
>
> (Rogers-Cooper, 2011: 4–5)

In whatever reading, there is the potential of a multitude to put power out of joint. This multitude is not the same as an audience of fragmented individuals or disaffected communities in whose lonely self-involvement and exclusion from others and outsiders are easy prey to elite demagogues. Their fragmentedness can find an expression of unity reflected in the fellow feeling of the audience roused by the 'leader' who makes sense of their world. In this, their knowledge consists of what Spinoza designates as the first of three kinds of knowledge. This first kind of knowledge formed from the senses is vague, incomplete and dominated by "imperial 'signs' that are perceived as a command" (Lucchese, 2009). To some extent this evokes Lacan's 'imaginary order' through which relations between fragmented sensations and perceptions are organised into unities as in a mirror providing a reflected surface image perceived as real, whole, seamless. The role of the demagogue is to present such a mirror reflection. Knowledge based upon the imaginary order, or aesthetic, of images may be true or false with little way of knowing – as in the magician's illusions created through 'smoke and mirrors'. In Spinoza's second form of knowledge the power of reason contributes the process of abstraction where the essential features – rather as in Husserl's phenomenological formulation, invariant structures are common to all variations of a particular object of consciousness define its 'essence' – of things serve as ways of organising the confusions of images perceived by the body. Thus a way of reducing the confusions is sought that give rise to

> notions which are called universal, such as man, dog, horse, etc. I mean so many images are formed in the human body – e.g., of men – at the same time, that they overcome the power of imagining, not altogether in deed, but to such an extent that the mind cannot imagine the small differences between individuals (e.g., colour, size, etc) and their fixed number, and only that in which all agree in so far as the body is affected by them is distinctly imagined: for by that was the body most affected by each particular thing, and this the mind expresses by the name of man, and predicates it of an infinite number of particulars. But it must be noted that these notions are not formed by all in

the same manner, but vary with each according to the thing by which the body was most often affected, and which the mind imagines or remembers most easily. For example, those who have most often admired men for their stature, by the name of man will understand an animal of erect stature; those who are wont to regard men in another way will form another common image of men, namely, a laughing animal, a featherless biped animal, a reasoning animal, and so each one will form concerning the other things universal images of things according to the disposition of his body. Wherefore it is not surprising that so many controversies should have arisen among philosophers who wished to explain natural things merely by the images of things.

(Spinoza, 1993: 67–68)

And of course, in more contemporary terms, in Rancière's discourse our current critical and liberal distribution of the sensible, which composes what might be called a progressive ethics and aesthetics of perceiving, problematises the notion of 'man', framing controversies around gender, race, ablism, and so on. It is through the common experiences of those affected that knowledge of discriminations is formed and shared as a condition for producing political, social, cultural demands. Sides are drawn as between the progressive and the reactionary where each may either listen to the other and try to see the world as the other sees it and the reasons for seeing it that way; or they can close down such communication and listen only to others like themselves and so formulate the other as 'enemy', 'evil' worthy only of contempt and outright hostility. As the fourth industrial revolution gathers pace, the capacities to reinforce the divisions by creating social media bubbles has attracted the manipulative strategies of political campaigners with competing views as to their effectiveness. However, to take a broader notion of the social bubble to include traditional news media as well as sharing the views of friends, neighbourhoods and workplace colleagues, then online campaigns can act to reinforce views. Certainly, that was the view of the billionaire Mercer family, Arron Banks the millionaire funder of the Leave.EU campaign and the UK Independence Party (UKIP) (Cadwalladr, 2017; 2017c; 2018).

Each campaign attempts to paint a picture in the mind of the audience, as Lippmann (1922; 10–11) advised. As he argued, reality is just too complex and people need simplifying stories, that is 'fictions' to be carefully distinguished from 'lies', as a basis for understanding the world and engaging with each other in it. These pictures provide perceptual gestalts that fill in the gaps, overlay the contradictions, obscure the relations underlaying manipulations involved in the production of elite wealth, and create separations that pose the need for frontiers to safeguard 'us' from 'them'. Rather like the scientific paradigms of Kuhn (1970) and of Feyerabend (1975) such fictions can provide ways of seeing that help navigate the world. Their trustworthiness can be tested or evaluated in many ways. Like maps they enable people to co-ordinate their activities, their plans, their destinations with each other. Their utility can also be assessed, for example, to the extent they enable the replication of activities required to produce desired outcomes, enable predictions or stimulate fruitful innovations. However, whereas scientific, or more general, academic or indeed educational ways of seeing are generated over time through critical debates between a multiplicity of competing views, the campaigns filter out competing views in order to school ways of seeing and behaving by castigating alternatives as the views of the 'mad', the 'bad' or the 'enemy'.

In Spinozan terms, "The more bodies that form a relationship, the more complex and multiple this relationship is, the more it contains common notions, and the more adequately our mind is capable of perceiving a multiplicity of things" (Lucchese 2009). That is to say, only by crossing the frontiers between ways of seeing can the extent to which frontiers are illusionary be seen and what is common between the so-called 'sides' be established. In that sense, as Lucchese (2009) summarises:

> A tyrant always relies on a dissolved group of separate, isolated individuals, reduced to enslavement by their own passions and, in a way, crushed by a general will that is already the final and transcendental cause of their own decisions.

It is because of this narrowness that Spinoza argues for a democracy where individuals multiply their associations with each other, freely and equally, as the basis for coming to forms of knowledge that reasonably represent the world.

At a fundamental level, for Spinoza – unlike Descartes – the mind and the body were not split from each other. This meant that by focusing on the body that thinks and speaks, Spinoza was thus able to make thinking and speaking a power that acted directly upon the world, through the world and so creating a common basis for the evaluation of ideas. This idea of the 'common' is quite different from the narrow 'common sense' of the Straussians such as Kristol described in the previous chapter. As the common expands to include ever-new perspectives a different form of the 'real' becomes 'visible', legible, actionable. That is, new gestalts, ways of seeing, ways of figuring the real, are possible. The great richness of language(s) then provides the ever re-figurable ground that provides thought and speaking with their resources for debate. With each figurable form a reading-trace sets aside one legible thing from another, a visible from an invisible, a real from an unreal, a sensible from a senseless, a figure from a background. There is thus an intimate relation between what is felt inside the body and what is exterior. Language joins this intimate touch with a perceived exterior. And language itself is both intimate and exterior, that is, it is *extimate* as Lacan would have it. In the extimate process a perceptual, nameable figure emerges, nicely described by Lyotard:

> Only from within language can one get to and enter the figure. One can get to the figure by making clear that every discourse possesses its counterpart, the object of which it speaks, which is over there, like what it designates in a

> horizon: sight on the edge of discourse. And one can get in the figure without leaving language behind because the figure is embedded in it. One only has to allow oneself to slip into the well of discourse to find the eye lodged at its core, an eye of discourse in the sense that at the center of the cyclone lies an eye of calm. The figure is both without and within.
>
> (Lyotard, 2011: 8–9)

The figure that is no longer repressed by posing frontiers between an elite-defined 'right' and 'wrong' way of seeing puts the power consolidated by elites out of joint. Rather than being confined to certain pastures rather than others the eye transgresses and grazes freely re-seeing what may not have been seen before, or creating a new picture from a multiplicity of pictures in a multiplicity of minds. In this process, what is being seen is the process of seeing itself:

> The painting is not something to be read, as contemporary semiologists would have it. Rather, as Klee put it, it has to be *grazed*, it makes visible, giving itself up to the eye like the exemplary thing it is, like naturing nature (to borrow Klee's words again), since it makes visible seeing itself. What is more, it makes visible that seeing is a dance. To look at a painting is to draw paths across it, or at least to collaboratively draw paths, since in executing it the painter laid down, imperiously (albeit tangentially), paths to follow, and his or her work is this trembling, trapped within four wooden slats, that an eye will remobilize, bring back to life. The "fixed-explosive" beauty lucidly required by *mad love*.
>
> (Lyotard, 2011: 9)

As Lyotard (2011: 9) puts it, the "power lies with the eye".

## The I of the researcher

It is through the body as the perceptual-I that the work of the researcher is accomplished. It is a work of perceptual grazing, creating spaces of inscription as a resource for debate and for re-mobilisation, the work of the researcher engages with the powers of individuals at the fundamental level of how people see themselves in their world as a basis for all their activities. How people relate to each other is critical.

A fundamental course of action for the expression of relational powers is working together as 'collaborators' or 'co-operators'. How that work is appropriated, valued and organised as a unit of activity – that is, an 'individual' – that realises potential provides a way of conceiving 'cases' to be researched. Cases, then, become defined in terms of the patterns of relationship through which activities result in organisations of powers that leave traces of activities and result in transformations, or outcomes, or productions as a consequence of collective aims to realise potential. This is not the same as regarding cases as single instances from a larger population, or indeed, as regarding them as so unique no generalisation is possible. Rather, the value of the case here is in identifying or mapping the conditions under which forms of collective action are generalisable to produce ever-greater common advantage. Or more accurately:

> It is cooperation itself that enables the individual: the social field is the terrain that enables any possible notion of the individual. And as we operate within a social field that prefigures our constitution as individuals, it is a fiction to insist on our mere ability to act on our passions as evidence of our freedom or free will.
>
> (Ruddick, 2010: 26)

However, co-operation is not the only political and social possibility. Within a field of powers and potentials that is the terrain for the possibility of co-operation between individuals as co-producers, there is indeed the potential of maximising freedom for all; but also only for some, or indeed, only for oneself as master of all. In this context what is perceived to be within the reach of the researcher to do?

The researcher is part of the field of powers and potential, a member of the social terrain – as an individual, a person – conceived in the broadest sense. A person's powers are assessable by making comparisons with other individuals, with groups, with crowds, with organisations, and in the last analysis with the State, just as a State's powers can be judged against other states and groups of states. A researcher's powers then become knowable when through the mobilising force of ideas new ways of seeing and thus comparing are created that enable new forms of social organisation, new forms of cultural productivity and production in their widest as well as most specific senses in catering for the needs of the body. Thus the eye of the researcher is a condition for the I that draws out, or educates, new potentials as grounds for mobilisation.

There is a term employed by Spinoza that covers this mobilisation towards some effect – *conatus*, which denotes a striving or effort, or an inclination, towards a persistence to become. Lenz (2012) calls it intentionality without objects. This can be distinguished from but compared to Husserl's notion of intentionality defined in terms of always being directed towards some object for some subject. There is perhaps a fruitful association of powers to be made. For Spinoza intentionality concerns the relation between the mind and the body first where the ideas of the mind are directed towards the body and only secondarily to some exterior and then only because we are all part of nature. More specifically, the striving for the continued existence of the body – the conatus – provides both the force and the criterion by which appropriate ideas concerning relations to, and the nature of, the objects in the world about are formed, rather than arbitrary ones, or ones that are desirable fantasies. It is through bodily interaction with the world about that objects, say a tree, can be educed to produce a fully educated picture or idea formed of experiences. Each sensual interaction:

provides, as it were, the cognitive contact to the tree, while the tree's positive or negative impact on my body determines my conatus to pick out the tree's properties relevant to my persistence. Generally speaking, my striving determines the contents of my beliefs, whereas the teleological structure of my striving determines this content in a normative way, since it can fail or succeed with regard to its desired contribution to the power of my being.

Lenz (2012)

There is a striving, a directedness towards, that focuses attention, that organises and concentrates powers of perceiving, thinking, acting in order to formulate understandings that contribute one's persistence in the world. A life then is structured ultimately towards self-persistence and this persistence is what drives attention towards others as people or things that contribute to one's continuing vitality. Vitality acts then as an embodied validity. Triangulation is typically the term employed by researchers to describe the process of adopting different perspectives on, or employing different methods – observation, interviews, focus groups, documentary analysis, questionnaires – to compare and contrast what is seen to be common and what is different. In order to build up a rounded image of something that then can lead to an idea about its nature – or essential structure – requires an attitude of investigation, a persistent curiosity where all the sensuous powers of the body are involved to pick out its properties from a variety of perspectives. I see something, I touch it, I squeeze it, I see if it can be pushed, lifted. I walk around it to build up a fuller profile of the features of this object. I employ memories of possible objects that it may be. I draw similarities and differences in order to nuance my understandings of what it is. It is like a chair, you can sit on it, but it has no back to rest upon, in that sense it is like a stool, but more than one person can sit on it so it is more of a bench, but much wider so that you can lie down on it like a bed. In this way of varying the picture in the mind of the object being perceived certain characteristics remain common while others fall away until one gets closer to being able to describe the essential characteristics of the object, that is, those characteristics that remain the same no matter how much the other characteristics are varied. So, although there are many different triangles all share the same essential feature of having three sides. Adding a fourth would change its nature and make it a rectangle (cf. Tragesser, 1977).

The more we can nuance distinctions, the more we can identify what does not change and how things do change under our manipulations, the more we can have confidence about our understandings of the physical and social worlds upon which our life, our persistence as a living body, depends. There is a social architecture – much like the triangle, or the chair – where powers are co-ordinated to produce specified objects, effects and affects; but unlike a triangle or a chair in that it is barely visible and nameable until a disturbance occurs and an alternative makes the taken-for-granted seeable, tangible.

When crisis threatens the known, critical to the striving to persist is an imagination able to grasp new framings or categorisations of 'objects', 'subjects', configurations, horizons and 'frontiers' between the 'inside' and the 'outside', the 'reachable' and the 'beyond'. In the moment when that happens, when something 'new' stands in relation to what had been defined as the only reality, the simply commonsensical, there is an echo of Rancière's 'the political':

> The political doesn't need barricades to exist. But it does require that there be two distinct and perceptibly opposed ways to describe the common situation and to count the players involved. This is also why it exists as moments, not as fugitive bursts. A moment is not simply a unit of time. It is another weight to be thrown on the scale that sizes up situations and the individuals capable of seizing them. A moment unleashes or strangles a movement.
> (Rancière, 2014: viii)

Articulating these conflicting ways to describe the common are the opposed dramatis personae configured to 'seize the day'. They are in a sense 'mirror groups' (Schostak and Schostak, 2008: 172) that stand opposed, each seeing in the mirror of imagination that divides the groups, what they conceive the other to be. In a world ranged between the gated affluent and the custodialised slum, attention is contrastingly divided and shaped to construct worlds that reflect the 'realities' each experiences. These realities define the limits to the powers of the one and of combinations of the many and of the totality. In the experience or moment of crisis what is perceived is the potential for the collapse of the established powers and their reconfiguration. In that moment, there is the glimpse of an equality between individuals where no one has more chance than another of seizing the moment and where there are those whose interests are to maintain their previously established privilege, those whose interest is to create new elites and those who see the potential to be seized for a socially just society. At any time, such a moment can be imagined just as Hayek and Friedman did – and like them it can be prepared for by constructing the ideas, forming the individuals and placing those individuals in socially, politically, culturally, economically significant places pre-crisis. As the bearers of the 'ideas lying around', established in places of power, they are ready to frustrate alternatives, to supply in a co-ordinated and well-disciplined fashion, '*the* solution', as in the Thatcher-Reagan moment of 'there is no alternative'.

As Mouffe (2018) correctly sees, it is about playing an hegemonic game, left, right, centre – or from 'out of the box', a position that collapses any left-centre-right political framework. The political left was not ready, or not capable, to exploit the financial crisis in which Lehman Bros collapsed leading many to see the collapse of capitalism itself (Quiggin, 2010; Keen, 2011). But it did not. The neoliberal ideas were well embedded (Earl et al., 2017). And the left was timid and fragmented, with western democracy being seen to be bound to capitalism which in turn was increasingly considered to be in crisis (Streeck, 2014; 2016). Thus neither the left nor the centre-right conservatives were ready for the Trump and Brexit populist campaigns leading many to see democracy in chains

(MacLean, 2017), dying, (Levitsky and Ziblatt, 2018) or indeed that its time may be over (Runciman, 2018). Such views on contemporary democracy are written with the question of either how to save it or what replaces it. Although the fate of western democracy is very much bound up with the fate of capitalism, democracy is not reducible to it. Capitalism has sought to tame it (Bouton, 2007), substitute for it through the 'market' as in Ludwig Mises view (Peterson, 2004), stand outside of it in 'moneyland' (Bullough, 2018) or eradicate it (Thiel, 2009). In each case, democracy and capitalism transform what it means to be a 'people', a 'citizen', an 'individual', a 'subject'. Capitalism in the first (steam) and second (electricity) industrial revolutions was able to transform people into exploitable 'big numbers', as pools of labour available for factory mass production processes. In the third revolution with the development of microprocessors, automation developed, replacing increasing numbers of workers and making them redundant. In the fourth revolution artificial intelligence holds the promise of making capitalists, as sovereign individuals, independent of 'the people', the state and thus of government (cf., Davidson and Rees-Mogg, 1997; Rushkoff, 2018) and so, making people, state and government redundant. Capitalism has only ever seen 'the people' as pools of labour, 'big numbers' only relevant for the production and exploitation of wealth; but with the downside danger that the people may rebel and take away their accumulated wealth.

Echoing the pattern of the industrial revolutions, democracy reduced to being merely big numbers is equally exploitable by those who have learnt how to nudge opinions, stir passions, and capture the 'will of the people'. Governments, however willingly or unwillingly, have effectively created machineries to do so: schools with their allied systems of discipline, surveillance, curriculum and examination as machines for turning people into 'big numbers' for employers, generals, politicians and religious leaders; a mass health and welfare system that was able to confirm a new post-war awareness of the value of people that has been progressively transformed under the ethos of the business model and privatisation into a mass market for 'big pharma', private health insurance and private hospitals; a mass custodial, control and policing system that leads to proportionally high numbers being incarcerated – for example, the US has 5% of the global population but over 20% of the global prison population (Stullich et al., 2016); and England and Wales have the highest imprisonment rate in Western Europe (Travis, 2017). Perhaps the neo-conservative Charles Murray's (1999, 2005) proposition for the development of a custodial democracy is being realised. In his view, as advocated to Margaret Thatcher and Tony Blair it is pointless trying to educate or civilise the 'underclass', it is better to custodialise them by restricting them to highly policed areas away from the rest of society.

What form of research can challenge this, rather than just feeding it?

In radical democratic terms, research becomes a living project as lived by Rancière where he speaks of his book – *Althusser's Lesson* – in the context of his life's strivings (Rancière, 2011: xvi):

> From the very beginning, my concern has been with the study of thought and speech where they produce effects, that is, in a social battle that is also a conflict, renewed with each passing instant over what we perceive and how we can name it. I have confronted the philosophies of the end of history with the topography of the possible ... Above and beyond the theses specific to Althusser, the book has its sights trained on the much broader logic by which subversive thoughts are recuperated by the service of order. The principle of this process of recuperation is the idea of domination propogated (*vehiculer*) by the very discourses that pretend to critique it.

If perceiving is naming, then what we call things matters. The specific target in his book is any thesis or discourse that calls the masses ignorant of the realities of their life circumstances, because, somehow, they have been deluded, and are blind to the realities. Those promoting such theories see themselves, or see some 'guru' or leader, as blessed with an insight, a vision of the real, who can 'cure' the blindness of the masses. In short, there is an essential inequality of intelligence imposed on the relation between the elites who 'see' and the masses who are 'blind' – in effect, the intelligent, the experts dominate the masses, the ignorant. Thus, "My book declared war on the theory of the inequality of intelligences at the heart of supposed critiques of domination" (Rancière, 2011: xvi). Similarly, then, research, education and politics can work together through their practices, their forms of organisation and their projects to create the conditions of an 'equality of intelligence'.

## Towards next steps to engage research with power

Engaging with Power means exploring possibilities for creating countervailing forms of organisation to undermine the insolence of elites who seek to undermine the intelligence of others for purposes of exploitation and control. How? McCormick (2011; 2015) refers to Machiavelli's praise of peoples' tribunes in the Roman Republic to check 'the insolence of the nobles' as well as his view that only a particular kind of tyrant can change a corrupt republic:

> Tribunes, Machiavelli insists, ought to be drawn exclusively from the common people; the wealthiest and most prominent citizens should not be eligible for a plebeian tribunate. Moreover, tribunes should be empowered to propose legislation in popular assemblies, veto partisanly oligarchic policies pursued by executive and senatorial elites, and legally prosecute before large-scale citizen assemblies wealthy and prominent citizens accused of political crimes. The kind of tyrant whom Machiavelli deems necessary to reform a corrupt republic is reminiscent of ancient Greek tyrannies: A usurper-cum-reformer of republics must crush senators and rich citizens, distribute their wealth to the common people, and expand the number of armed citizens within the polity. Having overthrown a republic grown

corrupt through oligarchic encroachment on the commonweal, such a Greek-styled tyrant lays the foundation for a more robust—that is, more egalitarian and martial—republic down the road through economic redistribution and military reforms.

(McCormick, 2015: 253)

The insolence of the rich, the corporate leaders and those who hold positions of financial and managerial power over others are the contemporary equivalents of Machiavelli's nobles. How to combat them? Machiavelli's answer is the search for a reformist tyrant. This view was echoed by Zizek (2013) when he called for a "Thatcher of the Left". It is essentially a restatement of the dominant political aesthetics that sees only a world under the thrall of various types of great leader. However, alongside this in Machiavelli's view is the 'common people' who are to be given a radical role in shaping a new aesthetics under the reformist Great Leader. This Robin Hood-like figure has not been forthcoming and seems unlikely to arrive anytime soon. Rather, there have been revolutions which in their bloody wake have rejigged the political aesthetics from monarchies and tyrannies to tamed democracies under the dominating influence of extravagantly wealthy and ruthlessly exploitative global oligarchs. More recently, there have been 'movements' focusing on social class and increasing economic well-being, the 'new social movements' of the 1960s and 70s that focused more on 'rights' of women, minorities, gender and the subsequent identity politics that led right-wing commentators to call 'political correctness'. Indeed, following the financial meltdown of 2007, as Mason (2013) put it, 'it's kicking off everywhere'. So, it was tempting to see commonalities in events as wide apart as the Arab Spring, the Occupy movement, Syriza, and the *Indignados*. Perhaps in all this fervour a new view of democracy, ground up, could be imagined and actualised? The social media technologies of the fourth revolution had had some success in leading to an Obama. However, the same technologies were employed in the Trump and Brexit wins. It seems that building from the ground is a slow and unpredictable process. What can be learnt from the successes and failures?

People have been played with an older political aesthetics that sees the world as 'friends and enemies', 'black and white', 'Man and woman', 'leader-led' and 'us and them' against a more recent liberal, internationalist and global one that has failed so far to fill the imagination of the majority. Whatever 'picture in the mind' succeeds, creates the conditions like a map for navigating around its 'natural' urban and architectural spaces, enabling directions to given and coordinating activities. A picture is the ground for evolving narratives of the 'way things are', the biographical experiences involved in navigating a life, the stories that can be told about episodes and how these fit with overall narratives about 'people', 'us–them', 'friends–enemies', 'nation–foreigners' and so on. In particular, a picture can be deployed to account for 'what is mine' and 'what is yours'. This picture changed radically, for example, following the enclosures of the 'common land' during the eighteenth and nineteenth centuries. The effect was to deprive the poor of the use of common land for growing and grazing as the rich accessed land that could be used for new techniques of farming. Echoing this, the openness of the digital spaces have been increasingly 'enclosed' by technology giants such as Facebook, Youtube, Paypal that are able to process benefit financially from freely given personal data and then track internet usage. Such pictures and how they command what people believe to be real set limits to what they can do. Just describing and analysing such pictures is not enough since the powers of the researcher to describe and analyse are essentially no different from any other actor. And any actor can enter into disagreement with the researcher. It is only when a principle of the inclusion of all viewpoints underlying research practices is adopted that the research and its implications for action becomes radical. This principle is gradually articulated when some 'other' – that is, an 'other' to those already included and their established ways of seeing – is seen, heard and acts as a source of re-viewing, re-configuring and re-articulating a world.

The political arises in relation to research and education at a moment where the rigidities of 'there is no alternative' weaken and alternative possibilities transform relations between people and dissolve borders fissuring categories to enable new forms of order to be imagined, thought, understood and taken seriously as realisable. It is here that the next step – as a process of education for new forms of relationship, new ways of seeing and knowing – is possible.

## Chapter 6

# Radical educational strategies

It is hard to imagine, even harder to realise in practice, but the development of an approach to learning that involves building education as the accomplishment of an equality of intelligences is critical to the emergence of a just society. Why? Simply, to ensure that all are included in voicing ideas, experiences, imaginative possibilities ensures also an aggregation of powers transcending the viewpoint of any individual. This is the condition for the education of what Spinoza saw as his third kind of knowledge. His views were, however, sufficiently ambiguous for Strauss to appropriate the idea of the third kind of knowledge to his view that only a few individuals would be capable of achieving this. However, this runs counter to Spinoza's argument concerning the emergence of democracy as the only form of politics that could support the fullest development of the powers of all and the freedom of all. As Lucchese (2009) has argued, there is a counter reading that, focusing on the free multitude (*libre multitudo*) as a complex of relationships and form of life rather than on the single individual, generates a power to know greater than that possible by the individual alone. It is this multitude as 'multiple individual' that enables education to be viewed as a process of the aggregation of powers, personally, collectively, co-operatively to engage in activities, critical debate to educe understandings as a basis for projects whether of day-to-day work, enjoyment or imagination. The free multitude is free only to the extent to which there is no suppression of the powers of a given individual by another who seeks the management and organisation of the powers of others for their own advantage. Such management and organisation of powers for the benefits of another, an elite, may be called schooling as distinct from educational processes that seek the free and equal expansion of powers. Under schooling, these powers of the multitude can be deployed to produce conditions of inequality whereas under education it is the conditions for freedom with equality for all. How the production of knowledge, understanding and learning is organised is critical (e.g., Goodson, 2003).

The challenge for educationists in the context of the domination by elites of schools and curricula designed to limit, shape, exploit and train people in the political, commercial and social interests of the wealthy is to create the conditions for all individuals to draw out and develop their powers freely and equally to engage in the arts of living. The arts of living critically involve the arts of *organising* for all social, economic, political and cultural purposes. In order to compose radical educational strategies that address these purposes, first a good mapping of what is at stake for individuals to act in the context of the prevailing forms through which their powers are organised must be made.

## What is at stake in the education of powers?

What is at stake can be seen in the conversation between Zizek and Kotkin focused on Kotkin's study of Stalin. Revolution is not enough, even though:

> the revolution was fantastic and it spawned a tremendous amount of dynamism and energy and craziness. Unfortunately, what happens in a revolution is the brilliant ideas don't take over. What takes over are institutions. The shards of the old regime become the building blocks of the new regime. Protest movements, massing in the streets, forming communes, chiliastic songs, right, this doesn't get you a parliament, an independent judiciary, an impartial civil service free and open media space. These have to be built. Institutions have to be built and instead of building free and open institutions during the 1920s, they build this dictatorship and it's on purpose it's not an accident it's not something circumstances caused. It was something that Lenin wanted and something that Lenin, Stalin and the rest of them were able to implant. Now you can argue that they were doing it because they were trying to create a new world, trying to overcome the injustices of the old world and that's correct. That was their motivation. They were not cynics, they were not just out for personal power, they were not killing people for the sake of killing people in some type of sadistic orgy. It was a revolution to bring about a new world. The institutions to bring about the new world were in conflict with the goals. The methods and the core idea of the reigning communists could never bring the freedom and the abundance and the happiness that the revolution had been about. This is a very tragic story.
>
> (Kotkin, 2015)

The motivation to overcome injustice is not enough. As the Arab Spring also showed, tragedy is too often the aftermath of revolution where even when the tyrant falls, as in Egypt, the institutions that remain maintain their grip (Roberts and Schostak, 2012). How can the building for alternative more equal, more socially just, freer futures be accomplished if the forms of organisation, the decision makers, and the values, the beliefs, the knowledge of how to run organisations, and the practices of people remain the same? Of course it can't. But what can an individual do when the crowds have dispersed? A person's powers circumscribe what is within reach, what is imaginable, what is thinkable, what is realisable. The management of powers is thus critical to the development of forms of governance whether for elites to discipline and control the mass or for individuals to generate organisations that respect the democratic principles and practices underpinning freedom with equality – or what Balibar calls *égaliberté* – for all. This contrasts with the kind of Modernity, of Reason, of Enlightenment that seeks to impose technical reason over the body, that sees the body as weak, a source of corruption, decay and wild passions, urges, instincts and drives that must have catharsis, be tamed, regulated, surveilled and controlled. It is this version of Modernity that has hijacked education to make it into schooling. It has given rise to the discourses of mastery that can be allied pragmatically with conservative interests to use reason in its most limited sense of technical rationality to dominate the mass as 'labour', 'citizen', 'herd', and 'underclass'. What is at stake is the diminution or, at the extreme, the crushing of one's powers.

If what it means to be a human is to be able to use all one's powers in creating the arts of living, then privileging one power – reason – above all others is a perversion, or in Lacan's pun, a père-version, invoking the role of the Father in the deviation of powers to meet the desires of the Father. In this sense, Father refers to all the forms of mastery over people that have the structural configuration of domination–submission. This pattern is repeated not just in traditional paternalistic families with the father in the position of power (as earner, as master of the household) but also in any hierarchical leader-led organisation from schools to business organisations to political and faith systems. It matters little the actual gender of the individual in the place of power whether in the household, community, economic, faith or political systems of organisation. The repeated historical challenges to the domination–submission structure, whether made in the interests of 'emancipating', 'enfranchising' and 'including' the working classes, women, and minority ethic groups and cultures, have made little difference to the broad frameworks of surveillance and control of populations that have hijacked the liberatory potential of education in the interests of elites. As pointed out by Bleiker (2000) the power to disobey is insufficient in the context of a multiplicity of discourses that variously privilege hierarchy, paternalism, nationalism, inequality, greed and self-interest. Instead, the 'emancipated' have largely been appropriated and co-opted into the maintenance of the overall structure of inequality.

The discourses of schooling whether they are of the 'right' or of the 'left' in contemporary politics have largely supported those forms of management and school practices that involve discipline, surveillance and promoting duty to the state through 'citizenship'. Under such systems all is prescribed: the role of examinations, the content of curricula, the work of the teacher, and the function of schools in preparing the young for wage-earning employment, or in later life in colleges or training centres the retraining of adults for new employment. In short, there has in effect been little other than a progressive subjugation of children, young adults and the older generations to the necessities of maintaining the hierarchical forms of organisation essential for elite governance in all matters of life. How then may powers be used differently in such a disciplinary context?

## Two logics of reason and power: Hierarchy or equality

Power may be used strategically for opposing purposes: first, as an aggregation of powers reified to serve elites or leaders in a society of inequality; second, as a fluid play of the combination of powers to serve all equally as a society of equals. The strategic development, organisation and use of powers is a fundamentally educational matter. Drawing out, arranging, combining and setting into motion powers for the formation of communities, societies, worlds: that is the highest matter for education.

In terms of reified power, a particular individual, group or class occupies the place of power (see Lefort, 1988) through the systematic intensification and aggregation of powers into vertically constructed Power. Disciplining the powers of others has the effect of organising subjectivity, consolidating identity and producing habits of compliance to those who 'have power' or are the agents of Power. In a hierarchical structure of Power, a sovereign emerges, that is, the one whose decisions and actions stem from no other power than his or herself. The sovereign is the one who decides upon the exception to the laws that others follow (Schmitt, 2005). The strategy of sovereignty is: "a kind of mirror image of the political theory of liberalism: not law, but exception, not judge but sovereign; not reason, but decision" (Kahn, 2011). Schooling in turn mirrors this approach to the extent that it produces the forms of subjectivity needed to naturalise obedience to sovereign decision as represented by a 'teacher' and the hierarchical apparatus through which sovereign decision is operationalised through the rules and systems of law, internal and external militarised forces and managerial systems in all the institutions of the state and private sector. It produces subjects that from cradle to grave are schooled to be subdued, submissive, disciplined, obedient. At best, people find their place and learn how to negotiate and how far to protest in order to win sufficient freedoms and rewards; at worst, they steal their freedoms and rewards through disobedience, disruption, violence.

The question of sovereignty and how it arises cannot be avoided. If there is no god to deliver the rules that humans must follow, then who or what occupies the place of sovereignty? If, as Spinoza formulated, "man is God to man" (Lucchese, 2009: 152) then the alternatives depend on how politics itself is perceived and structured. For the very rich, the answer lies in getting richer, so rich in fact that they are capable of being independent of others in all matters. This is the object of Davidson and Rees-Mogg's (1997) *The Sovereign Individual* that sits well with the broad neoliberal-oriented capitalism of Hayek, Friedman, Mises and the influential fictions of Ayn Rand as well as the neoconservatism of Schmitt, Strauss and Kristol and the populism of Bannon. This as we have seen is a mix that has been drawn into the hybrid *Californian Ideology* (Barbrook and Cameron, 1995; edmundberger, 2013) of Silicon Valley and worked its way into the Trump and Brexit campaigns and the rise of the hard right across Europe.

Democracy offers two broad strategic alternatives to the question of sovereignty. In each case, the people, rather than an individual or a god, are the occupier of the place of power as 'sovereign'. Under the first version democracy is either tamed (Bouton, 2007), managed (Wolin, 2008) and placed in chains (MacLean, 2017) by ensuring the elite rich are in all positions of political, juridical and economic power offering only an illusion of people sovereignty (Bernays, 1928; Lippmann, 1922; 1927); or, it is equated with the use of technical reason and thus the machineries of power are run by apolitical experts who deliver policy (Barber, 2007) because there is no alternative. Indeed, a hybrid of both combines seamlessly with the billionaire ideology of sovereign individuals; as well as the 'third way' (cf. Giddens, 1998) model associated with Bill Clinton and Tony Blair that combines a claimed degree of concern for social justice with acceptance of neoliberal market capitalism and the desirability of its billionaire entrepreneurs.

The second version of democracy begins to take shape when decisions that have been taken in private impact on the quality of life of others. For Dewey (1927), as a response to Lippmann's (1927) view that the public is a phantom, it is here in the consequences of decisions, particularly negative ones, that a public emerges to demand rights and redress. Dewey (1916, 1938; Mayhew and Edwards, 1936) focused on education as structurally necessary for the emergence of a democratic public. Recalling Dewey's (1916: 6) statement that, "the very process of living together educates", perhaps it is now that we can speak of the legacies of hope where the principles and practices of experimental social forms and their processes of education are critical – if not decisive – in the development of counter discourses, practices, institutions and forms of governance. Rather than schooling at all age levels in all institutions, being the engine of inequality can it become the ground for the promotion of democratic freedom with equality? However, as already discussed, there is a considerable machinery to confront and to dismantle if there is to be any serious challenge to the contemporary elitist status quo. Consequently: "as he grew older Dewey himself increasingly lost faith in the ability of democratic schooling, alone, to equip citizens with the collective practices that would allow them to make their society a better place" (Schutz, 2001: 267).

It may be, as Labaree (2010) states, Dewey won the arguments on points but, historically, he lost. However, given the continued interest in Dewey's ideas, he did not lose the educational debate (see for example the centennial special edition of the Journal of Curriculum Studies, 2016). If Dewey's vision of education and democratic living is to prevail, then democratic practices need to be systematically drawn into everyday relations and in particular into the organisation of all places where learning takes place. Only in such a way can elite-dominated forms of schooling that privilege the measurement of performance, competition and discipline be countered.

If there are, as it were, two contrasting 'architectures' reflecting the two streams of modernity (Israel, 2001; Mack, 2010; Ducheyne, 2017) for living together – the hierarchical, and the egalitarian – a decision must be made. If under the hierarchical architecture the strategy of schooling is to engineer learning in order to shape the powers of the young to meet the interests of the elites, then the challenge can only come from the radically asserted inclusion of powers that have been ignored, repressed, excluded in the processes of subjection. This challenge follows from the broadly Spinozan argument as explored by Balibar (1998) and Negri (1991) that there must be an equality of powers within and between individuals if freedom is to be attained personally, psychologically and socially. In short, freedom and equality are co-extensive – a relation named as *égaliberté* by Balibar (1994). This is initially understood by Spinoza in terms of what can only be termed a radical sovereignty to distinguish it from the sovereign of Schmitt, Strauss and indeed the market-driven sovereign individual of Davidson and Rees-Mogg. All are equally sovereign by natural right:

> it is certain that nature, taken in the abstract, has sovereign right to do anything she can; in other words, her right is co-extensive with her power. The power of nature is the power of God, which has sovereign right over all things; and inasmuch as the power of nature is simply the aggregate of the powers of all her individual components, it follows that every individual has sovereign right to do all that he can; in other words the rights of an individual extend to the utmost limits of his power as it has been conditioned. Now it is the sovereign law and right of nature that each individual should endeavour to preserve itself as it is, without regard to anything but itself; therefore this sovereign law and right belongs to every individual, namely to exist and act according to its natural conditions. We do not here acknowledge any difference between mankind and other individual natural entities, nor between men endowed with reason and those to whom reason is unknown; nor between fools, madmen, and sane people.
>
> (Spinoza, 2004: 45)

If radical sovereignty expresses a 'right' for each individual 'to do anything she can' then this 'can' is always placed into relationship with all individuals who also have a sovereign right to act differently from each other as conditioned by their own 'nature'. How can this provide a stable foundation for living? Spinoza recognises that such a formulation does not rule out acting due to hatred, conflicting desires and fear. However, if they are to avoid living miserably due to such conflicts and anxieties, people:

> must necessarily come to an agreement to live together as securely and well as possible if they are to enjoy as a whole the rights which naturally belong to them as individuals, and their life should be no more conditioned by the force and desire of individuals, but by the power and will of the whole body. This end they will be unable to attain if desire be their only guide (for by the laws of desire each man is drawn in a different direction); they must, therefore, most firmly decree and establish that they will be guided in everything by reason (which nobody will dare openly to repudiate lest he should be taken for a madman), and will restrain any desire which is injurious to a man's

fellows, that they will do all as they would be done by, and that they will defend their neighbour's rights as their own.

(Spinoza, 2004: 202–203)

In this agreement to live together the conditions for a public ethics is created, a public that, unlike a neoliberal or neoconservative public does not define itself in contrast to a private domain. Rather than reason imposing upon a recalcitrant body of passions and instincts, reason as a power of the body emerges as the body's creative solution. It is as much the internal desires, passions, powers of the individual as the external relations between individuals that are resolved through democratic reason. In this sense, it is the logic of a different architecture, a different political aesthetics to that of the hierarchies of elites or the iron cage of reason as Weber (2001) called it, shaping behaviours and constructing forms of organisation and designing environments that fulfil technical values of efficiency, cost-effectiveness or monetary profit maximisation rather than, say, happiness.

Under the logic of hierarchy, schools have been constructed to resemble iron cages ruled by a logic that takes little account of the body, the imagination, the spirit of debate. Rather, schooling under the dominant forms of modernity stemming from the Industrial Revolution has framed reason largely in terms of technical and bureaucratic reason. Elites require technicians of all kinds in all sectors to manage, administer and engineer projects that serve their interests. At one level, the transformations required to produce the worlds of iron cage modernity can be seen as a pedagogical challenge to old ways of seeing and acting. As an example, Hamilton (1980) identified a key ideological and material turning point in the eighteenth century. Indeed, he pinpointed it rather exactly – May 11, 1762. It was the moment when the classroom as a term was, perhaps, first recorded. Even if it is not the first use, it is a useful fiction. It was when "the Faculty of Glasgow University decided to convert a College 'Chamber' (living room) into a 'class room' for civil law." The university at the time was a centre of "educational and intellectual innovation". It was where key intellectual, educational and social reformers such as Adam Smith, Robert Owen, William Hamilton and David Stow met with members of the faculty. Hamilton sees the idea of the classroom as "an architectural unit" gaining dominance from the 1830s along with mass factory-style systems involving "lessons, subjects, timetables, grading, standardisation, streaming". This architectural unit and its factory-style systems still has global resonance despite dramatic changes in communications and production technologies. The concept of the 'system' is telling and has become a symptom of contemporary late capitalism with its focus on financialisation rather than production and its rapidly globalising forms that view nation states as tools for organising business rather than as a home centre from which to do business nationally and with the rest of the world. Hamilton points to Adam Smith's comment that: "Systems in many respects resemble machines …. A system is an imaginary machine, invented to connect together in the fancy those different movements and effects which are already in reality performed" (Smith, 1795: 44).

The school system as an imaginary machine progressively came together as a solution to the problem of charity schools not being able to cope with the numbers of poor people whose lives were being disrupted and displaced in the transitions from rural, artisanal and craft economies to an urban mass industrial economy (cf. Berman, 1982).

Under the metaphor of the imaginary machine, then, social and cultural logics underpinned by the rhetorics of rationality and modernity enabled the development of factory-like learning with its focus on masses, classes, surveillance, discipline and repetitive forms of learning that could be tested through mass forms of examination. The idea of the machine, the technical rational system, still has a central role in constructing the curricular imaginary in the twenty-first century. But rather than the factory it is the communications network designed to deliver, manage and assess 'learning' online that dominates thinking about the 'knowledge society' with its 'smart cities' and 'intelligent organisations' that form the policy makers' dreams of lifelong educational futures devoted to making individuals, communities, regions and nations competitive. The rhetoric of intelligent systems as opposed to the dumb machineries of the nineteenth- and twentieth-century mass factory systems is seductive. It produces ideas of schools being reformed and transformed by tailoring or individualising learning in ways that promote difference and diversity as well as equality. However, the vision has been easy to hijack.

A special edition of the Monthly Review (2011) provides an overview, in the USA, of the extent to which the logic of corporate capitalism has captured education. In summary:

> The hijacking of school reform by neoliberal corporate planners, private foundations, the U.S. Chamber of Commerce, the Business Roundtable, U.S. government strategists, and conservative-oriented education elites has led to an intensified attack on teachers, teachers' unions, teacher education, schools, and the kids themselves. The aim is to recreate the privileges of the powerful while forging a generation of technicians and passive followers, disciplining the lower classes to accept their place in the matrix. The gravitational pull of this narrative is so great that even radical reformers find themselves re-voicing the deceptive goals and phoney frames. If we are to take a thorough and honest look at the educational landscape before us, we cannot accept the standards and benchmarks established by the power elite, from the acceptance of capitalist development, meaningless and wasteful work, and ecological depredations as the only way forward, to the normalizing of white, middle-class discourse as the gold standard of excellence, anointed with titles like Standard English or Academic English.
> 
> (Ayers and Ayers, 2011: 1)

Just as Lowe called for an education of 'our masters' that would result in ensuring they made the right decisions, that is, the decisions desired by propertied elites who saw themselves as the possessors of intelligence and reason and thus the natural rulers of society, so contemporary schools are shaped by the modern versions of the political need for elites to manage the attitudes, behaviours, knowledge and skills of the various flavours of the mass that today comprise a given society. In the UK, this need has been articulated through the discourses of the market leading to increasing privatisation and 'marketisation' of schools, where each school is treated as if it were a business. Such privatisation occurs, not only in the UK but as a general, if 'hidden', global strategy (Balls and Youdell, 2007). For Benn (2012) there is a 'war' between competing ideologies. However, this war is being overwhelmingly won, it would seem, by the ideologues of the market who present a compelling narrative that there is no alternative. What can be done?

## Making moves that promote equalities

There are multiple 'Enlightenments' (Keane, 2016), 'modernities' (Eisenstadt, 2002). Each provides 'moves' that can be made in order to capture or justify or implement futures desired by particular individuals or interest groups. Rather than thinking under conditions of 'there is no alternative' to the twin ideologies of neoliberalism and neoconservativism, the move is to thinking under conditions of plurality which Arendt (1998) and others sees as fundamental to the human condition – it is for her the basis for politics as 'action' founded upon a principle of friendship (Nixon, 2014). Of significance for the argument of plurality is the idea of a radical enlightenment and alternative modernities that draws inspiration from Spinoza (Israel, 2001; Mack, 2010; Ducheyne, 2017). Spinoza's democracy of powers, where body is not separated from mind as in a Cartesian modernity, provides a way of rethinking the principles of association adopted to undertake political, economic and community forms of social organisation. As a consequence, there are multiple economic imaginaries (Gibson-Graham, 1996), a diversity of, or variety of, capitalisms (Jessop, 2011), just as there are alternative theories of markets (Harrison and Kjellberg, 2014; Bowman et al., 2014) – or indeed, different ways of framing 'world systems' (Wallerstein, 2004). It is not so much a question of which theory, which philosophical way of seeing, which interpretation is empirically 'right', but rather which one do we *want* to live with? That is why we must take decisions and make moves.

If there are choices and decisions to be made – and crisis demands decision – then returning to the critical imaginary of the factory as a place for the organisation of work, choices open up in terms of what work means and how it can be organised. The idea of the factory and consequently of work organisation was part of the revolutions of mind and practice that were taking place due to the ferment in philosophical thinking, debating and writing taking place from the mid-1600s in the works of Descartes, Spinoza and Bayle (Israel, 2001). For the capitalist:

> Work and labour are exclusively organised around the production of commodity exchange values that yield monetary return upon which capital builds its social powers of class domination. Workers, in short, are put in a position

where they can do nothing other than reproduce through their work the conditions of their own domination. This is what freedom under the rule of capital means for them

(Harvey, 2014: 64)

However, work and labour can be organised differently as Robert Owen and later developments of the co-operative movement demonstrated. Co-operativism has adopted many forms, some highly hierarchical in form and others highly egalitarian (c.f. Woodin, 2014). However, if this movement is reframed in a Spinozan rather than a Cartesian form of modernity the emphasis turns to an equality of powers engaged in projects of mutual benefit rather than a hierarchy of powers engaged in projects of exploitation and the politics of accumulation by dispossession (Harvey, 2006: 16). For example, drawing on Arendt's (1998) hierarchically ordered distinction between three fundamental kinds of human activities – labour, work and action – Dejours (1998; 2003) reframes the relationships, perceiving work as organically inclusive. Work for him involves both labour (in the sense of providing for biological needs such as gathering food) and action (in Arendt's sense of action to create social futures, that is, 'politics'). Thus the activity of work is not limited to transforming the natural world into an artificial human world through the use of tools to build houses, transport systems and so on but is at least embryonically a form of political action in terms of coming to agreements through debates about who is best fitted to design, manage, undertake the woodwork, the plumbing and so forth. In working and living together there are always many decisions being made about the best form of organisation to meet mutual projects for mutual ownership. In order to create the best possible result, different opinions and expertise have to be taken into account to come up with an agreed form of organisation – in short, there is already a politics of co-operation with democracy implicit, if not explicit in the process of working together. More specifically, there is an underlying educational process throughout the negotiations – people mutually learn from each other how to ensure the best outcomes for all are accomplished. This, in short, is an education as the basis for the development of common, public co-operatively created wealth, rather than the private in the form of 'human capital' where what is mutually produced is appropriated and owned as a means of enhancing the value of the individual in the competitive market place for jobs. Thus in the curricula of the common, it is the production of mutual value rather than objects whose predominant or only significance is in exchange value and their use in predatory practices for the accumulation of wealth and social privilege at the expense of others. If education engages in the creative work required for democratic forms of co-operation, it becomes an education against all forms of the politics of dispossession even where it is disguised by politicians as a virtuous politics of austerity.

Education becomes radically opposed to neoliberal, elite-driven forms of schooling through the organisation of work that returns to a broader narrative of co-operative, democratic endeavour to enhance the powers of the individual by drawing upon and contributing to the community structures, resources, heritages and processes upon which an individual depends for the enhancement of their own potential. Such educational narratives of plurality with mutuality and democratic co-operation run counter to neoliberal narratives of freedom only for the strongest who compete for personal profit and advantage by exploiting the common legacies of community to the benefit of capitalist elites at the expense of the rest. The multitude grounds the possibility of forming a plurality of relationships that move outside of the one-dimensional structure of a hierarchy. The radical move for the education of powers is thus to form new associations and categorisations that enable innovative forms of action based on discourses of openness, equality and inclusivity that are capable of undermining restrictive discourses. Such moves often take the form of a resistance to the dominating discourses, a struggle to counter them and a fight back to bring down the walls, remove the detention camps, in order to open and occupy freer spaces in which to create projects, work together and create visions of a freer form of society.

In the spirit of a Spinozan logic, to the extent that education assumes a diverse community of intelligences, each directed towards developing their individual powers to the greatest potential, then that potential is further enhanced if each individual is able to aggregate their powers with others for mutual benefit. The power of association is fundamental to engaging in mutual work to achieve mutual ends. Work in this sense has nothing to do with employment as defined under laws that give all ownership to the owners of private businesses or to a business as a legal 'person' since such employment involves giving up rights to shares in the ownership of anything produced unless otherwise stated. If what is at stake in any education that serves the individual rather than elites is the freedom to develop one's powers to their fullest potential, then those philosophies, schools, forms of organisation and practice that explicitly encourage the development of those powers can be sought out as a resource for contemporary circumstances. As Fielding (2009: 517) puts it we need to "reclaim and re-voice narratives of our radical past and weave our own emerging stories into the fabric of the future". Or as Harvey (2014: 90) puts it, as well as learning from the past there is "an obligation to write the poetry of our own future against the background of the rapidly evolving contradictions of capital's present".

Writing the future as a curricular strategy turns organisations into educational laboratories at first sight similar to Dewey's sense of the Laboratory School (1896–1904) in which he attempted "to release the 'powers' of individuals" and then "direct these individual powers to collective and socially productive ends" (Schutz, 2001: 268). This sounds at least to be quasi Spinozist except, of course, there are issues about how socially productive ends are chosen and how the direction towards these ends takes place. Dewey's pragmatism places thinking into a fall-back position from that of 'habits' that is, thinking only takes place when habits fail. In this sense habits are 'inscribed' corporally. This is not to say that habits are formed passively. Dewey (1916, section 2, chapter 4) made that:

a habit is a form of executive skill, of efficiency in doing. A habit means an ability to use natural conditions as means to ends. It is an active control of the environment through control of the organs of action

and "Education is not infrequently defined as consisting in the acquisition of those habits that effect an adjustment of an individual and his environment". From this point of view, the initial writing of the future is the writing of habits. It is only when there is an obstacle to their use that further thinking takes place in order to bring about a modification or the construction of entirely new habits. Growth, in this view, then depends on the formation of useful habits. Dewey's use of 'growth', as the Maussians who go by the name of Falafil[1] (2006) point out, has echoes of Spinoza's conatus and also of course, Mauss' 'body techniques' (Mauss, 1973). These two terms are useful for signalling the conservative weight and cultural specificity of habits as well as their potential for innovative growth. This is revealed in the culturally specific ways that people use their bodies whether in walking, chewing, swimming, coughing, spitting and in the almost infinite number of other activities they engage in. Mauss gives as an introductory example of the cultural specificity of these body techniques his observation during World War I of:

> the technique of digging. The English troops I was with did not know how to use French spades, which forced us to change 8,000 spades a division when we relieved a French division, and vice versa. This plainly shows that a manual knack can only be learnt slowly. Every technique properly so-called has its own form.
> 
> (Mauss, 1973: 71)

Interestingly, the 'thinking' applied here is of the puzzle variety, that is, what is the solution to ensuring the soldiers of World War I fighting trench warfare are able to use spades efficiently: change the spades according to the ones used in their specific cultures. It was not the sort of thinking that would be involved in questioning the purpose of the war itself.

Both forms of thinking – puzzle solving and challenging the puzzle itself – plus all the other powers of the body are involved in 'conatus' which is Spinoza's term for self-preservation. Self-preservation was involved therefore in the decision to use spades that were efficient in order to help increase their chances of survival. However, it would not take them out of the line of fire – only ending the war would do that. It requires another kind of thinking to examine the assumptions that frame the activities of the soldiers and undermine their capacity to make radically different collective decisions. In this kind of context, who has the right of using their power of thinking to decide about courses of action for their self-preservation?

Outside of war conditions and military control, in the peace time conditions of 'civil society', there are certainly many examples of people exerting their democratic rights of protest, pressure and indeed strike action in addition to the rights to vote in elections in order to shape policy. There is in that sense some progress in people's demands for democratic inclusion. However, within organisations, the household, the neighbourhood and on the streets the examples of democratic forms of social living and working are in the minority. Indeed, Rosanvallon (2013) argues that democracy as a regime has progressed whereas as a social form it has regressed and that: "The American and French revolutions did not distinguish between democracy as a regime of popular sovereignty and democracy as a society of equals". As against consent to inequality, there was as Rosanvallon (2013: 3) informs us in the words of Pierre-Louis Roederer, a key voice of the French Revolution: "The first motive of the revolution was impatience with inequalities". What then is the role of education to counter the consent to inequality that stifles and frustrates the freedoms all?

## Note

1 Pseudonym for Alain Caillé, Philippe Chanial and Fabien Robertson

# End of part one: Reflections on the research and educational implications of chapters 1–6

Realising the challenges to become a public

The challenge for both education and research, following chapters 1–6, is the struggle to realise an effective public rather than a phantom public (Lippmann, 1927). This involves rendering visible the invisible forms of issues and social formations impacting upon our lives in order to resist and struggle against obstacles inhibiting the development of socially just societies. Such forms are hard to see, indeed, invisible, not so much because of some inherent characteristic but the selective patterns of seeing that overlook, block or look-away from what already exists. This is distinct from strategies of distraction politically employed to shape and manage views and opinions. More fundamentally, it echoes Kuhn's (1970) 'paradigms' that organise ways of seeing the world. For him, change the paradigms and the 'facts' change. More broadly, a way of seeing takes the form of an 'imaginary' composed of how people relate, how society works. For example, Anderson's (1983) imagined communities involved 'seeing' a connection, an identity with millions of others they will never meet to form 'Britishness' or being an 'American'. Such forms of imagination contribute to what Rancière (2004) calls an aesthetics of politics through which the voices of individuals are defined as being countable or dismissible, as sensible or senseless. This is a sensual world built of all the things to which we perceptually attend and value in some way. It thus overlooks – or systematically inattends to – all the things that exist outside of the fields of attention. For example, in an experiment by Chabris and Simons (2010) by counting the numbers of ball passes between players, what is not counted and thus not seen is the gorilla that walks on stage. It is what Mack and Rock (1998) call 'inattentional blindness' or what Austin and Leander (2019) call 'visibility practices' involved in seeing and overlooking. What you don't look at, you don't see. Indeed, with regard to contemporary working practices, Taylor (1919: 40) the developer of 'scientific management' boasted that his work was so simplified, an intelligent gorilla could do it. In such approaches where performance is measured and monitored through the achievement of specific targets, what is specifically overlooked – and thus not counted in management – is not the gorilla but the human being.

Given inattentional blindness, the process of selective inattention becomes a strategy by which to construct 'not seeing' and thus rendering given phenomena invisible. So, in the empirical sciences adopting forms of positivism where only measurable phenomena can be counted as scientific objects, values and 'subjective' perceptions, intuitions, meanings, feelings and emotions are 'removed'. As in an often-quoted statement attributed to the psychologist Thorndike (1914: 141; cited by Hunsicker, 1925: 15): "If a thing exists, it exists in some amount; and if it exists in some amount, it can be measured" (Thorndike and Gates, 1929: 300). Hence, if it cannot be measured, it doesn't exist. Even in education, "If any given knowledge or skill or power exists, it exists in some amount" (Thorndike, 1922: 27). More generally, Thorndike (1940: 152, 161ff) saw monetary value as a convenient form of measuring preferences. As discussed in our earlier chapters, monetary value was politically convenient and underpinned economic social choice theory (Buchanan and Tullock, 1962; Urken, 1991) and games theory (Amadae, 2015) leading to forms of collective hardship and precarity engineered by shifty neoliberal policies of austerity. In the rush to emulate 'scientific procedure', what was too often overlooked or minimised, or indeed rendered invisible or inaudible as 'noise', was the sheer complexity of the human and its resistance to being reduced to the purity of clear and distinct categories necessary for logical and statistical manipulation. The weakness of such reasoning applied to the social worlds of everyday life was already nascent in Cohen's comment:

> In the end, the truth of a generalisation from a sample depends on the homogeneity of the group with respect to which we wish to generalise. A single experiment on a new substance, to test whether it is acid or alkaline, is much more convincing than the result of a questionnaire addressed to millions of army men to measure their intelligence. For the latter is not a simple quality of a uniformly repeatable pattern. In this respect the methods of social statistics are gross compared with refined analysis, so that when our analysis is thoroughgoing, as it generally is in physics, one or two samples are as good as a million. If what we are measuring is really homogeneous, one is sufficient. In the social field, therefore, statistics cannot take the place of analysis ....
> (Cohen, 1944: 134–135)

In the analysis of the social, and more specifically the struggle for a public, it is clear from the preceding chapters that what counts is not homogeneity but difference and change. What then is the nature of *analysis* that is required for research and also for education?

## Analysis, the place of truth and what *counts*

If research and education are principally concerned with augmenting the powers of individuals to know the truth about themselves and their horizons – horizons limited only by the dynamically varying and expanding 'perceptual' – then analysis begins for research and education with what is to be publicly counted, what has not been accountable and what cannot be measured but demands a public voice to express the fullness of being within perceived 'horizons' circumscribing worlds of experience that define the positions, locations and relations of subjects to each other and to their objects. What counts as being publicly 'visible', 'audible', 'sayable', 'demandable' within such horizons is equivalent to fully existing, that is, emerging, standing out (*existere*) in one's individuality, one's difference for others to see, hear and value. It is within these horizons that what is possible, probable, plausible, real and actualisable come to be seen as the basis for action in a world that realises the potentials of an individual and, more specifically, associations between individuals engaging in mutual projects. It is within an horizon that 'truth' takes its position of public as well as personal responsibility in relation to the evidences required to justify action. In that sense, truth has no meaning and no position without a public discourse capable of relating and accounting for the position of the subject standing with others having powers of action. If this is so, then the nature of the public capable of holding critical discourses as the foundation for a society of mutual benefit for all becomes the 'end' for the endeavours of education and research. To this end it is not the certitude of reason in that mechanical paradigmatic sense of tool kits of rational procedure that is the first significant step but 'doubt', 'suspending belief' and 'disturbing' the seeming certainty of what is counted as known, right, valid.

Rational procedure, by itself, is not a trustworthy guide unless it stems from a public capable of systematic, rigorous and critical reflection upon what is to count as the 'truth' of observations, experiences, ideas, explanations, interpretations and theories about the world. As the old software programmer's saying went, 'garbage in, garbage out' – if your evidence is rubbish, then no matter how systematic the logical, mathematical or statistical procedures the conclusions will reflect the inputs: trash. This essentially is what is at stake in the divisions between those (for example Bloom) who see education as a matter of instilling traditional virtues, employable skills, knowledge, 'common sense', and the 'right' beliefs as 'contents' needed to form and maintain a stable society on the one hand; and on the other, those (like Dewey) who value the continuous practices of critical thinking, discovery of knowledge and problem solving as processes essential for personal development as well as forming the creative, mutually supportive relations and forms of organisation fundamental to a democratically effective public.

Complicating – even hindering – the exploration of peoples' everyday life, there have been, and continue to be, unhelpful disciplinary battles as to the relative merits and epistemological significance of the quantitative and the qualitative approaches, producing a 'friends–enemies' relation between adherents of different theoretical perspectives, paradigms, methodologies. In each case, methodological decisions have to be made about what counts as the 'data' to be collected or recorded and what constitutes a viable method of recordings related to what happened as it was happening. And in doing this, what counts as 'analysis'? For example, Durkheim in his pioneering *The Rules of Sociological Method* published in 1895, analysis begins in identifying social facts.

> A social fact is every way of acting, fixed or not, capable of exercising on the individual an external constraint;
> or
> which is general over the whole of a given society, whilst having an existence of its own, independent of its individual manifestations.
>
> (Durkheim, 1982: 59)

The sense of constraint that marks the degree of independence of the 'social fact' depends on the perceptions, the understanding, the knowledge, the capacities to interpret as well as the prior experience of the individual. That is to say, all the powers of the individual in conjunction with those of others are involved in the manifestation of a social fact. Indeed, it is the powers exercised by individuals in relation with each other that constitute this 'constraint' that is both existentially intimate in its 'individual manifestations' and external in its generality over 'society'. In the pursuit of generality, the 'social fact' as something objective, where 'objective' is reduced to being measurable and testable, can be recognised in the various positivist approaches spread across the social sciences with perhaps economics being the most 'successfully' mathematised. In education, for example, as well as Thorndike's work, there was Cyril Burt whose influence – regardless of accusations of fraud (Kamin, 1974) – led to IQ measurement as a basis for selection into different tiers of schooling in the UK. Unsurprisingly, the selection favoured the middle classes and the wealthy, reinforcing and 'naturalising' their social and economic privileges. Herrnstein and Murray's (1994) *The Bell Curve* argued the view that the spread of ability across a population naturally followed the bell curve: few at the 'tails' either side of the mass in the middle. Thus, the elites cluster as a 'natural' grouping at the 'tail' representing the upper end of 'intelligence'. Rushton and Jenson (2005) summarised 30 years of such research extending it into racial comparisons 'proving' the broad inferiority of those categorised as African and Afro-American. Such work has provided a powerful tool for the segregation and selection of people in schools and in employment. Indeed, Murray (1990; 2005) recommended 'social apartheid' and 'custodial democracy' in order to separate and protect the desirable from the undesirable elements of society.

In this sense the invention of IQ is a division-creating category that works by suspending the complexity of individuals and organising research and education into debates about 'nature' versus 'nurture' that distract attention from the complex relations that enrich cultural, economic, political and social organisation experience and benefits. It is important, then, to be careful about how one justifies categorisations for research and educational purposes. Indeed, in political terms differences in ability were 'naturalised', 'proving' the superiority of elite white men, and European culture (see in particular Bloom, 1987; Huntington, 1996; Kristol, 1995; 2011; Murray, 2005) – a view consonant with and used to support neoconservative, sexist, imperialist, anti-immigrant and racist views.

At an everyday organisational level, measurable categories enable the production of management tools by which to engineer people, whether it is by Skinner's behaviourism on 'learning' that could be employed through social engineering to produce if not Thoreau's (2018) *Walden* published in 1854 of a utopian life of being in tune with nature, then at least a *Walden II* (Skinner, 1976), the product of scientists with their schedules of rewards for behaviours that can be progressively shaped – or nudged (Halpern, 2015) – towards those deemed by experts as 'desirable'. Perhaps the ultimate educational fantasy in this regard is expressed either by Reynolds (Reynolds and Stringfield, 1996), whose inspiration for 'high reliability' schools was the precision engineering required for nuclear power stations and the precision management required for air traffic control, or the educational views of Schreber's (1955; Schatzman, 1973) father who in the nineteenth century was influential in the German education system of the time as well as internationally, but unfortunately in rigorously applying his methods of microcontrol to his own children sent them mad and suicidal. These extreme versions of 'improving' the products of schooling aside, the controversies about how research can be employed to generate the evidence by which to 'improve' education can be seen in Hammersley (2007). However, 'improvement' is such a sly word. One always has to ask, in whose interests? And who is in a position to define these – elites, politicians, experts, parents … the 'public'?

The best that can be said of quantitative approaches when applied to people is that they provide a heuristics for decision-making; but it needs to be remembered that no matter how sophisticated the mathematical operations, they are necessarily based upon relatively crude analyses that are required to obtain measurements. The danger in the widespread application of management techniques in the public sector focusing upon measuring performance is that it can reinforce the corrosive view that experts should design the management of behaviour, influence consent to elite policies and manipulate political and economic choices. In such expert-driven systems what cannot be measured remains, however, as 'noise', 'blurs', 'nonsense'. It was this 'remainder' that was the fertile source for exploitation in the Trump and Brexit campaigns that blamed elites and their experts for the sources of popular discontent. The question then is how to include in any public debate the left out, the wilful actors who do not fit policy categories, who change their minds, misread, fantasise, sometimes lie, or, at least, disguise their real feelings and opinions?

What is missing, then, from the mathematised and behavioural accounts of how research and education should be undertaken is a sense of empowering relationships with others to organise, define robust evidence and act accordingly. It is through actively deploying a multiplicity of senses (seeing, touching, hearing, smelling, tasting), adopting different vantage points (in front, behind, below, above), manipulating objects to experience their 'hardness', temperature, permeability and so on and sharing with others these observations, that key unchanging or persisting features of the material and social world can be educed. Similarly with feelings, emotions, ideas, by sharing and debating with others comparisons and contrasts can be drawn out or 'triangulated' to ascertain what varies and what does not vary across different groups, forms of organisation and contexts. Through such a process public intelligence is effectively constituted.

## Towards public intelligence

To understand the social worlds of people requires exploring and analysing how they build, modify, transform and break relationships with each other and the objects of their worlds. To do that requires a different approach than that employing a model where all relationships are broken in order to create the conditions necessary for statistical research that depends upon homogenised and individualised categories to construct its research methodology and design. Since there are no social conditions that currently form freely that conform to the rigid controls of the laboratory experiment of the material sciences, then as Cohen (1944) rightly stressed, all such studies of the social world are limited, indeed, suspect. Critically what is left out is the agency, the wilfulness, the fantasy-driven decisions and, at best, the critical thinking, debate and struggle between people who have a multiplicity of different interests and demands about what kind of social order and forms of organisation are 'best' that neither rocks nor atoms exhibit. More specifically what has been ignored, or kept under wraps and deployed deviously, is the construction and use of power as well as the public's development of independent political 'intelligence', that is, their critical knowledge about how to resist exploitation and promote change. These dimensions of the human have, of course, been the stuff of poets, storytellers, diarists, historians, travel writers and those who seek to persuade that they have the answer to all the woes facing a people. However, rather than as audience to the stories of others, it is as members of an active public that the voice of each can be raised, heard and counted. Through mainstream forms of education and research, this power has been taken out of the equation by the mathematical formula and the behavioural schedules of stimulus and reward that shape behaviour and manage the manufacture of consent from the days of schooling, work and retirement until death: "It's the fundamental problem of why the left and liberals can't find a way of challenging what's rising up now. They gave in, and have given up talking about power. I think that's because power is quite frightening" (Curtis in MacInnes, 2019).

But the point is, it's not just talking about power but finding, expressing one's own power and joining with the powers of others that is frightening both for the left intellectuals as well as wider members of a society, particularly when:

> Information warfare is where we're living now. More specifically, it's story warfare. There's this battle in the US where our oligarchs are claiming they are the Joseph Campbell heroes. That they're the ones who are going through the three-act structure of going into the unknown. Charles Koch is taking on

the world. There's this weird thing going on where these traditional story structures really play bogus now.

(McKay in MacInnes, 2019)

Whether as the ideal – or fantasy – mathematised worlds, stories (Lippmann, 1927) or myths Campbell (1968) constructed and interpreted to support elite social orders (Schostak, 1986; 1993; Samuel and Thompson, 1990,) as discussed in the earlier chapters, these are supported by discourses, material structures, institutional mechanisms and forms of organisation that comprise the 'conditioning frameworks' that at national levels can be manipulated by elites "for impairing, and locking-in neoliberal reforms" (Grinspun and Kreklewich, 1994). Such conditioning frameworks are not limited to neoliberal policy, of course, but can be found under neoconservative or any hierarchically determined social order. The danger for researchers and educationists is that they become part of the conditioning frameworks, and thus tools of the domestic and global power elites. Focusing on the delivery of programmes or undertaking only those forms of research that meet such measurable 'quality' and 'impact' criteria as imposed by the UK's Research Assessment Framework (REF) criteria and more generally research and education directly funded by governments and corporations, there is the danger researchers and educationists become neoliberal and neoconservative 'fellow travellers', that is 'corporate professors' (Giroux, 2018). Given the difficulties of active engagement with the creation of 'public intelligence' as a challenge to elites, some may despair that achieving it is hopeless:

At every level, including our own, this is a seriously undereducated society. The problems it faces are intractable with the kinds of information and argument now publicly available. There is no obvious way of measuring this most serious of deficits. Some indications occur in the condition of our newspapers, after a hundred years of general literacy, and in the character of parliamentary and electoral debates. The way is open for weak minds to renounce in some despair, the whole project of public education.

(Williams, 1989)

How then can research and educational methods address the exercise of public intelligence capable of resisting and countering authoritarianism and the production of what Lippmann calls phantom publics (Lippmann, 1927) and Williams the "seriously undereducated society"? The following chapters turn now to addressing what has been devalued and most feared by research and education that has been driven by neoliberal, neoconservative and corporatist policy: the creative powers, the life, the dreams of ordinary people in its emergence as an effective public. It is to be argued that an effective public is coextensive with education and the production of research-based knowledge. If corporate forms of research have developed to exclude, devalue, tame or make invisible the hard to measure, then what are the conditions and methods required for undertaking a good analysis that does not leave out the hard to measure, the otherwise unseeable, inaudible, unspeakable and unfelt – and in particular, discourses of power? It is the idea of the public that involves the bringing together all possible views on a particular object – material, social, symbolic, ethical or, indeed, imaginary – that what is common, what is different, what is agreed, what is in dispute, what is marginal or what is excluded can be debated and assessed as 'valid' or otherwise. It is in this way, the following chapters will argue, that education and research as a function of public intelligence is constituted as a condition to avoid democracy being reduced to a spectator sport, where audiences cheer on the antics of their preferred players. It will not be easy:

*We cannot go back and change the beginning. But we can start where we are and change the ending.*

(Attributed to C.S. Lewis)

Part II

# What Can Be Done?

# Chapter 7

# What might turn social learning into social movements?

If democracy originated as a struggle against elite domination and exploitation then it continues as a counter to counter the ways in which truths, beliefs, attitudes, behaviours are structured by elites in everyday life to reinforce their power. For Crouch (2004: 2–3) "Democracy thrives when there are major opportunities for the mass of ordinary people actively to participate, through discussion and autonomous organisations, in shaping the agenda of public life, and when they re actively using these opportunities." However, democracy is not thriving other than as post-democracy where behind the "spectacle of the electoral game, politics is really shaped in private interaction between elected governments and elites that overwhelmingly represent business interests" (Crouch, 2004: 4). If 'post-democracy' is to be challenged, what new road to freedom can be constructed, and who is to follow it?

Consider this example, when the investigative journalist famed for his role in exposing Nixon wrote a book on Trump and an anonymous White House insider wrote an exposé on Trump's 'craziness' Trump's base supporters were hard to convince. A Trump supporter, Douglas Knight, was interviewed for his reaction:

> He was blissfully unaware that a book by investigative journalist Bob Woodward and a New York Times op-ed by an anonymous White House official were supposed to herald the end of his support for the man whom he voted for in 2016.
>
> "I hadn't heard nothin' 'bout it yet," the 50-year-old construction worker said. "You know, they're up north. It takes a little bit for news to travel this far."
>
> Even in the age of the internet and 24-hour cable news?
>
> "Oh yeah, it still takes time."
>
> Strikingly, when Knight did learn of the op-ed, the impact was minimal.
>
> "I don't pay a lot of attention to the news, 'cause they don't tell you the truth anyway," he said, echoing a sentiment common among the Trump faithful about the fourth estate, or the 'Fake News Media', as Trump calls it.
>
> Knight gave no credit to special counsel Robert Mueller's investigation into potential collusion between Russia and the Trump campaign.

"It's just bullshit," he said, rejecting not only the idea that the president colluded with Russia to sway the election in his favour, but the notion that Russia interfered in the election at all.

"The people of the United States ain't gonna let that happen," he said.

For Knight, none of the endless scandals that seem to shake Washington and east coast media on a weekly basis register. All that matters is that Trump "went in to make America like it's supposed to be".

(Pittman, 2018)

As Anderson (1983) argues, we live as imaginary communities constructed by the mass media then such illusory bubbles pre-formed by mass media – or nowadays social media – to present pictures of the nation as a common community as the basis for a national identity and culture create the conditions where counter evidence simply cannot be seen. If a common illusion is the basis for judging 'truth', then there is no 'outside' that can puncture this 'truth'. Of course, times has moved on from Anderson's discussion of the role of mass media in constructing the imaginary community supporting British nationalism. There is now the role of social media or alternative news media that Trump labelled "Fake News Media" to take into account. Nevertheless, the role of the imaginary community in being the ground of 'truth' remains. As the final arbiter in this exchange, it is the 'people' who stand against what counts as false news in their eyes. Perhaps to challenge the one-dimensional discourse overseen by 'the people' involves overcoming the fear that what is perceived as real is an illusion. Because, if it is an illusion, what is left? How can one live one's life? Indeed, Erich Fromm in his 1942 classic warned there was *The Fear of Freedom* that is the psychological fear of freely acting to challenge the conditions of unfreedom in everyday life. However, the conditions of unfreedom have first to be seen and the fears overcome.

## Learning 'truth'

Truth has always been problematic. And the Trump and Brexit campaigns heightened public debates about post-truth, truthiness – and of course trumpiness (Zimmer, 2010; Weber, 2016). It seems like a no-win debate. Each side 'sees' a truth the other does not. Each side has *their* heroes who speak *their* truth. It takes courage to challenge – a long-valued virtue (Foucault, 2006). However, the courage to speak the truth does not guarantee that the truth has indeed been spoken.

If it is the case that a one-dimensional discourse becomes self-fulfilling, that is, it is the grounds of its own truth, then those grounds can only be opened up through the admission of multiplicity, where no single source of perception dominates as the last resort for validating 'the truth'. In that sense, there is no 'people' capable of challenging a conformity of view and identity. However, a multitude with a plurality of views can take each other into account. There are then multiple learnings that are open to debate, challenge, cross checking and further learning to construct multi-dimensional accounts. Through imagination anything is possible – people, as well as pigs, might sprout wings and fly. However, for people to fly certain radical changes to their biology have to be accomplished. Without that advance in the biological sciences then the technologies of air transport will have to suffice. In each case, certain laws of material reality have to be educed, tested and realised in the material world. Under the schema of Spinoza's three kinds of knowledge, where the first provides knowledge based on imagination and the senses but can lead to falsehoods, the second, based upon the experiences of the first, is formed through what is experienced as common and validated in terms of being useful or convenient amongst individuals across a variety of perspectives, this is turn leads to the third kind that furthers the notion of the common in order to take it into the infinite realm of what is eternally true. This schema can be reimagined through an Husserlian phenomenological method that starts not from Descartes but from Spinoza. Husserl transformed the Cartesian doubt into the more neutral suspension of taken for granted understandings and beliefs concerning the truth or reality of something thought or perceived. In that sense, the ground of phenomenological knowledge is in the imagination and senses (first kind of knowledge) of individuals pursuing their everyday lives as they negotiate their relations to each other to establish shared understandings that are 'true' for all practical purposes (second kind of knowledge). Husserl recognised the contribution of pragmatist philosophers to understanding everyday life as the paramount reality (see, for example, the explorations of phenomenology and pragmatism in the special edition of William James Studies, 2016). Schutz drew on this 'paramount reality' for his development of a phenomenological sociology from Husserl's philosophical method. The idea of 'bracketing' this paramount reality by the ethnomethodologists Cicourel (1964) and Garfinkel (1967) stemmed from phenomenological readings. The philosophical method, for them it can be argued, provided the equivalent of the third kind of knowledge. Its purpose was to generate theory validated by identifying what is common across different viewpoints or what resists disruption and disturbance of taken for granted ways of thinking, talking and behaving as in Garfinkel's (1967) method of causing trouble. These, together with the success of grounded theory (Glaser and Strauss, 1967) in influencing the formation of theory from close observation of everyday behaviour, interaction and discourses provides some insight into ways of thinking through the development of Spinoza's kinds of knowledge in a modern context of research practice. A Spinozan, or more generally radical enlightenment, turn brings into focus the glossed over politics of knowledge creation that has been the legacy of reason reduced to producing a mathematisation of the world (Husserl, 1970), an instrumental rationality (Habermas, 1984), an iron cage of reason (Weber, 2001). A reflection on Spinoza essentially returns debates back to a politics and ethics of knowledge creation in that he saw the fullest realisation of what he called his 'intuitive science' – based on the third kind of knowledge – in the context of a democratic organisation of powers, that is, the actual powers of bodies, not some disembodied, virtual mind (cf., Lucchese, 2009). It is at least an interesting flight of fancy to wonder what might have become of Husserl's phenomenology and its sociological translations had he written 'Spinozan Meditations' instead of *Cartesian Meditations* (Husserl, 1960).

Spinoza begins with the observation that generally people prefer to live alongside each other rather than in isolation, no matter how barbaric the resulting society may be. To that extent they live as 'multiple individuals' rather than the solitary Cartesian 'I-Think'. And in living alongside each other in some form of social relation they converse, listen and debate. This provides a richness of viewpoint, experience and argumentation that is greater than that obtained by the individual alone. In the constant comparisons and contrasts – to borrow a common grounded theory phrase for the development of categories from data – between viewpoints concerning the objects of debate, lines of separation can be educed between that which is considered 'the same' and that which is 'different'. This knowledge of sameness and difference can be nuanced to identify – as in Husserl's *eidetic variation*, that is, variation in the mind – what is essential whether defined as being invariant in all possible variations; or that which is invariant across a range of specified viewpoints and contexts; or that which holds convenient family resemblances that are useful for broadly identifying socially significant patterns. This then takes in a range of 'objects' from the mathematically precise to the more difficult and often disputable definitions of the 'good', the 'beautiful' and the 'socially just'. The more something becomes disputable, the more it becomes politically significant as creating a dividing line between adherents of the different views. Nevertheless, if people prefer to live in peace rather than hostility, then they will seek creative solutions; otherwise, hostility may become war. Spinoza advocates democracy as the best solution to hostility and war. The formation of knowledge through its passage from first to third kind, then keeps its embodied, social and political nature rather than abstracting it into some controlled, idealised universe that can be mathematised. Knowledge, truth, generalisation across viewpoints and contexts are thus embodied social products. Knowledge and social learning are inextricable, coming into existence only when relationships with others are constructed that demand reciprocity, exchange, commerce.

There is in these interactions a play of values, subject positions and the creation of forms of organisation at least for the duration of a transaction of some kind. In democratic contexts, the relationships that develop depend upon trust or at least the belief that the trust in the other will be reciprocated and fulfilled in terms of mutual action for mutual benefit. In contexts that are not democratic, suspicion will rule as each attempts to out-game or impose views upon the other. There is then an intimate connection between political context of social learning, social action and the production of the goods and services that realise well-being and the common good. That is to say, work, and its forms of organisation, is also fundamentally connected to social learning, knowledge, social justice and the good society.

## The populist turn

The claim to govern rationally has been critical to the view that given the fall of the Soviet Union, the political philosophy underlying western liberal market democracies won (Fukuyama 1992). Mouffe sees in this the emergence of the post-political which is:

> the blurring of frontiers between right and left. It is the result of the consensus established between parties of centre-right and centre-left on the idea that there was no alternative to neoliberal globalisation. Under the imperative of "modernisation", social democrats have accepted the diktats of globalised financial capitalism and the limits it imposes on state intervention and public policies.
> 
> Politics has become a mere technical issue of managing the established order, a domain reserved for experts. The sovereignty of the people, a notion at the heart of the democratic ideal, has been declared obsolete. Post-politics only allows for an alternation in power between the centre-right and the centre-left. The confrontation between different political projects, crucial for democracy, has been eliminated.
> 
> This post-political evolution has been characterised by the dominance of the financial sector, with disastrous consequences for the productive economy. This has been accompanied by privatisation and deregulation policies that, jointly with the austerity measures imposed after the 2008 crisis, have provoked an exponential increase in inequality.
> 
> (Mouffe, 2018a)

As a result of the loss of alternatives able to speak for those who have not benefitted from – indeed, have been impoverished by – the processes of modernisation, the dominance of finance, the voiceless have been an easy target for exploitation by 'populists' who claim to speak on their behalf. However, the self-styled political 'moderates' were not able to hear, or ignored the overlooked demands. For some, the voices of protestors, such as those engaged in the Occupy movement, were just 'noise', incomprehensible and thus dismissed (Schostak and Schostak, 2013: 96–97). For others, populism represented an existential threat to democracy itself. Mounk (2018: 1), for example, saw it as a confrontation between 'the people' and 'democracy' with "authoritarian populists on the rise" and a "system of government that had seemed immutable looks as though it might come apart".

> First, populists claim, an honest leader – one who shares the pure outlook of the people and is willing to fight on their behalf – needs to win high office. And second, once this honest leader is in charge, he needs to abolish the institutional roadblocks that might stop him from carrying out the will of the people. Liberal democracies are full of checks and balances that are meant to stop any one party from amassing too much power and to reconcile the

interests of different groups. But in the imagination of the populists, the will of the people does not need to be mediated, and any compromise with minorities is a form of corruption. In that sense, populists are deeply democratic: much more fervently than traditional politicians, they believe that the demos should rule. But they are also deeply illiberal: unlike traditional politicians, they openly say that neither independent institutions nor individual rights should dampen the people's voice.

(Mounk, 2018: 7–8)

In Mounk's view democracy depends on the relation between liberalism and the people. Given that direct participation in decision-making is not practical in a nation of millions, liberal democracies have evolved hierarchical systems where representatives of the 'will of the people' – as defined by the rules and mechanisms deployed to register eligibility to vote and process the results of voting – take decisions and experts deliver the policies. However, liberalism and the institutions of liberalism can be subverted, displaced or removed by illiberal governments. In his argument, this relation is now being undermined by populist insurgents who draw upon the fears and angers of people in order to attack liberal values regarding immigrants, other faiths, other cultures, other ways of life, other identities:

Hierarchical democracy allows popularly elected leaders to enact the will of the people as they interpret it, without having to make allowances for the rights or interests of obstinate minorities. Its claim to being democratic need not be disingenuous. In the emerging system, the popular will reigns supreme (at least at first). What sets it apart from the kind of liberal democracy to which we are accustomed is not a lack of democracy; it is a lack of respect for independent institutions and individual rights.

(Mounk, 2018: 10)

In short, Mounk regards the people as the problem because they are a prey to illiberal, authoritarian populists who use the 'popular will' to undermine liberal democracy through the "populist disease" (p. 260). This he sees as a recent problem destabilising liberal hierarchical democracy. As a solution, he argues there needs to be a defence of liberal hierarchical democracy; or, as Mouffe would put it, a return to post-politics to ensure the mass does not have the means to express those demands that the elites at the top do not value, can not see, or do not want to take into account.

Frank (2018) reviewing Mounk's book presents a radically different view of populism. He traces a history of American populism from the time of Jefferson and Jackson but says

Populism's evil rightwing doppelganger is usually dated to 1968, when George Wallace and Richard Nixon figured out how to turn the language of working-class majoritarianism against liberalism. Rightwing populists have been building movements and winning elections in the US ever since.

He illustrates his argument that there is a 'good' populism with reference to Lawrence Goodwyn's (1978: vii) *The Populist Moment*, a history of the agrarian revolt of the 1890s that was "the largest democratic mass movement in American history". In short, populism itself is not the problem. Indeed, as Mouffe (2018a) points out, populism expresses a "democratic nucleus" at the core of their frustrations and demands. In that sense, by building upon the 'democratic nucleus' can a road to freedom be built?

## Democracy is the road to freedom

Goodwyn (1978: viii) describes how in the 1870s,

> the farmers increasingly talked to each other about their troubles and read books on economics in an effort to discover what had gone wrong. Some of them formed organisations of economic self-help like the Grange and others assisted in pioneering new institutions of political self-help like the Greenback Party.

This in itself did not lead very far. However, they:

> developed new methods that enabled them to try to regain a measure of control over their own lives. Their efforts, halting and disjointed at first, gathered form and force until they grew into a coordinated mass movement that stretched across the American Continent.

What were these methods?

Goodwyn saw the process of democratic movement-building occurring in four broad conceptual stages:

> (1) the creation of an autonomous institution where new interpretations can materialise that run counter to those of prevailing authority – a development which for the sake of simplicity, we may describe as "the movement forming"; (2) the creation of a tactical means to attract masses of people – "the movement recruiting"; (3) the achievement of a heretofore culturally unsanctioned level of social analysis – "the movement educating"; and (4) the creation of an institutional means whereby the new ideas, shared now by the rank and file of the mass movement, can be expressed in an autonomous political way – "the movement politicised."
>
> (Goodwyn, 1978: xviii)

But why do such efforts not occur more often? First because the established elites raise roadblocks at every stage and second because of:

that complex of rules, manners, power relationships, and memories that collectively comprise what is called culture. "The masses" do not rebel in instinctive response to hard times because they have been culturally organised by their societies not to rebel. They have, instead, been instructed in deference.

(Goodwyn, 1978: x)

Social movements are started, according to Goodwyn, by people who have reached a high level of political self-respect, are not resigned and are not intimidated. In a sense this repeats the hope for a leader, a leadership group, a vanguard that is expressed by Zizek's (2013) call for a Thatcher of the Left. This may appeal to those who believe there is nothing other than the eternal return of a master with the difference only that the master expresses an ideology of mastery over the masses that is more congenial to live with. Until, of course, the Thatchers of the Right can return on the backs of newly oppressed and aggrieved groups. Is there then, another way?

For Mouffe (2018) the answer lies in a radicalisation of democracy. This is to be accomplished by providing an alternative vocabulary to that of the right-wing populists by which to express complaints and make demands; by radical reformism; and by seeking broad alliances amongst groups and movements involved in diverse struggles who can at least agree on their common 'adversary'. In that way a political line or frontier is drawn between a 'people' and the oligarchic elites who repress them. She refers to *Podemos* in Spain, Mélenchon's *France Insoumise*, Bernie Sanders in the US and Jeremy Corbyn in the UK "whose endeavour to transform the Labour party into a great popular movement, working 'for the many, not the few', has already succeeded in making it the greatest left party in Europe" (Mouffe, 2018a). Thus, the strategy is to use what already exists and reform it through the force of the 'people' against their adversaries who also use what already exists in order to erode its democratic potential while reinforcing its authoritarian potential. This agonistic relation between adversaries is what for Mouffe defines *the* political. It is as true for the right as for the left. Populist movements of the right have sought to create the dividing line between immigrants and those who by birth and culture have a right to live and work in a given country. This in turn enables the frontier to be also placed between those liberal elites – who have advocated immigration and the immigrants who have threatened the livelihoods of the local communities they have 'invaded' and the multiculturalism that has 'diluted' national identity – and those who speak for the 'people' and their national culture, their language, their traditional values, their jobs and ways of life.

Building a left strategy involves maintaining democracy as the privileged signifier. If democracy is to count for people, then they have to be included. Democracy is not an entirely empty signifier, it is already – and always – shaped and pervaded by an embodied sense of freedom and equality. If people's voices are not included freely and equally, they will look elsewhere for their expression. What is empty is the place of power (Lefort, 1988). That has to be constructed by people aggregating their powers and creating forms of organised force that underlie discourses of legitimacy and the application of rules and laws. Under tyranny the place of power is occupied by the tyrant who is able to command all the forms of organisation under his or her will. If a revolution removes the tyrant, then there is a vacuum at the centre of power. How will it be filled? When the tyrant Mubarak was toppled only the symbol of power had fallen. What remained were the elites with their military (Roberts and Schostak, 2012). When a party in a democracy is voted out of power, what remains are the institutions that enable the peaceful passage of power as well as the electoral system that ensures regular voting and the institutions that enable protagonists and the 'public' to debate and formulate and critique alternative analyses and policies. That is to say, in each case there is a legacy that shapes the contents of what can or cannot be constructed in the place of power. For this reason, a radical reformist approach in a western-style democracy intends to start with what is available and to deepen the democratic practices, procedures and mechanisms of all forms of organisation as well as create the conditions for the emergence of any new forms of democratic organisation that are necessary for equality and freedom. Protest is not enough if the governing organisations and the ways of perceiving and realising the distribution of power remain untouched. Revolution removes the tyrant but if that still leaves the organisations of control in place then there has been no effective change. What is it that creates such inertia?

Wherever one looks in a society, even those that claim to be social and liberal democracies, there remain fundamental institutions and organisational practices that are hierarchical in their modes of operation and systematically limit freedoms. This is typically justified under a separation between the public and the private domains. This separation creates a political frontier that sets private and public into opposition. For the neoliberals the state, for example, has to set minimum rules to ensure fair market behaviour, enforce the laws of property and ensure the security of private individuals. Neoconservatives attack the liberal ideals of actively fostering multiculturalism, immigration, anti-discrimination in terms of race, gender, differences in abilities and in promoting social justice, health care and help for the vulnerable. Neoliberals and neoconservatives have sufficient in common to attack liberal elites and governments when taxes are employed to build the public sector that dispenses health and welfare. Campaigns can be developed to discredit the public sector in the eyes of the voters by blaming rising costs on 'benefit scroungers' and immigrants. This then moves towards Kristol's (1995: 359–363) right-wing populist ploy to capture the place of power in hierarchical democracies. Legitimate grievances of poverty due to lack of rights, lack of jobs, lack of health care can be taken up by mainstream politicians strategically deploying nationalist and anti-liberal discourses that typically evoke hostility to immigrants as the focus of blame, thus giving credence and strength to extreme right-wing nationalist movements.

The private–public divide facilitates hierarchical authoritarian leadership by locating freedom in the private domain and what Hayek called 'serfdom' in the public domain. However, a heads-I-win, tails-you-lose strategy can be set up by capitalist elites by leveraging public sector institutions such as education as a site of freely exploitable knowledge and trained labour, along with having the police, the judiciary and the military to enforce their rights to property, patents, copyright. In short, the public/private split enables elites to keep democracy out of the private domain. Corporations employing tens of thousands can, so long as they keep within the law, be run as private authoritarian institutions. And, of course, corporate elites along with other property-owning elites predominantly fill the highest posts of government and the legislature. The military and police, although state institutions, have strict hierarchical, discipline-based structures. Even in the more 'human-centred' professional domains of schools, health care and social care, hierarchical frameworks predominate. A walk through any village, town or city centre provides a clear architecture separating the private from the public. And even in the public, the underlying command is to keep moving, be temporary, do not linger too long. The public, in that sense, cannot be 'occupied'; and the private can only be occupied by legitimate owners of a given property. What then counts as democratic access and occupation? Such a question can only be answered by going outside of the private–public structure.

If in a Spinozan sense the prime experiences of freedom and resistance in relation to the world about are bodily then it makes no sense to create a private/public split. Rather, experience is sensually shaped by that which resists or bends to the whims and fancies of desire and imagination. That is, one can only come to know one's powers and what they can achieve when they are engaged in some real relation one with another and with the world about. Like language, that which is most intimate is also public. To call the intimate private and split it from the public is to miss their co-extensiveness, their dynamic interaction thus devaluing and shrivelling both towards one-dimensional forms: the homogenous mass for the public and the self-absorbed narcissist for the intimate. The challenges posed by lies, post-truth, truthiness and all their variants involved in deception undermines the mainstream institutions of reality testing: schools, university scholarship and research, investigative journalism, the arts. These are the core institutions that have come under attack by the right-wing media as sources of liberal elite values and the undermining of authority and the state. In particular, schools and universities have been criticised for their forms of teaching, their organisation and their curricula when these have adopted democratic forms, forms that challenge hierarchy, dominance by a particular 'traditional' canon of literature (Cox and Dyson, 1975; Bloom, 1987), and the centrality of the headteacher or principal along with the teacher in maintaining discipline, setting performance targets and engineering school improvement (Reynolds and Stringfield, 1996). The institutions of education are focal points in mass society for the struggle to provide the grounds for reality testing and truth. What counts as truth is always under contest and the strategies for engaging with truth testing is not as simple as drawing a political frontier between the varieties of post-truth and a settled body of truth maintained and developed by jealous guardians of truth.

In the intimate, yet public, process of reality testing and truth assessment all the powers of the body are involved in generating valid knowledge to inform decision-making and guide action. Those powers include participation with others in particular, through debate, to share and test experiences, beliefs, values and understandings in the development of common projects as well as evaluating the positive and negative social impacts of individual projects. There is, then, participation one with another, a constant attentiveness towards each other. It is grounds for a form of surveillance that the early revolutionaries saw as essential in the guarantee of democracy. It is through such attentiveness that the public is formed as surveillance of government by the people, not by the government over the people (Rosanvallon, 2012), and more recently: "new social movement organisations often function as 'Watchdogs' in their specific policy areas. For instance 'whistle-blowers' are people or groups that call attention to certain types of problems" (p. 63). It is not just the idea of the watchdog that is of critical importance in the emergence of the public in democratic movements and society:

> Listen, for instance, to one Bergasse, who served as a member of the Constituent Assembly in the early days of the French Revolution: "Public Opinion," he wrote, "is truly a product of everyone's intelligence and everyone's will. It can be seen, in a way, as the manifest consciousness of the entire nation." Today, the Internet embodies in an almost material sense this pervasive force. Everyone can participate, and no one can control the result.
> (Rosanvallon, 2012: 68)

Here, Rosanvallon does not develop the comparison with the Internet. However, the current architecture of the Internet dominated by search engines and social media corporations that exploit their access to Big Data, deploy algorithms to undertake high-frequency trading to manipulate market prices and target and influence opinion is rather shaping everyone's intelligence and will rather than being a product of it. The degree of democratic effectiveness of a public is dependent upon the material architectures that shape it. The Internet corporations have profited from an imbalance in the relation between public access and private exploitation. They can build a profile of individual use by tracking Internet usages and analysing the content of messages. In a sense it mimics the architecture of the city in terms of its public and private spaces. The key difference is that corporations, in creating the spaces for individuals to communicate globally, have the power to track private use. This is a key difference with the way Jacobs saw the role of the 'eyes' of the street in managing strangers:

> A city street equipped to handle strangers, and to make a safety asset, in itself, out of the presence of strangers, as the streets of successful city neighbourhoods always do, must have three main qualities:

> First, there must be a clear demarcation between what is public space and what is private space. Public and private spaces cannot ooze into each other as they do typically in suburban settings or in projects.
>
> Second, there must be eyes upon the street, eyes belonging to those we might call the natural proprietors of the street. The buildings on a street equipped to handle strangers and to insure the safety of both residents and strangers, must be oriented to the street. They cannot turn their backs or blank sides on it and leave it blind.
>
> And third, the sidewalk must have users on it fairly continuously, both to add to the number of effective eyes on the street and to induce the people in buildings along the street to watch the sidewalks in sufficient numbers. Nobody enjoys sitting on a stoop or looking out a window at an empty street. Almost nobody does such a thing. Large numbers of people entertain themselves, off and on, by watching street activity.
>
> (Jacobs, 1961: 35)

By manipulating the public/private distinctions, the Internet oozes into the private lives of users thus creating the conditions in mass society to undermine knowledge, mutual understanding, freedom and equality as the fundamental dimensions of democratic life. There is, then, a democratic nucleus in Jacob's eyes of the street that ends at the pay-walls, gated communities and corporate towers that see the mass as exploitable, external and as insignificant as ants. Nevertheless, the democratic nucleus of the eyes upon the street is in the equal freedom to see. The securest knowledge of what is going on is democratically produced and such knowledge is essential in the on-going struggles for freedom and equality. How then to reimagine roads to freedom?

## Towards reimagining democratic life

What drives revolution is the idea of a new beginning, not merely a return to the same. Since the desired future state does not arrive by itself fully formed, the organising principles of the desired future must be prefigured. Given the essential relation between freedom and equality for democracy, in his history of the eighteenth century revolutions, Rosanvallon (2013: 11) distilled three key principles for the development of a society of equals: singularity, reciprocity and communality. A key focus is economic exchange underlying reciprocity:

> When individuals exchanged the fruits of their labour, they affirmed both their status as *independent equals* and their relationship as *interdependent equals*. In other words, people in the eighteenth century believed in the possibility of regenerative exchange. They spontaneously dreamed of ushering in a new world of a sort that Marcel Mauss would much later describe in his Essai sur le don: a world in which "the economy" is a process that mingles lives together with things, that recognises the dignity of individuals while establishing

equivalence through transactions. One cannot understand the spirit of equality in the American and French Revolutions without recognising the idea of the market as both an expression of liberty and a vector of equality. The market was seen as an institution of equality. The eighteenth century thus theorised the *liberalism of reciprocity*.

(Rosanvallon, 2013: 26–27)

It would seem the liberalism of reciprocity is an important formulation for rethinking and transforming practices in contemporary market democracies. Reciprocity of this kind forms horizontal relationships of equality. The more this is done, the less hierarchy can be sustained. However, there are further steps to go before a society today can be formed through publicly driven knowledge creation, value and ethics sustaining the political and social visions of free and equal individuals.

# Chapter 8

# What is happening today in terms of social learning becoming social movements?

Education has the capacity to undercut the institutional supports to inequality and elite power by creating a different field of relationship between free and equal individuals learning and working together to create their social projects in common. Making an educational link to work is a key dimension to the realisation of futures through knowledge. This process is inhibited as soon as education and work are displaced into private domains where democratic practices can be suspended in order to be pervaded by hierarchical forms of organisation.

When Dewey established his 'laboratory school' (1896–1903) it was with the ambition to change society for the better. Although in his later years he had increasingly lost hope this would happen through education, the idea and the practice of democratic schools, typically at the fringes of mainstream forms of state and private schooling, has a substantial legacy that continues to develop, at least in the margins. For a period in the 1960s and 70s, there seemed to be such a flowering of progressive ideas and ideals that reactionary conservatives such as Kristol (1995), Bloom (1987) and the authors of the 'Black Papers' (Cox and Dyson, 1975) wrote of the need to return to traditional values, curricula and forms of discipline. To avoid fundamental changes in society that they saw as negative, *Dark Money*, as Mayer (2016) called it, funded the emergence of a 'counter-intelligentsia'. More widely, 1968 became known as the year of revolutions, at least, if not revolution, then a year of global "social movements, ones that profoundly changed the world without seizing political power" (Katsiaficas, 2018). The youth movement had spilled over into the streets, it seemed everywhere, threatening authority, if not succeeding in accomplishing revolution. Lennon's song 'Give Peace a Chance' became a countercultural anthem of the anti-Vietnam movements. As Mason (2013) said of the twenty-first century movements it was 'kicking off everywhere'. People were active in the anti-Vietnam War protests, the civil rights movement, the Women's Liberation movement, the Black Power movement, there was the Prague Spring, and in France millions of workers were on strike with students as *Mai '68* became a moment when revolution was possible and the reverberation of which can still be felt (Leclercq, 2017).

Moreover, the pop youth culture supported by a globalising focus on music gave a vocabulary by which to express the demands for change which promoted a more generalised intergenerational aesthetic, a gap that also threatened the national frontiers of previous generations, a mood summed up in the 1971 Lennon song, 'Imagine', imagining a world of no countries, religion, possessions, hunger. With a different vocabulary enabling a different way of seeing, one can learn differently, knowledge is constructed differently, issues that had not been seen can be named and addressed. In the way that Kuhn (1970) described how the 'facts' changed after scientific revolutions, so the world is perceived differently through different discourses of the real. But then there came a time the dreaming had to be stopped.

## The policing of the political frontier

Whether it was the police in Paris (Davis, 2018), in Chicago (Mailer, 1968; Kusch, 2008) or elsewhere in 50-odd countries (Katsiaficas, 2018), in 1968 they stood with shields, batons and gas between the protesters and the elites targeted by the protests. It was not the first and has not been the last time. What is dangerous for wealth and power elites is not so much the protest, but the shifts in the ways the world can be seen that protests symbolise with the consequent impacts upon the public. What if the public came to see the world differently?

In the view of Hayek (1949), to conquer politics, it was necessary to conquer the intellectuals, a view that came to influence those who funded and led conservative foundations. Mayer (2016) describes the view of William Simon, president of the Olin foundation that:

> Only an ideological battle could save the country, in Simon's view. "What we need is a counter-intelligentsia … [It] can be organised to challenge our ruling 'new class'—opinion makers," Simon wrote. "Ideas are weapons—indeed the only weapons with which other ideas can be fought." He argued, "Capitalism has no duty to subsidise its enemies." Private and corporate foundations, he said, must cease "the mindless subsidising of colleges and universities whose departments of politics, economics and history are hostile to capitalism." Instead, they "must take pains to funnel desperately needed funds to scholars, social scientists and writers who understand the relationship between political and economic liberty," as he put it. "They must be given grants, grants, and more grants in exchange for books, books, and more books."
>
> (Mayer, 2016: 102)

Thus the foundation invested in broadcasting, funding right-wing authors such as Allan Bloom (1987), Dinesh D'Souza who castigated 'political correctness' in his *Illiberal Education*, as well as funding professors such as Samuel P. Huntington's John M. Olin Institute for Strategic Studies (Mayer, 2016: 105).

And of course there were mass right-wing outlets ready to spread the word. What the key works had in common was a view that liberalisation was essentially an attack on people's freedom to live and speak as they wished. It was summed up in the term 'political correctness' that both named the frontier between the right and left in politics as well as aligning large sections of the public with the right wing who blamed the discontent, resentment and sense of not being heard on the policies and discourses of the liberal left.

Political correctness became a weapon with which to police politically liberal social movements, liberal academics, liberal media, the arts and left wing, democratic politicians and policies. In 1991 the New York magazine published an article under the title "Are You Politically Correct?" (Taylor, 1991). The article described Stephan Thernstrom, a Harvard University professor, as having been hounded by students for having "used the word *Indians* instead of *Native Americans*" and other similar terms. The article then developed its themes in relation to the pernicious ideas of '60s radicals and authors like Simone de Beauvoir, Jacques Derrida and Jacques Lacan. They provided, the article claimed, the tools for a critique of language and power so that "any attempt to assign meaning to art, literature, or thought, to interpret it and evaluate it, was nothing more than an exercise in political power by the individual with the authority to impose his or her view." However, the Thernstrom case that was a pretext for the article was not true. Indeed, Hellerstein and Legum (2016) wrote that "In a 1991 interview with *The Nation*, Thernstrom himself told reporter Jon Weiner that he was 'appalled' when he first saw the passage. 'Nothing like that ever happened,' he quipped, describing the author's excerpt as 'artistic license'". In short, as Weigel (2016) put it, in political correctness, the right invented a phantom enemy. With this enemy in mind, people could line up one side or another. Enough lined up with Trump to make him president.

Much has been made of his 'base' being working class white voters as shown through analyses of opinion polls (McGill, 2016) who strongly backed his anti-immigration and refugee views. Moreover, the support of white evangelicals grew despite allegations of hush money paid to a former Playboy bunny girl, shady business deals and Russian connections amongst his close associates. The 'base' is not necessarily homogeneous. It is composed of many interest groups and communities – evangelicals, male white working class, older white women who lack qualifications, National Rifle Association and gun owners broadly (despite or because of the dangers of shootings and extreme right – re-branded Alt-right – movements (Neiwert, 2017)). Even included with this assemblage were 'Hispanics for Trump' and although the African American vote was overwhelmingly for Clinton (88%), there was a small percentage who voted for Trump which included: a higher proportion of African American men with a college degree (16%) than women (6%) and men without a degree (11%) than women (below 5%) (Durkee, 2016). This is only possible if there are multiple writings and multiple readings where each can find an interpretation that speaks to them personally, that enables them to justify their vote within their everyday theatres of conversation and debate where learning what is common and different takes place (at home, the neighbourhood, the workplace, places of socialisation and entertainment, the street – any place where debate or conversation is structured to enable 'fitting in', 'standing out' or 'excluding'). Trump enters those theatres of debate in many ways, whether it is through his appeals to anti-political correctness or 'common sense' – it gave him the aura of 'plain speaking', 'talking like us' not despite but perhaps because of his 'inarticulacy' (Leith, 2017). There was then a strong anti-Them appeal, that is anti those elites who use their expertise power in ways that belittle, hoodwink, exploit and as a result undermine those who see themselves as the ordinary, real Americans (Graham, 2017).

Similar strategies to defuse the negative, diabolic connotations of racist, anti-immigration, anti-faith views were employed in the Brexit campaigns and were taken up by Marine Le Pen's National Front in France (Crépon et al., 2015) and across Europe (Mondon and Winter, 2018). The history of the political role of appeals to 'common sense' is long (Rosenfeld, 2011). Talk of common sense about 'immigration' for example, allows racism to be denied (van Dijk, 1992; Capdevilla and Callaghan, 2008). Such strategies of de-fusion enable otherwise disparate individuals and groups to line up against a common enemy or adversary. It is a strategy Laclau (2005) calls establishing a relation of equivalence. There is, then, amongst otherwise disparate individuals at least one significant relation that places them on the same side against others. In that sense, there is no implicit ideology underlying the strategy. Thus for example Mouffe (2018) makes use of this strategy to argue for the construction of a left populism. Where the right drew upon such issues of unemployment and provided a vocabulary born of fear, racism and nationalism, the left could provide a different vocabulary by which to explain causes and provide alternative visions of work and community. In short, there are repressed voices looking for forms of expression and understanding.

## Crying out and not being heard

In America it was with the death of Mohammed Bouazizi in Tunisia that had set in train what came to be known as the Arab Spring, according to Micah White (2016), that the "cycle of revolt that eventually led to Occupy Wall Street began". This was to say, as one of the self-proclaimed inventors of the Occupy Wall Street strategy, they were inspired by what they saw as the tools for protest and change that had been deployed by the protestors of the Arab Spring. But before those events, in Iran, a young woman – Neda – with thousands of others took to the streets following the fraudulent elections of 2009. Her name is also the word for 'voice', 'calling'. During the protests she was shot. Film from mobile phones and cameras was uploaded onto the Internet. She became a worldwide symbol of the call and the demand for freedom, not a particular freedom, nor the policies of political parties, just the ordinary freedoms that represented the everyday ambitions of people, male and female, across the generations, classes, communities and faiths so that 'We are all Neda' (http://neda.webnode.com/). This coming together around a powerful symbol expressed a democratic demand for ordinary freedoms.

In Tunisia, on December 17, 2010, Mohammed Bouazizi, 26 years old, set himself alight. A policewoman had confiscated the cart he used to sell his vegetables. He felt humiliated by the authorities who refused to return the cart. Video clips of the protests that followed were posted on the Internet, spread across the country and the widespread protests that led to the revolution began (Roberts and Schostak, 2012). These protests began with a video posted on Facebook on January 18, 2011 by Asmaa Mahfou calling for people to meet at Tahrir Square on January 25, 2011. She said that she would not set herself alight as four other Egyptians had done but spoke passionately of the need to rise up and fight the corruption to regain dignity:

> I'm making this video to give you one simple message. We want to go down to Tahir Square on January 25$^{th}$. If we still have honour, and want to live in dignity on this land we have to go down on January 25$^{th}$. We'll go down and demand our rights, our fundamental human rights. I won't even talk about any political rights. We just want our human rights and nothing else.
> (http://www.youtube.com/watch?v=SgjIgMdsEuk&feature=player_embedded)

The people came. And they stayed until Mubarak resigned on February 11, 2011. What was displayed, in what came to be known as the Arab Spring, for the world to see was the power of people acting together and the tactics they used.

There was, however, a prior non-violent 'curriculum' participants could draw upon. It consisted of the work of Gene Sharpe (2010), the *Otpor* of Serbia, who developed strategies based upon non-violence to resist Slobodan Milosevic (Henley, 2015) that the *April 6 Movement* drew upon for its support of a strike called for April 6, 2008 by workers in the Egyptian town of El-Mahalla El-Kubra as well as the 'We are all Khaled Said' following the police killing of a student. From the strategies they used, the world could learn.

Characteristic of the Egyptian protestors was their insistence on peaceful means. This, in Sharpe's terms, is critical because "dictators almost always have superiority in military hardware, ammunition, transportation, and the size of military forces. Despite bravery, the democrats are (almost always) no match" (Sharpe, 2010: 4). Thus although Otpor had begun with a day of rage they chose a non-violence path inspired by the work of Gene Sharpe (2010) in developing a conceptual framework for a peaceful strategy where the immediate tasks are:

- One must strengthen the oppressed population themselves in their determination, self-confidence and resistance skills;
- One must strengthen the independent social groups and institutions of the oppressed people;
- One must create a powerful internal resistance force; and

- One must develop a wise grand strategic plan for liberation and implement it skilfully.

(Sharpe, 2010: 7–8)

From their experience of employing the tactics to achieve these broad tasks, members of Otpor, Srdja Popovic and Slobodan Dinovic instituted in 2003 the Centre for Applied Nonviolent Action and Strategies (CANVAS) which "advocates for the use of nonviolent resistance to promote human rights and democracy." (http://canvasopedia.org/about-us/)

There was then a body of work to draw upon for the Egyptian protestors. There was also the Internet, social media and the mobile phone that provided a key resource for dissemination of news as well as the ability to co-ordinate activists. Al Jazeera were broadcasting live from Tahrir Square. Much of what follows drew upon the recordings made everyday by Schostak during that period and written up for lunchtime talks at Manchester Metropolitan University as well as conference papers.

The power of the Internet led to the Egyptian authorities denying access to the Internet and despite Vodaphone being compromised on January 25, 2011 and 'forced' to send propaganda, the foundations for face-to-face work to keep the protests going had already been laid. Even when violence was used against the protestors by the police as well as Mubarak 'supporters', the protestors drew strength from the anger, the injuries and the killings to return in even greater numbers. That the police had 'melted away' was a common observation of commentators on Al Jazeera and elsewhere. When pro-Mubarak supporters appeared on January 31, there was speculation that these were composed of, or stimulated by, the police. Several police identity cards were found upon captured pro-Mubarak supporters and shown to Al Jazeera reporters lending credence to this view. That the military did not fire upon the protestors, that the protestors persevered in remaining peaceful, determined, that they showed they could defend themselves against attack, that they defied the nightly curfew and consistently turned up in greater numbers each day, transformed Tahrir Square into a symbol of unity. It drew together people of all ages and it became a family event, giving at times the sense of a party atmosphere. Considerable attention was given to the range of people who came – engineers, doctors, workers, middle classes, working classes, men, women, Christians, Muslims, non-believers. Again, much was made of the fact that no one person represented them all. There was no leader. There was no political party that would take the lead. Mohamed ElBaradei, thought of as a possible leader, appeared for half an hour or so to make a speech at Tahrir Square. In his expressed view, this was protest begun by the youth movement that spread throughout society. There could be no leader. The Muslim Brotherhood said that it would support but not lead. When Wael Ghonim, a Google executive and well-known blogger, went missing on January 27 and was then released from custody on February 7, he refused to be accorded the title of 'hero' and thus a symbolic leader of the revolution. The real heroes, he said, were the people. His emotional interview on release, however, contributed to a sizeable turnout at Tahrir Square and other cities. The increasing size of the protests, particularly at Tahrir Square, was a significant factor in focusing attention both locally and internationally – there was the Million Man March on January 30, and the crowds flooding the square on 'the day of departure', February 4. After Ghonim was released on February 8 there were further large crowds, with the trade unions joining in on February 9, involving strikes around the country and finally after Mubarak's disappointing speech on February 10, the next day thousands more protested and Mubarak resigned.

The consistent claim being made for this leaderless unity – focused symbolically on Tahrir Square, then, was that it was an expression of the 'people'. Some commentators talked of a 'raw' demand, a demand for freedom, for social justice, for rights of free speech, for a more democratic future. In Laclau's (2005) approach to understanding political struggles key terms like 'freedom', 'human rights', 'social justice' are universalising signifiers, empty of contents. They become a site of contestation as different groups, with different interests, seek to place their 'contents' and thus construct the 'meaning' of the term. The task for the protestors – widely seen as a youth movement – was to show that their demands were not limited to a particular social group or age group. Conversely, the task of those against the protestors would then be to show that the interests of the protestors were limited and thus not universal. This struggle to manage the contents that would be associated with the key terms very much involved the control of the media, particularly in terms of what could be seen and heard. During the protests, state television showed optimistic peaceful views of Egyptian society, Mubarak going about his presidential duties and quiet scenes on the streets. Attempts by Mubarak to employ the rhetoric of 'my people', symbolising himself as father and the people as children were seen to be patronising by the increasingly large crowds in Tahrir Square and in the major cities where protests were also taking place. It was a contest between competing constructions of 'reality'. Al Jazeera, which gave continuous coverage of Tahrir Square and events as they were happening in other cities, was criticised and its office closed and its reporters harassed. It was stated that foreign journalists were actually spies and troublemakers, particularly from Israel. Coverage, however, continued. Indeed, a large screen was eventually put up in the Square for people to see broadcasts. Although the Internet was disrupted and mobile phone coverage taken down this was partially restored during the latter days of the protests. Twitter messages of support continued throughout the period, indeed Google helped by improving its speak2tweet technology.

Twitter had played an important role, both in the early developments and the period during the protests. It enabled a shared sense of solidarity, emotion and hope that is expressed in the following twitter messages – a few amongst many hundreds if not thousands that were sent at the time – that were recorded on February 6, 2011:

You can't imagine how I wish to be in #**Tahrir** again! We're making our history guys ... don't listen to anybody now ... Just go on

Christians, Muslims hold hands in Cairo, some holding up crosses and Korans

At times, **Tahrir** looks like a European flee market. At others, a rock concert. And yet others, a war zone

Egypt state TV says 6 youths representing **Tahrir**Sq protesters participating in gov talks w/ opposition

RT Just interviewed novelist Ahdaf Soueif in **Tahrir**: "Egyptians have found their voice again"

The world is watching. We see you. We see your bravery. We are your witnesses and we are in awe.

Witnessing is powerful. What was seen was the moral force of countervailing powers built widely from the population transformed into a public voice demanding freedoms, rights and democracy. How such witnessing is constructed is critical. In this case, what was witnessed was the use of media by both the protestors and the government of Mubarak. The disjunction was itself powerful.

The witnessing builds community internally as well as externally. The more from different groups with different perspectives who witness and share their witnessing, the more a generalised knowledge of the 'truth' about what is happening develops creating the grounds for a countervailing power. As Sharpe (2010: 22) notes, 'democracies' consist of a multiplicity of groups – "families, religious organisations, cultural associations, sports clubs, economic institutions, trade unions, student associations, political parties, villages, neighbourhood associations, gardening clubs, human rights organisations, musical groups, literary societies, and others." As a member of different groups, each individual's body is complexly, dynamically directed towards other members, perceiving, giving and processing information to form understandings about groups and how groups relate to each other. In that sense, a given individual is intersected by horizontal relations to a multiplicity of organisations that internally may be vertically, that is hierarchically, constructed. Theoretically, at least, those horizontally constructed relations that connect individuals, say as an employee, a soldier, inside a vertical organisation, have the potential to subvert the hierarchy of that organisation. Does the soldier, for example, experience a higher duty to friends, family and neighbourhood than to the dictator? If so, then there are grounds for the development of a countervailing power.

For their definition of power Popovic et al. (2006: 24) quote Gene Sharp (1973: 27) that: "Political power is the totality of means, influences, and pressures – including authority, rewards, and sanctions – available to achieve the objectives of the power-holder, especially those of government, the state, and those groups in opposition." This could be made wider still by employing the concept of a '*dispositif*', typically translated as 'apparatus'. It was a term employed by Foucault and further developed by Agamben (2009) to include everything –

language, discourses, cultures, knowledge, tools, machines, organisations, architectures, in short anything that humans construct – that could be assembled to address an urgent problem. As such *dispositif* is much more than the usual use of the term 'apparatus'. In this sense, a dispositif can be assembled hierarchically for elite purposes, or it could be assembled horizontally for purposes of challenge, reform and radical change (see Schostak and Schostak, 2013). In their insistence on leaderlessness the protesters made it impossible for 'leaders' to deal with them. As in the 'Nuit Debout' movement in Paris, police authorities found there was no one to talk to who as a 'leader' could ensure rules were followed. Without a leader there is no one to blame, no one to sacrifice, no one to undermine the movement. The lesson of leaderlessness is therefore a key tactic of protest movements. Coordination of activities could be communicated easily and almost instantaneously through the Internet and mobile phone – not by a leader, but by individuals from a multiplicity of positions connecting in an always available network, 'tweeting' about what was needed and what was happening when and where.

This is counter to the forms of what may be called the hidden curriculum of all the dominant forms of organisation across society that promote the necessity of leadership and submission to teams and superiors within a hierarchy. The schooling of children typically underwrites this order as a foundation for the development of 'character', 'identity', 'subjectivity' and 'citizenship'. Its counter can only be in the formation of democratic organisations where leadership is systematically constrained and subverted by the voiced demands of the people. Just as the capitalist right were able to draw inspiration from Friedman's (1962: xiv) view that a crisis is a time of opportunity, so can the democratic left.

## A crisis for the left?

When the financial crisis of 2008 broke with the collapse of Lehman Brothers on September 15, it seemed that the credibility of the neoliberal project was in ruins. It potentially offered social movements and left-wing parties a focus for popular change. Indeed, when the Occupy movement burst on the scene around the world, Mason (2013) and others could say countervailing forms of organisation were kicking off everywhere.

What they were kicking off against was outrageous. It was a financial system so out of control that the weight of debt born by debtor nations, who had bought into the illusions sold by banks and hedge funds, was so huge it was impossible to pay off. To prevent the collapse of the world market by failing banks, they were supported by tax payers' money. This in turn led to austerity measures being put into place across Europe and the cutting of public sector services to pay to save the banking system. During 2011 there was the threat of the crisis deepening due to possible defaults by Ireland, Portugal, Spain and Greece. Indeed, a default on the loans by Greece was seen as having consequences far in excess of the Lehman Brothers default that set off the 2008 crisis. Many European and other banks were highly exposed to the Greek debt (Varoufakis, 2015a). For many commentators, the measures being undertaken to resolve the situation were scandalous, their effect being to asset-strip the public. Even in the midst of crisis by 2011 it could already be seen that the wealthy had in fact increased their wealth (Rapoza, 2011) at the same time as the rest grew poorer, more vulnerable, more anxious, indeed fearful (c.f., Oxfam, 2010). Neoliberalism and the practices of speculation that created the conditions for the crisis have not collapsed but simply continued. The chance for fundamental change by mainstream political parties did not take place.

There has, however, been the erosion of public space as the private sector tightens its grip with each austerity measure, public sector cut, with loss of jobs and the privatisation of publicly owned organisations. In effect, there has been an increasing crowding out of voice and democratic organisation in all the key areas of work and governance in everyday life. A private business has no obligation to adopt democratic principles of organisation and management. With increasing privatisation, so long as it adheres to state laws, even the nominal accountability to the electorate required of public sector organisations is irrelevant. With the dominance of neoliberal forms of management focusing on performance indicators across the private and public sectors and with the deregulation of labour markets, the weakening of the trade union movements through the use of laws regulating collective action, the increasing threat of lay-offs and the lack of employment opportunities for youth, voice has been structured into subservience, passivity, redundancy and superfluity. In this context voice is reduced at worst to noise, at best to mime or mimicry, parody or protest. As described in Schostak and Schostak (2013: 96–98) Camille Rivera, a member of Occupy Wall Street, described people's anger during a debate broadcast by Al Jazeera in 2011 saying "big banks and corporations need to take responsibility, that people are tired of going into their pockets and suffering from what is not their responsibility but the responsibility of our government to help us create jobs". An economist, Charlie Wolf, was then asked whether he agreed: "No, it just sounds intellectually fallacious. Listening to Camille just a second ago made no sense, if this was something said in a class I would have kicked her out the classroom". The complaints, viewpoints and demands of ordinary people and protestors are heard to be senseless because they threaten the exclusive rights of governing elites to command Power in their interests. However, as illustrated in the TV 'debate', voice can be staged through talk shows. Politicians and Chief Executives can meet the people and 'listen'. Surveys and media 'polls' can be undertaken to 'consult' with the public. The voice of protest can be mimed and mimicked by 'representatives' of 'the people' at great rallies, marches and broadcast studios. Rather than access to the actual structures, mechanisms and procedures through which real decision-making and action are realised, all is reduced to mime, mimicry and parody of the real thing – staged by the mainstream for spectacle.

In this context, Occupy like other movements can be marginalised in the longer run (Schram, 2015). Nevertheless, the continuities of struggle create the conditions for further possibilities. As Micah White (2009) wrote in his open letter to students, listing some of the campus occupations that had been taking place against increases in fees and pointing out that "the student movement has the potential to spark a cultural insurrection against consumer capitalism". Thus:

> I call on you, students of the "first world," to shift your struggle and link arms with us as we build a mental environment movement capable of smashing corporations, downsizing consumer spending and building egalitarian communities. We need your passion, your knowledge and your skills. Together, the future is ours.
>
> Join us!

This call to build 'a mental environment' is essentially a call to bring several issues-based movements together. White went on with others to organise Occupy Wall Street drawing upon the legacies of Sharpe, Otpor and the Arab Spring for their tactics. It became a model for other Occupies. In the UK in 2010 there was the formation of UK Uncut to protest against public sector cuts and influencing Starbucks to pay £20m in tax. In Spain there were occupations of Puerta del Sol in Madrid and of Syntagma Square in Greece as their Tahrir Squares. Rather than a protest against the cruel acts of tyrants and their police, it was protest against the IMF and European Bank demands for State austerity measures impacting on the lives of the youth, the elderly and the poor. Both led to political movements, Podemos in Spain and Syriza in Greece. There is clearly a democratic nucleus in the various demands which can result in a 'mental environment' for change that as Galbraith argues:

> In truth, the protesters of Greece and Spain and Italy, the voters of France, and sympathisers of the Occupy Movement in America do not clamour for growth. What they most want is to protect institutions and essentials that make their lives tolerable, safe, and attractive. These are health care, education, local public services, culture, the environment, and the right to retire in modest comfort at a reasonable age.
>
> (Galbraith, 2016: 37)

What hope is there for genuine widespread reconstruction to meet these wants? Despite limited successes and the spectacle of things 'kicking off', the global system has not come crashing down.

Can we rethink a return to the 'golden age' (1947–1971) – a time where working class people experienced increasing living standards, improved education, better health and a higher quality of life than their parents – without being thought of and rejected as being nostalgic for myths? For Pettifor (2014: 97) contemporary crises have been "a crisis of ignorance and political impotence in the face of a set of ideas serving the interests of a few" underpinned by the economic incompetence of academic economists of the mainstream. In her view this would mean a return to Keynesian informed economics. To do this there would also need to be a move from unrealistic, indeed, harmful targets applied through the technologies of discipline towards a democratically managed approach in the interests of all, not just the financial elites. In short, democracy needs to be brought into people's lives so that their demands can be taken into account realistically. There are many actors who need to be brought on to debate in all the forms of organisation where people engage each other at work, in schools, communities, the institutions of government, policing, the military: in short, in all forms of relationship. Protest is not enough. The work of prefiguring the future has to begin at home, the streets, everywhere.

## Towards prefiguring the future

The complex of expectations, habits, routines underlying people's freedoms to act in their everyday lives with a degree of confidence about the results of their decisions and to build their futures are so taken for granted that it often takes some unexpected problem to notice their existence. It is perhaps only when a freedom has been lost that it is seen to have been vital. How, then, is blame organised? If unemployment is blamed for the loss in income that supports independence and freedoms, then blame may be laid with immigrants taking jobs and those who welcomed them by opening the frontiers. If crime increases then blame may focus on cuts to police forces or lack of discipline in schools, poor parenting, a loss of spiritual values as expressed by particular faiths. Such reasons formed the populist bedrock advocated by neoconservatives such as Kristol (1995; 2011), exploited in the Trump and Brexit campaigns and by the extreme right across Europe. What is at stake becomes more apparent as discourses focus increasingly on equating nationalism with race and faith, legitimise practices of discrimination and result in creased surveillance and protectionist policies that threaten everyday freedoms, security and livelihoods. What is prefigured as likely futures, begins to look increasingly like a nightmarish past (Faulkner, 2017; Giroux, 2018). Unsettling similarities are noticed with the rise of Nazism in the 1930s (Albright, 2018). With for example the cruelty of immigration policies in the UK and the US that split families and effectively denied the right to a family life, the threats to UK jobs as businesses make plans to move to Europe and the cost of living and employment impacts of a protectionist trade war unleashed by Trump, what is lost in terms of freedoms begins to hit ordinary people in their everyday lives. In the UK and the US increased awareness of the impacts of Trump and Brexit led to an upswell – particularly among the young – of more radically left politics challenging the grip of capitalist-friendly democrats in the US and Labour in the UK. The grassroots Momentum movement in the UK was significantly instrumental in the rise of life-long radical socialist Jeremy Corbyn as the Labour leader. And in the US, grass-roots activism increased the popularity of Bernie Sanders as a life-long supporter of socialism promoting the fight against the rise of the right and calling for an international alliance. It is essentially the strategy of left populism set out by Mouffe (2018; 2018a).

The creation of alliances between committed activists, however, is not enough. Creating a political frontier between right and left parties that canvass the votes of a 'public' whose lives are entangled with and vitally dependant upon authoritarian corporate worlds who can threaten their livelihoods leaves them as targets to be manipulated one way or another. A greater change is needed.

It is in the impact of impersonal institutions, corporations and 'phantom publics' constructed by media on the intimate lives of people that both the fear of freedom, as Fromm (1942) called it, and the demands for freedom begins. It should not need the suicides, murders and sacrifices of ordinary people to bring this to consciousness in whatever democratic 'spring' that occurs next. The demand for freedom is experienced intimately as vulnerability faced with the impersonal might wielded by leaders, oligarchs, their supporting governmental institutions, law enforcement, military and managerial cadres. For that reason, democracy has to be prefigured in the most intimate of relations: first as the ground for the emergence of democratic relations with others in all forms of organisation, and second as the condition for an effective public. This then helps to define the next steps for a 'grass-roots' democracy that moves beyond identity politics, issue-based 'movements' or 'protests' by attending to the key sites of prefigurative action: education, work, the street and the more intimate family contexts of home and neighbours.

# Chapter 9

# How do you get from social movements to public space?

Public space is the arena of debate concerning the multiple 'goods' and demands for the 'good' that ground alternative notions concerning the 'good society'. In the 'babble', who can make their voice heard and how? Balibar's (1994) concept of *égaliberté*, defined as the co-extensiveness of freedom and equality, responds to this question in the double perspective of intimacy with the world about in both its natural and social dimensions. What it means to be free is experienced both in happiness and fear and together they help define the 'good'. As an example, take the concept of freedom explicitly held in the notion of free market economics. It is the freedom to be selfish as expressed by the Ayn Rand mantra of greed is good. It means that individuals are free to be greedy in a game of survival of the fittest. It is through unfettered selfishness that there is the greatest development of the powers of individuals and thus the greatest probability of securing happiness. The losers, of course, will not feel so free, indeed, under the domination of the winners who become their corporate and political masters they may fear not only for their standard of living but their lives. The winners, however, are relatively few in comparison to the masses who to varying degrees lose out to the powers of accumulation of the winners. The resulting inequalities mean that the losers have less or even no freedom to act against the influence, the coercion, the violence of the winners. And the winners come to fear the potential unrealised power of the masses to act as an overwhelming collective. It is essentially this logic that led Spinoza to view democracy as the best political framework to bring about the equal development of the powers of all individuals. Hence, in Balibar's terms, *égaliberté*.

Given contemporary inequalities individuals combine in protests, social movements, and more formal organisations to address issues and achieve greater equality. In these struggles the political frontier is clearly established between those who win from the system and those who lose. There is then the potential for a greater alliance to emerge from the different combinations of individuals focused around a given interest. They are in that sense equivalent in their opposition to the same elite powers. To get what they all want they must first recognise this and then act upon that recognition to join together. Managing the emphasis given to multiple interests, however, always has the danger of the greater alliance falling apart into its constituent bits. To avoid this, each interest group must be able to voice their views, argue for their demands, and contribute to decision-making in ways that embed their interests equally in any strategy, tactic and particular contributory actions undertaken. In this way nobody has to give up, downgrade, or put on hold their particular interests. Such democracy is not easy. It would be much easier to have a leader able to discipline and silence disagreement. However, the argument for democracy is that in enabling the full potential of all powers the aggregate benefit is much greater than if one or more were inhibited. Similarly, in ensuring all voices are heard there is a much greater chance that the multiplicity of perspectives on the complex issues being faced will generate more comprehensive solutions. It is for such reasons that Rancière's (1999) counsel to be 'faithful to the disagreement' is so significant. A decision, policy, course of action that does not faithfully take into account the existentially defining disagreements between people will be attacked and eventually fall apart. Space, then, needs to be created that enables people to come together in order to debate their differences in ways that encourage the development of mutually pleasing solutions. As first approximations, that space may be physically conceived like a meeting hall, a broadcast studio, a public square; or, it may be virtual, digitally constructed to enable conversations and debates. However, the space is much more complex in that it must in some way contain all who live. How?

## Prefiguring democracy in the theatres of debate and struggle

In all individuals there is an inner theatre of debate and struggle, whether that is of reason over the passions, faith over reason, the will versus the bodily drives or wanting many contradictory things at once. How to decide? Various religions, schools of philosophy, psychology, psychiatry, psychotherapy and psychoanalysis have emerged in pursuit of an answer to variants of the question: how best to live? How to be happy? How to be fulfilled? Democracy does not give *the* answer, but at least offers a vision of the conditions under which better answers can be collectively found.

There is a Spinozan psychology to the extent that his ethical, theological and political reflections focus around the powers of the body and the idea that the body produces of itself. That is to say, there is no mind–body split with mind inhabiting some virtual or spiritual realm distinct from the earthly realm of flesh and blood. That idea that the body produces of itself and its relation to the world about is best accomplished through a democracy of powers. To that extent, continuing the logic, the body is a theatre of powers staging ideas of itself in relation to its environment. This is an intriguing possibility, since the psychology involved does not look for a Lacanian-like master, nor for a silent 'analyst' but for a debate where knowledge is produced through a cooperation of powers. Those ideas will be more comprehensive and at ease with the body and the physical universe the more that each power contributes freely and equally to its production. Thus, through aggregating the powers of one body with those of others better conceptual understandings can be created as a basis for living well in the world.

If this is so, then the key theatre of struggle and debate is this body of multiple powers and its immediate relation with others whether in the family, the classroom, the place of work, the neighbourhood, the community centre, the organisations of the market place and the streets where friends and strangers alike pass by or stop to watch, daydream and talk. How is all this potential for relationship, exchange, commerce and passage to be managed? If *égaliberté* is the principle under which the greatest benefits for each individual are to be obtained, then the democratic society that would deliver this has to be prefigured in each and every theatre of debate and struggle. In this sense, democracy as an idea composes spaces of equality where all are free to enter. Critical to understanding it is that *relationship* is the essential democratic characteristic, not number. How people relate to each other not as numbers but as related living beings is what builds democracy.

There has been an influential belief that somehow the differences between people, whether of interests or of knowledge and skill, can all be ironed out if the numbers are big enough. It has underpinned the development of statistical procedures by which to understand, predict and control. In the natural sciences and their applications in engineering mathematical and statistical developments have been behind major technological and medical advances that could be exploited industrially and commercially. These triumphs have led to significant schools of social scientists, economists, political theorists and psychologists modelling their methodologies on those of the natural scientists. To do so, they have had to reduce the complexities of psychological and social life to variables that can be isolated in some measurable frozen state long enough to satisfy the assumptions the methodologies need. The fascination with the power and authority of large numbers has continued through the twentieth and into the twenty-first century. It seemed to offer the promise of a rational approach to the political management and economic exploitation of masses.

An early pioneer in the development of modern political, social and economic theory was Condorcet's essay of 1785 which is often cited in relation to theories of social choice. Simply, "His metaphysical research program or paradigm was based on the assumption that individuals have the cognitive ability to judge right from wrong and that such judgments could be true or objective like theoretical statements in physical science" (Urken, 1991: 213–214). The theory, often referred to as the Jury theorem, showed statistically that the decisions collectively made by large groups can be 99% correct even when the competence of individual decision makers could not be taken for granted. Condorcet's motivation, as Urken goes on to describe, was "to mobilise expertise to deal with social problems" (p. 214). If it was doable then he could argue that a 'polity' could be created where the people could be trusted to make correct decisions in democracy. There were, of course, problems in the early theory but further development in relation to risk in games theory and by Buchanan and Tullock's (1962) placement of property as central to rational decision-making in social choice theory became central to twentieth-century approaches to neoliberal government and market theory as discussed in chapter 3.

What is lost in any chance-, risk- or greed-based theory where individuals seek to maximise benefits or at least operate according to what they are satisfied with on balance is 'relationship to others'. That is, individuals are not isolated choice makers, but always in a complex of relationships. Statistical models founded upon randomisation strip individuals of relationship in order to construct probabilities and correlations in a mass population. In a real sense, masses have been created – communities fragmented to create pools of labour for mass production, with mass consumption generating Big Data that can be exploited. The more one dimensional and fragmented the life of people becomes, the more they fit the models. The more insecure people are, the more choice-making can be modelled according to whether a choice increases or decreases risk. The greedier they are, the more their choices can be modelled according to the probabilities a choice increases obtaining what they want. That is, if they are to behave rationally. Rather than democracy being reduced to individual rational decision makers who can be aggregated to express a 'will of the people' once every few years in elections and referenda, democracy as a way of living seeks to work with powers in continuous relationship whether these are at any given moment antagonistic, agonistic or co-operative. To understand people acting in relationship, however, those relations have to be preserved, not broken, in forming appropriate analytic models that counter the strategies of massification and fragmentation in social life. What then is studied is not abstract models of the behaviours of fragmented, individual rational choice makers in massified populations but the concrete multi-layered networks of relation that are fundamental to a life worth living.

A principle power in everyday life, then, is the power of individuals to form associations in order to aggregate their powers as a basis for action by sharing understandings, triangulating perspectives to gain greater objectivity about what is common and what is different as a basis for co-ordinating activities. Elites have typically found the power of association, among those they wish to manage, to be problematic, even dangerous. Through such associations opinion, knowledge and visions for a future society can be formed that are very different from the manufacture and engineering of consent and desire that became central to both government and business in their respective appeals to a 'public' as voter and consumer discussed in our earlier chapters.

Indeed, as Rosanvallon (2012) argues it was the power of publics, composed of watching and listening individuals everywhere sharing and debating, able to turn the tables on elites, that was critical for what was to count as 'democracy'. This was the lesson of revolutions which continues to provide lessons:

> The truly visionary terms in which the revolutionaries of 1789 celebrated the ubiquity and power of public opinion suddenly take on new significance. Listen, for instance, to one Bergasse, who served as a member of the

Constituent Assembly in the early days of the French Revolution: "Public opinion," he wrote, "is truly the product of everyone's intelligence and everyone's will. It can be seen, in a way, as the manifest consciousness of the entire nation."

(Rosanvallon, 2012: 68)

In that sense, public opinion as the ever dynamically constructed will of the people was the key agency for democracy in inhibiting the will of the elites. Nevertheless, the will of the people, their 'common sense', their 'collective learning' can still be 'gamed' in the interests of the elites, particularly by convincing them of the necessity of leaders. In that case, how can people ensure politicians take note of people's experience, knowledge and opinions and do what they demand?

Insights can be drawn from an alternative reading of Machiavelli. Although he is popularly known for his advice to princes, McCormick (2006; 2011a; 2015) sees his work as a practical manual to constrain the insolence of the nobles. It is clear from his arguments that the mechanisms employed by the institution of modern governments are inadequate for the development of democracy – elections, however free, are not enough. The key Machiavellian tactics to remedy this include:

- the formation of tribunes exclusively from the common people "wielding veto, legislative and accusatory authority" (McCormick, 2015: 252);
- choosing executive officers by lottery;
- ensuring "political courts comprised of large subsets of randomly selected citizens" (McCormick, 2012–2013: 880);
- restricting periods of office so that none can build up a power base that biases; decision-making.
- And, corrupt republics "should completely eliminate over-weaning oligarchs via the violent actions of a tyrannical individual" (McCormick, 2015: 252).

If these stand as criteria by which to assess the functioning of contemporary democracies, then all are corrupted by elite influence. At present, democracy, if it exists outside of the corrupted versions of contemporary societies, exists only in the hollows, the spaces between the apparatus of elite organisation, control and surveillance. It is here where Rosanvallon's (2012) 'counter-democracy' may contribute to thinking how to prefigure in everyday forms of organisation the Machiavellian-like necessary steps towards democracies that are fully functional in terms of acting through the will of the people. By 'counter-democracy' he means

> not the opposite of democracy but rather a form of democracy that reinforces the usual electoral democracy as a kind of buttress, a democracy of indirect powers disseminated throughout society – in other words, a durable democracy of distrust, which complements the episodic democracy of the usual electoral representative system. Thus counter democracy is part of a larger system that also includes legal democratic institutions. It seeks to complement

those institutions and extend their influence, to shore them up. Thus counter-democracy should be understood and analysed as an authentic *political form* ....

(Rosanvallon, 2012: 8)

All of Machiavelli's tactics to constrain the insolence of elites fit well with the broad concept of a democracy of distrust. But what are these forms of subjectivity and social organisation that, in short, seek to stand between the 'common' individual and the 'sovereign individual' exploited by Davidson and Rees-Mogg (1997) to justify capitalist accumulation?

Rosanvallon (2012) points to three dimensions of counter-democracy: 1) powers of oversight and surveillance, 2) the sovereignty of prevention, and 3) the powers of people to judge. For these powers to be effective the public must operate a continuous vigilance. Although surveillance is typically thought of as operating from the top down, as a power of the public it is from the ground up. In this category can be placed the activism of the so-called 'new social movements' – as distinct from the class-based movements – that are formed around alternative collective identities focused on sexual minorities, the generations, feminism, discriminatory 'political philosophies', practices and organisations; as well as activism based around particular global issues such as environmentalism, climate change, consumerism; or more geographically specific concerns such as regionalism and movements for independence and cultural recognition. Each in their way exert a force of surveillance keeping the powerful in check. Unfortunately such vigilance and surveillance can also be employed for purposes of exclusion and suppression as in Theresa May's policy of building a 'hostile environment' for so-called 'illegal immigrants' that spilled over into discourses of hostility against anyone seen to have a 'foreign' name, language, accent, skin colour. Staff of schools, universities, the health service, employers, landlords were all drafted in by law to act as if they were immigration officers preventing access to health, work, education. The hostility extended to anyone in receipt of benefits whether 'foreigners' or British 'benefit scroungers'. Indeed, with anti-terror laws teachers and lecturers were expected to identify and report perceived fanaticism. According to an Amnesty International (2017) report the UK had amongst the most draconian laws in Europe considered to be 'dangerously disproportionate', threatening human rights. Indeed, on the European scale the reinforcing of frontiers – virtual and physical – have brought about a 'fortress Europe' (Amnesty International, 2014). The public, in that sense, have been conscripted to oversee virtual frontiers as between 'legal' and 'illegal', 'friends' and 'enemies', as well as the 'virtuous hard-working people' and the 'lazy benefits scroungers'. The political frontiers between each are policed in the wider Rancière sense, as well as more narrowly in the sense of police officers. Thus of critical importance are the criteria by which vigilance and surveillance are undertaken as well as who is to undertake it.

In constructing a public, for example, suppose only billionaires were legally allowed to debate and vote on the merits of having a system of taxation. Given that the very rich, the super rich and corporations routinely fund political parties, contribute advice to committees, become politicians and indeed political leaders and presidents, this is not too far fetched to suppose. Moreover, the rich and corporations are global in their influence. It is, as in the case of the response to the 2008 financial crash, not a surprise that the rich would prefer not to pay tax, or at least, as little as possible; nor is it a surprise that they prefer the 'bloated public sector' to pay instead through a combination of selling off public assets and privatising public services, austerity measures that mean benefits are cut, wages are frozen or stagnate, the power of the trade unions is dismantled, working age is increased, and tax payers money is used to pay off private debt. Illustration of all this can be found in the case of Greece (Varoufakis, 2015a; 2017). Now suppose a different case, one where the public is defined in terms of the proposition "no taxation without representation" – the slogan, as it happens, employed in the 1700s by American colonists objecting to not being included in British parliamentary decision-making. That would mean only people who paid tax could comprise 'the public will'. At least some billionaires might well be excluded! However, all those who work, including migrants, legal or otherwise, so long as they paid tax would be able to vote in order to be included in the will of the people. In each case, the public is defined by who is included and who excluded. The composition of the public, then, has a dramatic effect upon what constitutes a 'people' whose 'will' has to be counted in policy-making debates. In what ways might excluded demand enter public space?

Those excluded from entering a public space, where debate can be heard and decision-making can be registered through voting, can only have legal recourse if there are established procedures that can be interpreted in ways that open up legal protections, or there are some 'higher', that is, more global and thus more inclusive levels that have some influence, even jurisdiction over the lower levels. That is the case in the sense of international courts where accusations, complaints and pleas can be heard and adjudicated in ways that have consequences for member nations. Between elites and the rest there is a continuous struggle concerning who to include and who to exclude. In this struggle, the democracy of suspicion can be only too effectively manipulated by elites paradoxically simulating being on the side of the 'common' against governing elites. It is a world where 'facts' can be played to suit the purpose – there are always 'alternative facts' as Kellyanne Conway, Trump's presidential counsellor, put it (Revesz, 2017). This takes us into a Goffman-like world (Goffman, 1970) of cynical games of impression management where what is true or suspected to be false loses relationship with reality and, indeed, reality itself becomes constructible to fit the purposes and interests of the moment. This is the world of post-truth and trumpiness explored in earlier chapters. It is a world where truth, in a Lacanian-like sense, is at work elsewhere leaving a hole in the sensuously and discursively constructed realities misguiding people in their judgements as to the reasons producing the circumstances they face.

To discover that the scene has been set up, all it needs is to walk around the props, see that the otherwise solid walls of buildings lining a street are simply fronts with nothing behind. Whether it is a scene set up for filming or the scene created for a president who needs to present a view to himself and his audience that really the crowds at his inauguration were greater than Obama's (Bump, 2017); or perhaps a scene set up by Egyptian state TV showing calm, business as usual and empty streets while Tahrir Square is filled with dissentful hope for change. Truth is prefigured in the dissonances. Not so much seen as glimpsed awry, at the edges of a play of consciousnesses striving for an object. Each individual directed towards a 'something' to be figured in the consciousness of another for mutual recognition. If this something is to become a knowable object capable of truth testing, then each reflection on the phenomena appearing in consciousness requires a persistent honesty countering that of impression management. The courage to be honest in one's own reflections enables each representation to be critically assessed by other reflections, by one's self and in dialogue with others, over time and from multiple perspectives. This 'courage of honesty' is a key prefigurative principle. Through it a moment can come when ruling illusions are burst. Something of this was described by Yurchak (2005) during that moment of *glasnost* (policy enabling debate) and *perestroika* (openness) contributing to the fall of the Berlin Wall and the collapse of the Soviet Union. Just through: "Reading journals, watching live television broadcasts, and talking to friends who were doing the same quickly produced new language, topics, comparisons, metaphors, and ideas, ultimately leading to a profound change of discourse and consciousness" (p. 3). In these acts, there is a *dramatis personae* at play, a developing nucleus of actors engaged in mutual processes of discovery and creation. As more are drawn into the work of reflection of the *dramatis personae*, the more the discoveries and creativity. This provides a second key principle for prefigurative practices: share with others.

As occasions to share with others multiply, differences arise. Each difference constitutes a challenge requiring an honest exchange of views if through the dissonances something new is to appear. Perhaps in this moment there is both exhilaration and fear: the exhilaration of new vistas to explore; the fear of losing old certainties. It is a moment of crisis, that is, a moment of decisive splits that demand decisions on unfamiliar terrains. There is something of the ambiguous figure in gestalt perceptual experiments where a drawing is made in such a way that either the figure of a duck or of a rabbit, but not both at once, can be seen. In the oscillation there is a dizziness, perhaps a vertigo over newly opening spaces without the appearance of a ground. How can decisions be made in such an unbounded, place-less moment? Is there in that Kierkegaardian or Derridean sense, only the madness of the decision which amounts to the leap of faith? Or is there some other principle?

The ground of these crisis questions is always in the embodied experiences of people as they meet, exchange perspectives and work through the challenges each present to the other. We are each a protagonist to the other. In this there is already a mutuality of experience: we meet in the resistances we present, each profiling our differences and thus come to know each other as real or objectively profiled through our differences, the resistances we make to each other. Through the honest exchange of perspectives, the perspective of the other makes the world 'strange' for me. For Schutz (1964) the stranger offers the possibility of new grounds upon which to build new experiences. In that sense, it enriches one's own grounds for knowledge about the social world as a complex of worlds that are the 'homes' of others. In the act of following a stranger, systematised in a sense as ethnographic research or as a challenge by artists to taken-for-granted routines, new places are entered, different vistas as seen, the familiar profiles are given new configurations. To follow a stranger is to act transgressively in a world divided by private and public. Even to think of doing so is 'creepy'. Yet, it has a history in art including Poe's 'The Man of the Crowd', Baudelaire's *flaneur*, and the *dérive* of the Situationists. Each involves an experience of anonymous encounters whether deliberate or with permissions following, merging with crowds as a 'body' in itself, meandering or drifting amongst crowds in streets. Each drift or following presents a challenge to one's routines, pathways and taken-for-granted patterns of attention. It has even become a teaching exercise:

> "Follow a stranger" is one of the instructions I've been given by Serbian artist Miloš Tomić in what is billed as an alternative tour of the city, and I really enjoy it, while also feeling as if I'm doing something a little bit wrong.
> (Kent, 2018)

Even in ethnographies following strangers may be done openly with the permissions of 'gate keepers', or it may be done covertly, particularly if those strangers – in the form of gangs, secret societies, – represent a danger. One criterion for knowing the world of strangers is learning how to pass and be accepted as one of them. What in each case typically does not happen is dialogue of free equals between the follower and the followed. It is an asymmetrical relation. While it remains an asymmetrical relation, it does not build a free and equal public space. Strangers opening up to each other in inclusive debate is thus a third prefigurative principle for the creation of a public. This principle creates the conditions for the emergence of a positive sense of the other as real through the resistances offered; and through those resistances each is better known to each. Such knowledge reveals what is at stake in the challenges made both for a past that can either be frozen to be played for ever as the criterion for reproducing the present or rethought to lead to a future that can be co-constructed for mutual benefits.

In the meetings between an ever-expanding *dramatis personae*, the powers of each in the co-construction of what resists enables choices about either building walls to contain and exclude to protect old ways of life; or opening places to include, meet and create new ways of life. This fourth prefigurative principle pursues inclusivity of the stranger to build mutuality as a principle of friendship, where friendship includes but is more than having particular friends. It is the pervasive tenor of attitude and feeling about one's fellow human beings. It counters the hostility that is essential to building walls – whether composed of bricks or laws – in order to provide an ever-present symbol of enmity. There is as Rancière (2005) has pointed out a hatred of democracy, at least by those who would be threatened by it. Unlike Trump's divisive walls and May's policy to create a 'hostile environment', democracy directly promotes the powers of individuals to act as agents in free, friendly, honest and open association with each other to reflect upon the present and project a mutual future. Given the contemporary arrangements where individuals are predominantly employed to work in the interests of elites, this project for the future depends upon how work itself can be rethought and reorganised as a democratic project.

## Work and education as prefigurative public spaces

Work provides for the vast majority of adults their major experience of collective life, of being co-dependent on the work of others (c.f. Goodson, 2005; 2014). However, this co-dependency can be variously masked and manipulated. Corporate rule and the control over the mass organisation of work has reduced collective experience to 'employment' where labour can be hired and fired and the products of work are owned by the corporation. Every aspect of 'work' can be specified and managed through measurement, resulting in a gap between how work is really organised to be completed and how it is to be specified, measured and managed for the purposes of 'efficiency' (Dejours, 2003; Deranty, 2008). The difference between the specified definition of work and the realities of actually accomplishing work is most clearly spelt out in disputes when workers threaten to 'work to rule'. Following the specified practices of the rule book means that work cannot actually be accomplished. Work demands much more than the performance-related specification for its accomplishment. It requires a particular knowhow, an 'eye' for detail, a 'feel' for how things are put together that cannot be measured. When two or more people come together to explore a mutual project they at least require the personal characteristics to create a common space to act together, express their views, argue about who will do what, how and when, engage with disagreements, make decisions and determine the appropriate forms of organisation to achieve common purposes in the creation of the finished product or service. Such activity lays the foundation of a curriculum for social learning grounded in the working relations of people. As such, as Dejours (1998) argues it is already embryonically democratic as each recognises their co-dependencies. Work becomes employment only when those co-dependencies are subsumed under hierarchies where the employed have no claim on the products of their labour.

The recognition of co-dependencies as a basis not only for work but for fundamentally changing society was seen by Robert Owen, one of the most influential forerunners of the co-operative movement. The enduring impact, however, was brought about by the 28 original co-operators who created a shop in Rochdale in 1844. They were not rich like Owen but had saved up their money over a period to time to open the shop and ran it according to key principles which became known as Law First. In the 1844 publication of the 'Laws and Objects of the Rochdale society of Equitable Pioneers' after stating their immediate practical aims they stated their broader ambition:

> That as soon as practicable, this society shall proceed to arrange the powers of production, distribution, education, and government, or in other words to establish a self-supporting home-colony or united interests, or assist other societies in establishing such colonies.
> (Laws and Objects, 1844: 3)

The early practices, the values and principles underpinning them, and the broader ambition provided an enduring model that has spread around the world. Their contemporary version is published on the Co-operative College Website: 1, voluntary and open membership, 2, democratic member control, 3, member economic participation, 4, autonomy and independence, 5, education, training and information, 6, co-operation among co-operatives, 7, concern for community. The values that underpin these are: self-help, self-responsibility, democracy, equality, equity, solidarity. Self-help thus does not mean individualism in its neoliberal sense. It is through self-help that the individuals are co-dependent as a 'people', a concept captured in the title of the first historical account of co-operativism by George Jacob Holyoake in 1858. The core purpose of co-operation was "Self-Help by the People". In pursuing self-help by the people, the interrelationship between work, meetings and education in an atmosphere of equality was clear:

> The Store very early began to exercise educational functions. Besides supplying the members with provisions, the Store became a meeting place, where almost every member met each other every evening after working hours. Here was harmony because there was equality. Every member was equal in right, and was allowed to express his opinions on whatever topic he took an interest in.
> (Holyoake, 1858: 22)

There is a promise in equality that goes well beyond immediate working relations. It casts a restless critical eye over all forms of discrimination – gender, class, race, faith, abilities and so on. For example, the values and practices of the co-operative movement have found critical expression in women's rights (Khanna, 2013) and co-operatives have a long history of development by African-American pioneers (Bhatt, 2015). However, although it can be argued that a co-operative is prefigurative of a democratic public, the public cannot be reduced to the concrete practices of co-operatives. Rather the co-operative in its work and educational dimensions is always experimental, resulting from engaging together under conditions of freedom and equality. If it is not, then there is the danger of the corruption of principles of equality and freedom of debate by vested interests as new viewpoints are sifted out. What is prefigured is the quality of critique and the freedom to participate and organise that is expressed by what Rosanvallon (2013) describes as the 'society of equals' that arose in the discourses of the eighteenth- and nineteenth-century revolutionary thinkers.

## Towards the public as the society of equals

Democracy and institutionalised democracy are not the same thing. Institutionalised democracy is in a sense the formalisation through laws of the compromises reached between those who demand freedom with equality for all against those who instead insist on separating their own rights to the freedom to accumulate private riches, privileges and powers from equal access to such wealth, privileges and powers for all. The actual institutions that arise police the boundaries between those who have most and those who have least. However, it was early realised, according to Rosanvallon (2012), that there needs to be "an organ of oversight and initiative distinct from the representative assemblies" that could, as proposed by one Charles-François-Chevé in 1840, be "a permanent investigative body and a diligent workshop for the development of new and better methods, a clearing house for popular demands and a tireless laboratory for future improvements" (cited by Rosanvallon, 2012: 100). There is in this proposition a prefiguration of what Dewey proposed as the purpose of the school as an educational space for experiments in social creativity, innovation, that is, a laboratory for social innovation. As expressed by Mayhew and Camp who were teachers in the school, it was: "a cooperative venture of parents, teachers, and educators" (Mayhew and Edwards, 1936: v). Dewey saw it addressing the relation between the individual and the community:

> The problem of the relation between individual freedom and collective well-being is today urgent and acute, perhaps more so than at any time in the past. The problem of achieving both of these values without the sacrifice of either one is likely to be the dominant problem of civilisation for many years to come. The schools have their part to play in working out the solution, and their own chief task is to create a form of community life and organisation in which both of these values are conserved.
> 
> (Dewey in Mayhew and Edwards, 1936: xv)

Dewey's laboratory school as part of the heritage of democratic schooling (Fielding and Moss, 2011) along with the ideas and practices of the co-operative movement and other forms of community valuing freedom in relation to equality provide historical legacies that can prompt reflection on how prefigurative practices in all forms of organisation might be constructed to promote the knowledge, values and critical practices required for an effective public able to address key issues in the relation between individual freedom and community. The public, in that sense, is a 'permanent investigative body' and each organisation – schools, workplaces, families and so forth – in society is potentially therefore 'a tireless laboratory for future improvements'.

# Chapter 10

# Towards the creation of public spaces

All over the world, people are anxious, concerned about their futures. Millions are in movement from war zones, from tyrannies, from poverty zones, to find some decent life for themselves and their families. Who can say the real numbers that compose the 'collateral damage' of long-range cannon fire, missiles, bombing raids and drones? There has been and continues to be a global failure to grasp the tragedies of lives sacrificed. This failure is not a failure of leadership, but a failure of the public and how the public is constructed, organised and enacted to create its leadership. In a moment of time when climate change, environment and natural disasters are increasingly common on a scale and frequency rarely recorded, it is not a failure of leadership but a failure of public force capable of countering the short-term profit that the exploitation of the aftermath of disasters brings for elites. The demand for cheap goods and services is more effective than the demand for freedom, equality and a world safe for all. But it cannot be the case that people are not capable of caring.

On Independence Day in America, a woman called Okoumou clung to the Statue of Liberty – a symbol of welcome for those fleeing oppression or looking for a new life in the pioneering days following the revolution that was the American war of independence. It was a protest. She fell asleep on the statue: "I was thinking of Lady Liberty above me, you are so huge, you have always been a symbol of welcome to people arriving in America and right now, for me under this sandal, she is a shelter." When she awoke there were the police:

> "I said 'Don't come up.' He said 'I care about you.' I said, 'No, you don't, you could shoot me the way you shot Claudia Gomez and killed the trans woman,'" she said, referring to Gomez, a 20-year-old Guatemalan woman shot by the border patrol in Texas last month, and Roxana Hernández, from Honduras, who died in Ice custody [that is, the Immigration Customs and Enforcement agency] in May after reportedly spending five days in a form of chilled detention dubbed the ice box.
>
> Okoumou said she feared she would be shot or tranquillised, and shouted to the officer that "my life doesn't matter to me now, what matters to me is that in a democracy we are holding children in cages".
>
> (Walters, 2018)

Outside of protest, what power has a courageous individual got to stop the police in a democracy from obeying orders authorised by government policy to hold children in cages?

Two countervailing forms of organisation were clearly at present, at least symbolically, at the protest on the Statue of Liberty, first in the demand for the form of democracy that listens to, represents and takes account of all voices in decision-making; the second, the demand for quiet obedience to the prevailing political order of winners and losers conveyed by the police officer. For the first demand, there is no electoral mechanism equivalent to the market place that is sensitive to particular demands expressed by voters so that resources are automatically allocated to satisfy those demands. If there were, there would be no unheard injustices like "children in cages". For the second demand, in contrast, all the levers of legitimate power are placed in the hands of the winners who compose the government enabling them to define what is 'fair', raise the resources for example in the form of taxes, to implement and enforce policies that large proportions of a population voted against and others did not vote on at all either because they feel their voices do not count or because they have no right to vote. In such conditions and circumstances, what is required to address the lack of access to power and resource in order to construct a public where the demands of all individuals are equally and effectively counted in making and enacting decisions?

## Effective oversight

What is required first of all is the public means to oversee instituted power in all its forms – government, corporations, the rich – that promote and maintain undemocratic discourses, relationships and practices in all forms of organisation. Fundamental to anti-democratic practice are narratives that are sustained by variants of Plato's 'noble lie' that people are naturally classifiable into: rulers/leaders/entrepreneurial heroes at the top who decide upon the public good; that is then delivered by managers and experts on the one hand and enforcers and defenders on the other who protect the public good; and of course, at the bottom, the workers who in following orders engage in the necessary labour to produce the wealth of the nation. The noble lie underpinning contemporary discourses of neoliberalism and neoconservatism seek to justify wealth inequality and political hierarchy through discourses of merit based on intelligence, talent, risk taking and hard work, none of which hold up to scrutiny (Stiglitz, 2012; Marwick, 2013; Dorling, 2015; Bloodworth, 2016). Instead, the lie displaces attention from and covers over unfair allocations of resources and distributions of reward for work undertaken. The result is to place democracy and the physical world under threat. Rather than the 'good and just society' built through the benevolence of wise rulers there is a world suffering wars, poverty and environmental destruction. Instead of work and education increasing the standard and quality of life equally for all, work, social and political life is characterised by, for example:

- Demeaning work
- Deskilling of labour
- Deconstruction of dignity of selfhood
- Degrading services
- Debased and disintegrating knowledge
- Denial of expertise
- Destruction of environment
- Dispossession of people's productive and creative powers
- Decimation and Dissolution of the discourses, practices and forms of organisation necessary for democracy

all resulting in a:

- Dramatic increase in profits for the elites.

Much more can be added from the experiences of individuals but the list is enough to indicate the need for effective exercise of strategic, critical oversight of the acts of powerful elites inside and outside of government. This means that effective oversight is not limited to ensuring the governmental delivery of winning programmes but ensuring those programmes do not impact unfairly upon people's lives as well as constraining the anti-democratic insolence of elites outside of government to create and maintain organisations where democracy is excluded. These include the so-called private domains of the market, the 'domestic' domain of the household and the *in loco parentis* spheres of education as well as the sealed-off military/police/secret service domains of the State. If a society composed of these domains is to be considered democratic, then each becomes a legitimate focus of public oversight. It can be argued that some should be excluded, but if so, it is no longer possible to claim the democratic nature of society. If any part impacts upon the lives of individuals but cannot be scrutinised and held up for public judgement and action, then the democratic nature of society is undermined.

Each of these 'domains' becomes a site for prefigurative struggle. The struggle begins in scrutiny, a scrutiny that prefigures the ideal of state of democracy as providing the criteria by which to critique contemporary real discourses, practices and forms of organisation. In this, two key 'organs' of scrutiny are: investigative journalism; and critical academic research and scholarship. The first investigates those who want to keep their activities hidden or those whose lives and views are in some way ignored or overlooked by the mainstream or indeed actively repressed by elites. The second sustains continuing debates about the philosophies and theories justifying policies, forms of organisation, policy and practice. The two can contribute to developments in each by combining investigative details on particular instances of 'wrong doing', more generally researched case studies, ethnographies, evaluations and surveys as a basis for evidence construction and the building of theory and argumentation in relation to the evidence. Together they can contribute to the development of radical research methodologies that are explicitly democratically informed in all dimensions of project design and stages of implementation (Schostak and Schostak, 2008; 2013).

These 'organs' of scrutiny are necessary, but the broader scrutiny must come from the involvement of a wider public as witness. As Rosanvallon described in his study of the French and American revolutions, it is the potential of the public as 'eyes' everywhere that constitutes the power of scrutiny. Testimony can come from anywhere. And developments in the Internet and communications technologies in both software and hardware have added to this potential. On the one hand, as investigative journalists like the Guardian's Carole Cadawalladr (2017; 2017a; 2017b; 2017c) can bring to general awareness the problematic use of social media by elites to influence voting; on the other, high-profile hackers like Julian Assange can break into secretive organisations in order to leak data that is capable of challenging and undermining official narratives; or employees like the ex-CIA employee Edward Snowden can leak information on a huge scale; or in more limited terms employees may break ranks and provide eye witness accounts of the impacts of draconian policies on the vulnerable, or negligence and shady practices in their places of work.

All such witnessing contributes to building pictures in the mind that counter official or elite endorsed narratives. The more such counter-pictures are cross-referenced and resonate with biographical accounts and the personal experiences of life across the domains of social life, the more the evidence builds. The Internet, as Rosanvallon (2012: 68) suggests, offers the potential for the realisation of the public as a collective intelligence by sharing personal experiences, entering into debate and forming critical judgements. For example, the #MeToo campaign (Khomami, 2017) of women sharing experiences through social media of unwanted behaviour and sexual abuse from men has not only raised sensitive and critical issues but is able to challenge dominant discourses of 'natural' sexual conduct, bring charges in particular cases and more generally contribute to changing attitudes, mind-sets and behaviour.

A combination of investigative journalism, critical academic research and public witnessing provides the grounds for building evidence-based narratives that are able to bring into dramatic relationship individuals and organisations across the domains locally, regionally, nationally, internationally, globally. In this sense, such processes of linking witnessing, scrutiny and judgement creates the conditions for a change in the political aesthetics (Rancière, 2004) underpinning perceptions of what is 'natural' by creating alternative views that undermine the mantras of 'there is no alternative'. The power of witnessing and of communicating what is witnessed is the fundamental power of the democratic public. As Spinoza (2004) argued, the legitimacy of any government ultimately rests upon the powers of the people and that a democracy based upon the co-extensiveness of freedom and equality for individuals is the fairest expression of those powers. Indeed, each witness has the capacity to judge for his or herself whether or not their freedoms are being restricted by the powers of others as well as to communicate this judgement to others. Each witness is thus able to cross-correlate their experiences and form a more general judgement as to the impacts of the powerful on curbing the freedoms of the vulnerable. Etienne de la Boétie (1552) perhaps most plainly put it when he concluded that the god-like tyrant – the Atlas of Rand, or the contemporary financial masters of the universe – will fall at the very moment when people realise their collective power and refuse to obey. Zizek (1991) wrote of the moment when Ceausescu lost his grip on the imaginations of his people, the very moment when he was no longer a giant in their eyes.

To begin to see what is at stake in the narratives that constrain the imagination, one can, in Zizek's terms, 'look awry'. In doing so, what is left out of mainstream discourses about what is real can be brought to awareness and be the foundation for alternative perceptions and readings (Schostak and Schostak, 2013). Such 'new readings' open the way for alternative educations that may create the conditions for learning to explore countervailing forms of organisation for new visions of community and global society. For example, in Smith's key work, *The Wealth of Nations* (1776), there was already an alternative reading that had been suppressed, particularly in the work of neoliberal economists and their influence on the professional training of young economists in universities (Earl et al., 2017). Thus re-reading Adam Smith:

> as I suggested several years ago, there is a second model of order in the Wealth of Nations, a model of the economy as a system of power. Smith understood the deep forces of organisation and control at work in the economic system. He realised how market forces operate only within, and give effect to, the structure of power and, especially, how those with access to and (in some sense) control over government use it. Market order is achieved only within the structure of power. Both the market and power govern whose interests will count in the economy. Markets are structured by power, and market solutions are power-structure specific. Power and market relations both constitute sets of variables in a general interdependent system.
>
> (Samuels, 1977: 192)

More explicitly, therefore, Samuels concludes: "Smith includes both market and power models in his conception of how society works out resolutions to the problem of order" (Samuels, 1977: 193).

It is here that government is essential as a countervailing force to the market. In Smith's terms it provides the 'police order' through which markets can be regulated (see, Smith, 1762: 290). By 'police' he did not just mean the police force but its older connotation of 'policy', an approach later developed by Rancière (2004) to describe the controlling effect of all the parts of a given social order. Thus, as argued above with the dominance of the private sphere over all aspects of life, democracy has been both crowded out and hollowed out in all the major spheres of collective life – work, education, play, community and government – giving rise, to a police order that is equivalent to corporate order. The eyes of the public thus can act as a countervailing force to the emergence of elite power, generating another form of 'police order' where the 'distribution of the sensible' is under the gaze of the freely seeing eyes of the people as equals. In that sense, a critical public is a condition for the production of what Rosanvallon (2013) describes as the 'society of equals' that was fundamental to revolutionary discourses before, during and after the French and American revolutions in designing the reforms necessary for the new Republics.

Indeed, even now, the society of equals can be excavated as it were from where it lies implicit in the market narrative – whether of Adam Smith or of Hayek or Friedman. This narrative is driven by useful assumptions concerning freedom and equality that can, as it were, turn the free marketeers' narrative on its head. It begins with the impossible idea of perfect competition. This exists only when all firms – whether buyers or sellers – and their customers are free and more or less equal in their power to affect market price. It is this that gives modern neoliberal free marketeers a fundamental plank for their argument for a small state. The state should only exist to the extent that it ensures the conditions for the necessary assumptions grounding market competition to operate without interference, without bias. Under those conditions resources are allocated according to a balance or equilibrium point between what suppliers are willing and able to offer and what buyers are willing and able to purchase. Any monopoly power or government dictate will reduce the markets ability to optimise the allocation of resources to meet what consumers demand. Of course, this condition is nowhere met nationally or globally. If the neoliberals' strategy to achieve it was to place their acolytes in places of power (see Norton 2004; Harvey, 2005; Klein, 2007) while waiting for a suitable crisis that would throw the old elites into confusion but would enable the neoliberal ideologues to provide the 'solution', then the comparable strategy is to seed the adherents of the 'society of equals' in places of power: schools, universities, businesses, political think tanks, political parties, transnational organisations in finance, economics, law. It is in these places of struggle that the 'eyes' of the public can be educated, trained and mobilised. For a while, not long, admittedly, it seemed that the crisis of 2008 would enable a counter revolution. However, there were in effect no others in place who could provide a sufficiently clear and consistent alternative. Instead there was in the imagery of the critical books that appeared in the following years the continuation of the walking dead, that is, the same institutions that had bled dry the public sector as well as the citizens as consumers, workers and voters were simply continuing to find new sources of 'blood' to feed on (Keen, 2011; Quiggin, 2010 Crouch, 2011).

## Sites for prefigurative action

A key contemporary expression of the 'society of equals' can be seen in the aspirations, if not sufficiently the practice, of the co-operative movement. With its discourses of co-operation rather than competition, of equality and equity rather than hierarchy, of democracy rather than authoritarianism, it, at least in terms of values and ideals, presents a distinct alternative to neoliberal managerialism and elitism. They represent a model for prefigurative organisation.

The principle of co-operation begins with the freedom to associate with whoever one wishes under conditions of equality. Conversely, the freedom to associate is also freedom to disassociate and to reconfigure. This inherent dynamism underpins the potential power of co-operatives as a 'movement'. Given its potential for reconfiguration to invite new viewpoints and meet changing circumstances it is not surprising to see that:

> co-operative strongholds and clusters can be located around the world, including Mondragon in Spain, Trentino in Italy, Davis in California, USA and the network of Desjardins credit unions in French Canada .... While the largest 300 co-operatives have an economic power equivalent to the Canadian economy, it has been estimated by the UN that co-operatives have supported at least half the world's population and this fact helped to justify designating 2012 as the International Year of Co-operatives.
> (Woodin, 2014: 2)

Significantly in the UK during the nineteenth century co-operatives also established schools that later were brought into state schooling until by the 1980s their days were over. It was not until 2008 that the first Co-operative Trust school at Reddish Vale, Stockport was set up when the then Principal of the Co-operative College, Mervyn Wilson, saw the opportunity of using conservative legislation intended to promote free schools and academies to promote instead the development of a co-operative schools' sector. This has risen to about 600 schools, making the movement the third largest association in the UK after the Church of England and the Catholic Church faith schools.

There is the clear potential for co-operative schools to create what Dewey termed laboratories for social experiment to explore the "problem of the relation between individual freedom and collective well-being" (Dewey in Mayhew and Edwards, 1936: xv). The organisation of schools, learning processes and practice and curricula could all be formulated to prefigure the vision of a fully democratic society. In this endeavour much can be learnt from the experiences of democratic schools, that in a sense were living examples of democratic experimentation (see in particular, Fielding, 2005; 2009; Fielding and Moss, 2011). Education, in all its forms, has a radical role to play in creating the sites for prefigurative action. This role has long been known and typically subverted by elites of all kinds. Schools are made to fit the kinds of societies they service.

Just as Robert Lowe (1867) called for an education of 'our masters' that would result in ensuring they made the right decisions, that is, the decisions desired by propertied elites who saw themselves as the possessors of intelligence and reason and thus the natural rulers of society; so, contemporary schools are shaped by the modern versions of the political need for elites to manage the attitudes, behaviours, knowledge and skills of the various flavours of the mass that today comprise a given society. A special edition of the Monthly Review (Ayers and Ayers 2011:11) summarised the extent to which corporate capitalism and its power elites had captured and hijacked education, "normalising white, middleclass discourse".

To counter such 'hijacking', forms of research that shift power back to teachers, students, learners of all ages and communities to make decisions can be employed. Action research in conjunction with radical methodologies (Schostak and Schostak, 2008; 2013) can be employed. The action research 'movement' has its roots in the work of Kurt Lewin (1946) and in the UK in the Humanities Curriculum Project of Lawrence Stenhouse (1975) who used the term 'teacher as researcher'. In its critical radical democratic forms it can provide a countervailing force through prefigurative action. Schostak's 'listening and talking project' (the following is drawn from Schostak, 1989; 1990) focused on problems as they arose in a 'first school' (taking children from 5 to 8 years old) and how they were to be resolved. In doing this it prefigured both a shift of power to teachers and children as well as framing decision-making as productive of democratic forms of practice and organisation. The problems that served as subjects for mutual learning through discussion – or as the children called it sorting it out, or talking it through – were often unanticipated and as much to do with social and emotional problems as academic problems. That is to say, they did not easily form neat subjects, or require skills as set out in the levels of attainment expected in national testing. In short, the agenda of concerns arose from the everyday experiences of the school as a community within a wider community. That is to say, the educative process began by systematically reflecting upon the everyday curriculum of a given individual or group. The teachers built up an extensive archive of recorded examples of how problems developed and were solved. It became the basis of their own learning as well as for school policy formation. Here is an early videoed example:

> scene: it is a first school classroom, there are just under 60 children in a large room which has been used as two classrooms. There are two teachers and one welfare assistant. It is nearly dinner time and the children have just cleared up their work. One of the teachers has just praised them and the excellence of their work and clearing up their work quickly and neatly. She goes on to say:

TEACHER: Before we have our lunch, could I just speak to you for a moment?
PUPILS: Yes

T: Um ... Quite a few people have come and said that other people are bothering them. I think people came and said me that Alan was bothering them and people came and said to me that Mary was bothering them. What do you think you should do in that situation? What do you think is the best thing to do, Jill?

JILL: Go on the carpet.

T: Go on the carpet and sort it out. You can just say to the person "You are bothering me, please come with me on the carpet and we can sort it out." Now, what are you going to do if you can't sort it out, it's too hard? What do you think you could do then? Jane?

JANE: Come and fetch you.

T: Yes, come and fetch some help and then we'll, we'll help. There's no point in coming and saying to me "Alan did this and Mary did that", because I'm not going to sort it out for you ... OK? So, let's try that and see how it goes. Alright? The project idea began simply enough. A teacher had made the observation that quarrelling children were very often seen shortly after hand in hand as friends, as if nothing had happened. How did they sort out their problems? This was a school that took children from the nursery age of 3 through to the primary or 'first school' period from 5 to 8 years old. As the project evolved it became clear even very young children could engage in 'sorting it out' across a wide range of activities, whether these were behavioural issues, resource issues arising when scarce resources were wanted by several people at once, or whether it was about what to do when class work had been finished and the child did not know what to do next. Each time, the teacher would say something like, 'now that's an interesting problem, how can we sort it out? Have a think about it and come back and tell me when you have a solution.' What was remarkable was that children, regardless of age, became increasingly creative, self-responsible and self-organised in every area of school life. In order to research the ideas more fully, a new school was found where the staff agreed to experiment with the new way of working. Again, it was transformative. Indeed it resulted in an evidence-based policy development for the school. The school had box files of transcripts from audio and video recordings of classroom activities and discussions. From this they developed policies for the school grounded in the evidence as shown from an extract from their school policy on social development:

1   At every stage create opportunities for children and teachers to be explicit about problems and possible solutions.
2   At every stage encourage the children to contribute to the solution of problems. <*At a whole school level the tape of the football assembly is a good example of both of these. The children were given the opportunity both to lay out the problem, and to discuss possible solutions.*>

3 Encourage the children to say what they are thinking. The teachers and other staff too need to say what they are thinking. <*There are plenty of examples on the tapes of the children having the opportunity to say what they are thinking. The whole talking-out procedure is designed to do precisely this too. As far as staff are concerned the democratic mode of discussion and decision-making is designed to that end, but the principle also applies between staff and children.*>

4 Make time in the school day, in and out of the classroom, for discussion with the children. <*Look for opportunities for ordinary friendly social inter-relationships and chat between staff and children. It is important that our focus is positive not negative, and problems will then be reduced to their proper perspective.*>

5 Make sure that the solution of problems is one of our priorities. The rationale is that personal and social development is of crucial importance to the development of any learner, child or adult. <*This very much needs to be read in conjunction with 4. The evidence of the fourth year children on the interview tape reinforces the importance of this. Learning in groups is clearly tied in with their social learning.*>

Point 2 referred to the constant problem that during playtime the children who were playing football would sometimes kick the ball over the wall used as a goal that separated the playground from the houses behind. The neighbours regularly complained. The children involved discussed the problem and came up with several possible solutions. However, each solution would involve stopping other children from using that part of the playground when they were playing football. To address this issue the children called a general assembly of the school and put the possible solutions to them. From the assembly children then posed questions before voting on possible solutions. A solution was agreed and put into practice. It worked. The whole event had been videoed and became a key piece of evidence concerning how to build the practices and forms of organisation necessary to solve both personal and larger social problems within and outside of the school. The children had an impact on the curriculum of the school in terms of subjects tackled and projects created as well as the forms of teaching and learning relationships that emerged. Many parents were intrigued and were also drawn into the processes. With the emergence of the co-operative schools movement such initiatives could be drawn into wider forms of community development. Perhaps the model is that of Mondragon where work and community are integrated into a broad model of co-operation (Lafuente, 2012; Quigley, 2013). Broadly, attempting to live together generates issues across the currently compartmentalised areas of work, education, community, family, street and market place of products, services and entertainment. As people move from one site of daily life to another, issues arise. These issues are the stuff of curricula. Imagine if Okoumou, instead of having to cling in protest to the Statue of Liberty, had real mechanisms of liberty for 'sorting it out' with protagonists.

**Prefigurative curricula for the formation of a 'public'**

The Humanities Curriculum Project (1967–1972) based its curriculum on controversial social issues drawn from everyday life. Due to their controversial nature, debates between protagonists were inevitable. For that reason, the rules for debate became the focal point for what counted as curriculum, pedagogy and classroom relations. All were to be able to express their views, but views grounded in argumentation from evidence. All should have an equal chance to voice their views. And the teacher's sole responsibility was to ensure the rules of debate were followed. As to the answers or conclusions given, the teacher should remain neutral. Hence the idea of the teacher as neutral chair was born (see Stenhouse, 1975). An early statement of the approach to teaching stated the following essential characteristics:

1 The fundamental educational values of rationality, imagination, sensitivity, readiness to listen to the views of others, and so forth, must be built into the principles of procedure in the classroom.
2 The pattern of teaching must renounce the authority of the teacher as an 'expert' capable of solving value issues since this authority cannot be justified either epistemologically or politically. In short, the teacher must aspire to be neutral.
3 The teaching strategy must maintain the procedural authority of the teacher in the classroom, but contain it within rules which can be justified in terms of the need for discipline and rigour in attaining understanding.
4 The strategy must be such as to satisfy parents and pupils that every possible effort is being made to avoid the use of the teacher's authority position to indoctrinate his own views.
5 The procedure must enable pupils to understand divergence and hence must depend upon a group working together through discussion and shared activities. In such a group, opinions should be respected, and minority opinions should be protected from ridicule or from social pressure.
6 In sensitive issues, thought must be given to preserving privacy and protecting students, e.g., illegitimate children, children from broken homes, children of prostitutes should be borne in mind when discussing the family or relations between the sexes.
7 Above all, the aim should be understanding. This implies that one should not force pupils towards opinions or premature commitments which harden into prejudice. Nor should one see particular virtue in a change of view. The Object is that the pupil should come to understand the nature and implications of his point of view, and grow to adult responsibility by adopting it in his own person and assuming accountability for it. Whether

or not the pupil changes his point of view is not significant for the attainment of understanding.

(Stenhouse, 1969)

This is a statement of characteristics that is struggling to be a prefigurative strategy. Values of Enlightenment reason and the use of debate for the construction of adult public responsibility are both explicitly and implicitly built into the characteristics of the project's approach to teaching and learning. By replacing 'values' with 'powers' in the first of the characteristics above, "rationality, imagination, sensitivity, readiness to listen" are transformed from being subject to an external framework to being active demands. But what can be seen now in the text, and what may not have been seen then, was its use of teacher authority imposing an authorised version of reason, bending to the constraints of classroom discipline, external parental authority, underwriting the liberal virtues of tolerance and assuming individual responsibility and, of course, framing the text. There are, in this, echoes of a Cartesian or Lockean-like split between reason and the need to discipline bodies. Tolerance, of course, can be particularly problematic. As one HCP member said, what do I do with the views of the fascist at the back of the class? This continues its contemporary resonances with the rise of the Alt-Right, anti-immigrant and racist discourses, with their political successes in promoting 'fortress Europe', Brexit and Trump. Nevertheless, however critically one reflects on the text, it remains a powerful point of departure for thinking about prefigurative sites of struggle both in schools and outside in the community, across communities, across political frontiers of all kinds.

## Towards research as productive of prefigurative sites for action

New rules are required. Not new in the sense of never having been thought about before but new in the sense of research, work and education as mutually coextensive prefigurative activities. Necessarily combined they produce dynamic realities rather than being a neutral set of procedures rooted solely in some illusory pursuit of 'objective' knowledge or evidence that is frozen in its Platonic truth. Rather than privileging observation and measurement of empirically given realities there is a form of 'oversight' that includes imagination and the play of ideas, values, feelings, desires in assessing what is now in relation to what could be, how it could be and why it should be. Democracy is not just about hope but about getting there. The role of education and research is to contribute approaches for doing this across all the activities of social life. In doing so, they contribute to the development of a critically mutually informing public. This public is necessarily outside of any formally constructed institution, since all such institutions are subject to the public gaze.

Rosanvallon (2012: 111) makes a useful distinction between those democracies where the public space is seen as a domain of reflection and expression; and those where the public space is reserved only for those forms of organisation where voting takes place to elect representatives who then participate in the organisation in order to represent the range of views from the wider society. If research and education are to be productive of critical domains of reflection and expression then prefiguring the conditions under which demands are heard as legitimate across a public is essential to ensuring liberty for all. What are the next steps?

# Chapter 11

# New rules for research, social learning and creating a socially just world

The lessons to be learnt for engaging in research, education and action for social justice are very much to do with how public powers are constrained by elites and vice versa. That is, is the research purpose to find ways of shaping the values, views and behaviour of people in the interests of elites, or free people in the interests of creating a critical public? Bluntly, most university research is financed by a state, corporate or private charitable funding body; and mainstream education is typically funded by states, charities, philanthropists. How the funding bodies are themselves financed and managed matters, just as the political ideology and the way the state's power is constructed matters. Since research and education are critically shaped by the resources provided by their funders, it then matters how the research and education agendas are controlled and shaped. How independent of the funders are research and education?

There needs to be, for example, the resource to finance time to be spent in research and educational activities, the tools and materials to be used, access to or even building locations where research and education can take place. The rich can buy both time and resource to achieve their purposes. There is, of course, and always will be, research and education in the margins, outside of work: the lonely research scholar stealing time; the struggles of the self taught and the possibilities of mutual help as in the students who taught each other without a teacher at the School of Barbiana (1969). The choice, put crudely: is it the enlightenment project of a Freire (1972) or the profit-making agendas of Big Pharma that leads research and education? Posing the question *thus*, takes away the wriggle room.

The ideal first rule for democratically informed research and education would, in our view, always by guided by Balibar's principle of *égaliberté*. That is, research and education are both to be conducted by people who engage with each other and decide on mutually enriching agendas freely and equally. All other rules follow from or are framed by this principle.

### Formulating the rules

The world is not ideal. But the rules of engagement can be created prefiguratively. This can be done either directly or indirectly. Both have a subversive and reconstructive intent. The first is open and is to be preferred if it exists as a realistic option. The second recognises the games playing configurations of elites opening up the espionage-like world of Goffman's (1959; 1970) impression management and strategic interaction. He described open contexts where all actors have information of what is going on; one where only one side knows what is going on; contexts in which one side suspects what is going on; and another of mutual suspicion that the other is concealing information about what is going on but neither are saying. The question here is how to move from stealth architectures that deliberately conceal and from architectures that knowingly or unwittingly prevent knowledge sharing.

There is a wide range of areas under which open approaches to research and education can be undertaken: economic, social care, learning, entertainment, security and so forth. They arise under co-operative endeavours where freedom of participation and mutuality is key to the relationship between people. What emerges is a prefigured general public having open access to knowledge. For instance, the talking and listening project described in the previous chapter began in the curiosities of two teachers, a newly appointed head teacher and her deputy: how was it that children who were in angry dispute one minute were later found hand in hand as best friends again? What did they do to resolve their problems with each other? In order to answer this question a simple project approach had to be designed that: 1) treated children as equals to the process since they were the insiders of the process; 2) suspend the authority of the teachers so that all they could do was watch, listen and ask; 3) trust the children to engage in child-chosen courses of action. Under these conditions the result of every interaction had to be by agreement. If it wasn't, then a complaint would be made and those involved had to 'sort it out' by 'talking it through until there was a mutually agreed solution' and then seeing if the solution worked. The idea spread around the school by example. Others saw what was happening; a public expectation grew that this was the way to do things. And of course, the head and deputy head teachers encouraged other members of staff to try it out not only with children but with each other. This meant that the two senior teachers also had to suspend their own authority with the staff as soon as the staff raised their own issues that had to be 'sorted out'. The simple beginnings, in this school and in a second school that was influenced by it, prefigured an open public as a real political-like body that was increasingly outside of the official organisational hierarchy of the school as teachers, other school staff, the children and parents deployed the broad principles and practices to reflect upon all activities – personal behaviour, learning activities, curriculum matters, organisation of activities and so on. In the sense employed by Bergasse, the mutual relations between the children and the adults in their lives became a public, a collective body of eyes, ears and talk through which a guiding public opinion was dynamically formed as a product of the free interactions of each. The public, in that sense, is a force to be reckoned with.

It did not last, of course. After several years and under the relentless pressures of neoliberal policies along with staff leaving through retirements or to go to new jobs, the schools as experiments in democratic social learning had to end. However, ideas and legacies continue in memory for future experiments. In that sense, the public does not forget, nor does it go away. For Spinoza, there was a kind of immortality about the public in the sense of being independent of any particular individual that composes it. People are born, people die, the public continues. There continues to be the triangulations of seeing, hearing and conversing that compose the public as the ground for the development of knowledge – that is, the third form of knowledge in Spinoza's sense as formed from the collective practice of democracy itself where "by consulting, listening, and debating they grow more acute, and while they are trying all means, they at last discover those which they want, which all approve, but no one would have thought of in the first instance" (Spinoza, 2004: 376). For Spinoza it is through the network of relations that rationality is expressed. In that sense, there is always the potential for conflict between government, the public and the multitude that compose it. The elites composing governments do not easily suspend or give over their authority, their power, their leadership privileges. The government thus strives to manage who counts and what counts in decision-making and policy implementation. There is therefore a mutually subversive problematic relation between the multitude and the public on the one side; and on the other, the government and the wealthy who largely compose it. The nature of the opposition is nicely expressed in Hardt and Negri's (2009) reflections on Rancière's approach to the political:

> For Ranicière "the whole basis of politics is the struggle between the poor and the rich" or, more precisely, he goes on to say, the struggle between those who have no part in the management of the common and those who control it. Politics exists when those who have no right to be counted, as Rancière says, make themselves of some account. The part of those who have no part, the party of the poor, is an excellent initial definition of the multitude, as long as we add immediately that the party of the poor is by no means homologous to the party of the rich. The party of the rich makes false claim to universality, pretending in the guise of the republic of property to represent the entire society, when in fact it is based only on an exclusive identity, the unity and homogeneity of which is guaranteed by the ownership of property.
>
> (Hardt and Negri, 2009: 45)

Thus, where the rich create an exclusive identity around the notion of property, the poor are open, being defined as:

> a formation of all those inserted in the mechanism of social production without respect to rank or property, in all their diversity, animated by an open and plural production of subjectivity. By its very existence the multitude of the poor presents an objective menace to the republic of property.
>
> (Hardt and Negri 2009: 45)

The last sentence can be substituted for our purposes to include saying that democracy, education, research, knowledge and striving for social justice are inextricably linked in ways that present a menace to "the republic of property". In this context, the rules of research and educational engagement move towards the covert strategies of subversion. Democratically committed teachers and researchers have a key subversive role in this interface between the official institutions of the political and social order and the people. The teachers in the listening and talking school were open in what they were doing but, in the long run, its subversive implications for the wider society meant that it could not be sustained under the pressures of governmental policy

## Engaging subversively

Postman and Weingarten's (1969) *Teaching as a Subversive Activity* summed up a mood that pervaded progressive education in the 1960s and on into the 70s until it met the full reactionary force of neoconservative educational policy under Thatcher and Reagan in the 1980s. Underlying Stenhouse's Humanities Curriculum Project (HCP) was the subversive strategy of the teacher, the neutral chair. Similarly, Bruner's Man as a Course of Study (MACOS) with its emphasis on inquiry, evidence, argument, discussion, and process not content could be regarded as subversive of traditional or neoconservatively defined content and teacher-driven learning. In one sense their 'subversion' was open. However, not all teachers or all researchers operate in contexts that are tolerant of such 'subversions'. What then?

HCP, MACOS and the example of the listening and talking project all shared in practice the common principle of getting people on board, working openly together. HCP and MACOS had resources that could be shared through community networks of like-minded teachers. The listening and talking project involved the whole school with wide support from parents – as evidenced nearly 25 years later when one of the schools was the focus of a 'take over' by an academy-led consortium: the community fought it on the basis that it would threaten their unique culture and ways of teaching and learning. They were outflanked by the heavier guns of party politics and the private finance behind the government's policy of creating business-run consortia of school academies. Each consortium was comprised of multiple schools represented in their combined buildings and lands which thus for business investors offered the considerable prize of asset wealth. What has been learnt in the process from set up to failure is that some residue remains. It is in that sense an on-going struggle that has successes and failures only for the networks of the multitude to set up challenging projects elsewhere in other circumstances with other readings and articulations of the twin-born concepts of freedom and equality appropriate for the time.

It is within any individual's powers to form an association with any other in order to aggregate their powers. Such potential to form or dissolve associations between people is fundamentally subversive of organisational continuity as well as hierarchy. It is also potentially creative beyond the capacity of any one individual involved in the association. Hierarchies drive the productive benefits of the aggregated powers upwards rather than allocating them equally across the combined members. Thus, a key motivation to join with others is the mutual benefits that can be accrued that are greater than those that one individual can produce alone. The recognition of this, once it happens, can be highly subversive. As an example, Schostak drew on principles and ideas from HCP, MACOS, *Teaching as a Subversive Activity*, the *School of Barbiana*, and many other such examples of progressive, radical, anarchist approaches to take them to their limit as an exercise in open democracy in the context of student teacher education. In simple terms, the first task of the group as a whole (approximately 20 – although the ideas were later tried out with groups of around 100) was to decide collectively how to work together. It seemed reasonable to ask, as a group of relative strangers to each other, what the rules of engagement should be. In one group, after something of a silence, one young man spoke up and said, we don't really need any rules because we can just use common politeness. After asking if all others agreed, one young woman responded: "no we need some rules to shut him up. He always dominates and no one else has time to make a contribution". That response opened up the debate about what made for reasonable rules of debate. Thus following the nature of the comment these could be called rules for constraining dominance. If it remained at that, it would be insufficient. What the rules finally focused around was time to make contributions, with each having an equal chance to contribute if they wanted. As one person said, some people talk quickly. Sometimes the topic of debate moves so fast it is difficult to catch up, or difficult to formulate a contribution in time. The rules that were produced usually reflected this demand. Although they varied and were simple in format they typically included:

1. Right to make a contribution and be heard.
2. Each should have a turn.
3. There should be, what came to be called, the five-minute rule: anyone could raise their hand and say 'five minutes' and the room would stop debating and be silent for five minutes. It was argued this was necessary to give people time to reflect and formulate ideas and responses.
4. At the end of each session there should be time – say 10 minutes – to go round the room for each person to say what they wanted to say but had not been able to for some reason.

Rule '3' was never precisely timed. It was more symbolic of the need for a reflective pause and simply lasted as long as was needed. Rule '4' was not one that suited timetables! It was always used and always exceeded official seminar time by 40 minutes or more. Each final contribution – and not all made a final contribution – always stimulated further debate. Next came the question, what do you want to talk about?

As student teachers this was not normally a problem. There was at least a shared interest in some variant of the question: what do we do when we get in a classroom? This kind of question was appropriate for a course module titled 'professional preparation for practice'. Other more focused courses on special educational needs, or with a particular subject focus as the teaching of maths could just as simply begin with, for example, 'what do we do as a maths teacher when …'. The answer that follows is essentially a research question. Here each individual generated their own specific questions and designed an approach appropriate to exploring the question. Since teacher training involved periods of practice in schools and since in the particular degree being followed, a long-term relationship between school and student involved a day a week observation throughout school term times, there were plenty of opportunities for students to collect data and to act upon understandings built up through the research during periods of actual teaching practice.

Drawing upon the legacy ideas of HCP, MACOS and other curriculum development projects, as well as standard practices of scholarship, it was clear that bodies of evidence, archives of content and library references could be drawn up and tailored individually for each student by the student in discussion with others – of course that included lecturers and their resources. Today, with Internet content providers, discussion sites and social media, the possibilities for such development multiply exponentially. The students keyed naturally into the whole paradigm of the reflective practitioner, the qualitative researcher, the action researcher undertaking data collection through: reflective diaries, interviewing and transcription, observational records, and the collection of documentary evidence. Although the initiative was subversive of hierarchies and traditional expectation of student–lecturer/pupil–teacher expected relationships it was also reconstructive in the sense of creating new relations, practices and rules for researching, education and social learning for the participants. Everyone learnt from each other through sharing during seminars that were held under variants of the rules of debate described above. In most of the courses, it was decided sessions should be recorded and made available as material for critical exploration. Thus it would be reasonable to conclude that a key subversive-reconstructive rule is to drive a subversive initiative by the constructive interests and curiosities of associations of individuals who have a broad focus in common.

## Building a subversive-reconstructive ethics

Alongside HCP there had to be an evaluation. A conservative, traditional purpose of evaluation is to assess how well a project is delivering on its agreed aims and objectives. Barry MacDonald reluctantly – so it was claimed by himself and others – took on the role. Since HCP was novel and democratic in its forms of operation it seemed to MacDonald that the evaluation should also be innovative in order to capture the experiences, practices, understandings, forms of knowledge and forms of organisation being produced in the course of the programme. His approach came to be known as democratic evaluation (MacDonald, 1987). Its purpose was to ensure the representation of a full range of voices: from the lone voice through to the majority voices and the elite voices. In such an approach each can be treated equally as providing alternative perspectives founded upon reasons, rationales and experiences of impact. In that sense it echoed the role of the neutral chair in providing an arena for rational debate. In other contexts to that of HCP, that were more likely to involve largely hostile political environments, the strategy essentially evolved to find ways of putting as much in the open public as possible. In short, if funders actually wanted to know what was going on, they might well have to face some unpalatable truths about people's views, experiences and the impacts of innovations upon lives. In order to do this, principles for procedure were drawn up and agreed with funding bodies, organisational leaders and all participants involved in the fieldwork. These were always re-written and tailored to circumstances with each new project. They provided an 'ethical' framework in the sense that they were there to assure people that there were procedures in place to protect them. Such protections, it was hoped, enabled them to feel confident in speaking openly. The following was written for an evaluation of junior doctor training undertaken by Jill and John Schostak (during the period 1998–1999). Although the principles for procedure had developed over time from its origins in the practice and evaluation of HCP, the essential concerns remained much the same:

**Principles and procedures for the evaluation**

These principles and procedures are open to negotiation before potential participants agree to take part in the research. Their purpose is to offer an ethical framework in which this research is conducted and reported. The principles outlined below attempt to address issues relating to the rights and responsibilities of the researched and the researchers; they offer a blueprint for the relationship between the researchers and those implied in this enquiry.

Three principles underpin this code of conduct: confidentiality, anonymisation and negotiation. Described in detail below, these three principles are used to regulate the flow of information within the research up to the point at which it becomes public. That regulation endeavours to take into account the rights of individuals engaged in the research, in particular their right not to suffer professionally as a consequence of their involvement or decision not to participate with the research.

1. No individual will have privileged access to the data, unless that individual is the sole source of it (e.g., interview data). Nor may any individual prescribe the use of another person's contributions.
2. Those researched will be offered anonymity where they consider it appropriate, as will institutions.
3. The researchers will seek the permission of respondents to create or use audio records.

4  The researchers will treat everything seen and heard as relevant to the research but its use will be subject to negotiation.
5  The researchers will seek only reasonable access to the work and experience of the participants. Explicit permission will be sought to attend meetings or events considered relevant to understanding the contexts in which junior doctors and their consultants may operate.
6  The account will attempt to include, fully and fairly, the perspectives of participants, and to make explicit the range of opinion concerning any major issue.
7  The researchers will assume that they can freely approach any individual, group or institution involved with the junior doctor training they are researching.
8  The researchers will seek access to all documents, materials, opinions and practices relevant to the speciality training being researched. No private documents or materials will be examined or copied without authorisation. Copies of confidential material will be held in locked files until released, returned or destroyed.

We will be happy to discuss and amend these "Principles and Procedures" in pursuit of an agreed framework for the account of the study.

The principles offered a degree of protection both to the participant and the researcher. Each point or 'rule' can be decoded for its more political implications. Put broadly, they are essentially rules to regulate the use of powers of individuals in relation to each other and to the potentially hostile environments inside and outside their places of work. This can be extended to non-covert research undertaken in any form of organisation in societies. Its purpose is to be as open as possible while offering the cover that is felt to be necessary by participants.

Point '1' directly addresses power relations. Those in power – whether teachers, managers, consultants, directors – have sometimes thought they had the right to demand direct access to interview recordings, observational records and names. This point is a constraint to their authority, their insolence in assuming rights over the privacy of others, and their capacity to bully the researcher. Point 2 extends the 'cloaking power' by providing a degree of plausible denial, particularly when there are many involved in the research: 'no, it wasn't me who said that or our institution where that happened'. If such 'cloaking power' is not given, then the research stops there. Permission, as in point 3, particularly when 'signed off' in terms of written records, provides protection to the researcher as well as protection for the legitimate use of data. Stenhouse, in one of his later projects after HCP, extended the protections further by offering the opportunity for interviewees to see and edit transcripts of their interviews on the agreement that the edited script would be placed into a publicly available archive for future researchers. In the days of typewriters, whitening fluid to correct 'errors' and box files, this was found to be excessively clumsy. However, in the age of the Internet it could be rethought and revived. Point 4 is particularly interesting. It directly addresses the 'eyes' and 'ears' of the researcher as a member of a public. What is seen and what is heard is more than likely to influence the writing of the research. Thus: "if you don't want me to know, don't say it or do it" because in some way it will influence. Can that influence be negotiated away? Probably not. This then gets to the edginess of the rules of engagement. At some point in the research something problematic is highly likely to be seen and heard. What does the researcher do with that experience? In instances of abuse and criminality the answers are clear. However, there are greyer areas that are neither but reveal vulnerabilities or operational secrets or a myriad other possibilities that for some reason the speaker or actor does not want to be recorded but still wants the researcher to know about. What then? It could be resolved through discussion. However, the details that then emerge in the discussion may compound the situation. Such 'unmentionables' may indeed be revelatory of the real functioning, values or purposes of a group or organisation that once known will inevitably have an influence on thinking and writing. Hence, there is always the preemptive strike: "don't tell me, don't do it". But if told and seen, then the work of dealing with the influence begins and probably ends in constructing strategies of plausible denial where statements are couched in generalities, or quasi-fictional accounts are created and openly presented as being built upon multiple observations of different but comparable cases to illustrate typical interactions, forms of operation and so forth that because they are 'fictional' are plausibly deniable by actual people and organisations at the same time as providing more general insights across a range of typical cases. Points 5 and 6 extend the range of access as well as increasing the possibilities discussed in point 4. There is in a sense an underlying game of inclusion and exclusion going on. The question is, how as a researcher can I include as much as possible while offering to exclude? Certain exclusions will reduce the full range of viewpoints accepted as an aim in point 6, which puts a moral pressure of sorts onto the participants and the organisation to open doors. What is ostensibly an ethics framework is beginning, in practice, to look increasingly like the rules of a strategic game of hide and seek. At the back of this there is a public of 'eyes' and 'ears' who want to know, of which researchers, evaluators, workers, learners are all also participants. There is 'the public right to know' about the operation and the impacts of all forms of organisation on the everyday lives of 'the public'. The strategy of creating a 'private space' where seeing and hearing has to stop forms a political boundary or frontier. This frontier becomes particularly problematic when decisions made in private, behind closed doors in meetings, impact on the lives of others. Points 7 and 8 continue the theme of freedom of access in tension with private no-go areas even to the extent of destroying data. In short, all the principles and procedures are constructed in such a way to manage the politically tense frontier between the private and the public, between what is to be kept hidden and what can be seen, heard, said and how it can be spoken about in public in a culture of suspicion, dangers and hostilities.

The experience of creating such ethical/political protocols for research, curriculum development, teaching and evaluation developed from HCP and its evaluation. In 1988 John Elliott, an original member of HCP and then the Centre for Applied Research and Education (CARE) which was founded at the University of East Anglia by Stenhouse and MacDonald, drew on this experience to call for a code of practice at an invitational seminar of the British Education Research Association (BERA). In 1991 Helen Simons, who had been a member of the HCP evaluation team, along with Caroline Gipps, was invited to develop guidelines which were accepted in 1992 (BERA, 2018: 38). It is now a booklet of about 30 pages of detailed guidelines. How are these to be read?

Similar guidelines are produced by other associations and institutions around the world. In each case, they can be read either as rules for conduct having a quasi-legalistic quality, or as a map by which to navigate the political frontiers between the demand for a public to know and the countervailing too often elite-backed power to hide in the privacy of the shadowy. What is valued as intimate is a freedom that all may equally demand. It is as such, therefore, in the eyes of the public a universally valued good. However, the frontier between them is potentially a point of contention when the public becomes voyeur and eavesdropper. The legitimacy of intimacy as a public good is not equivalent to the private as a domain where decisions are made that impact on the public good. In that sense the private arises as a legitimate target for research, investigation and public censure. This does not, as a consequence, stop debates about 'fairness' and 'justice' relating to people being rendered vulnerable in the process of exposure. How to handle these frontiers is a fundamental political and ethical issue for researchers, investigators and educators to be continually debated and negotiated with each and every project.

## It's the truth

What then are the rules for determining the nature of the data collected under frameworks negotiated across the political frontiers of intimacy, privacy and the public? Rules of relation rather than rules for isolate pristine, clear and distinct atom-like 'facts' that hide nothing about their construction. The Brexit and Trump campaigns clearly raised doubts over the questionable relation between facts, beliefs, interpretations and the relevance of experts for bringing resolutions. As Dewey (1927: 3) pointed out, "Many persons seem to suppose that facts carry their meaning along with themselves on their face". And not just their 'meaning' but their truth also. If this supposition is appropriate in the hard sciences where facts and the truth-value of theories are determined by agreed procedures common among scientists – the ruling 'paradigm' as Kuhn (1970) called it – in the social sciences there is a different logic, not one attuned solely to the neutral 'fact given' observation of phenomena, but one which engages with inventing principles, conditions, practices, relational logics, discourses and rhetorics for the design of future social forms and identities. In this, it matters whose interests dominate. Dewey argues:

> The alternatives before us are not factually limited science on the one hand and uncontrolled speculation on the other. The choice is between blind unreasoned attack and defence on the one hand, and discriminating criticism employing intelligent method and a conscious criterion on the other.
>
> (Dewey, 1927: 7)

This is essential to any notion of education and research that is not about turning people into obedient servants. What intelligent method and what criteria? In rejecting any form of social instinct to explain the reasons why people associate with each other, Dewey takes

> his point of departure from the objective fact that human acts have consequences upon others, that some of these consequences are perceived, and that their perception leads to subsequent effort to control action so as to secure some consequences and to avoid others.
>
> (Dewey, 1927: 12)

He sees the idea of the public emerging embryonically in the recognition and the attempt to regulate indirect consequences:

> Those indirectly and seriously affected for good or for evil form a group distinctive enough to require recognition and a name. The name selected is The Public. This public is organised and made effective by means of representatives who as guardians of custom, as legislators, as executives, judges, etc., care for its empirical interests by methods intended to regulate the conjoint actions of individuals and groups. Then and in so far, association adds to itself political organisation, and something which may be government comes into being: the public is a political state.
>
> (Dewey, 1927: 35)

For most people, becoming a member of such a public is limited since the expert positions of Dewey's public are few and in an inegalitarian society largely filled by the upper classes. The only time they enter the state as a public, then, is at election time, a time when they are dependent upon the access to 'knowledge', 'evidence', opinion – that is, the means for social learning – are carefully manipulated and fashioned by the competing elites through their preferred communications media. Moreover, this proposition concerning the constitution of the public furthermore, leaves the way clear to regard massive corporations as equivalent, legally, to private persons, able to associate, influence and act. The inclusion of corporations in the sphere of the private adds a degree of ambiguity since inevitably the acts of the corporate person are heavy with consequences particularly as billionaires as individuals are also able to act and hide their actions through the corporate apparatus. The move is not far to see the intertwining if not the coalescence of corporate with The Public and the state – that is a form of corporatism - – that Mussolini defined as the kind of fascism he wanted to see exist, or indeed Schmitter (1974: 86) who saw a rescued concept of corporatism "as a system of interest and/or attitude representation, a particular modal or ideal-typical institutional arrangement for linking the associationally organized interests of civil society with the decisional structures of the state." In short, given Dewey's (1927: 17) notion of the public as embryonically the state, it can easily be defined in corporatist terms. How to prevent this?

To establish the truth of a situation, its circumstances and the contexts that enable its production take an ever-vigilant public asking questions, debating, sharing insights, establishing what is 'known' and what can be problematised in a perennial quest for the good society. This public is founded from the totality of the living who can be conceived as a multiplicity in continuous interaction. The productions of this multiplicity can be reflected upon as a public, as a strange unity of the multiple. This multiple-unity presents itself as *the* 'will of the people' demanding rights and access to knowledge as a basis for legislating for the social good. The multiplicity, of which we are all members, cannot ultimately be controlled by ethical codes, guidelines, protocols, legislations. Rather it is the source of the critique through which such frameworks are constantly challenged and revised in the light of changing circumstances and contexts. Hence the public is always less than the multitude. Thus there is always a demand to be met from the myriad voices of the multitude to include the voices left out of the 'will of the people'. Each voice overlooked, repressed or denied reduces the potential for truth, validity, reliability, objectivity and generalisability. The 'truth' of social and personal realities then is increased in reliability, validity, objectivity and generalisability to the extent that the range of different perspectives to be included in the debate bearing upon a particular 'reality', draws ever closer to the whole range that represents all views. Mapping that range is critical. Listening for the significance of each voice involves implementing as a fundamental rule the principle of *égaliberté* in order to constrain the insolence of elite views that claim to have privileged access to the truth, the right interpretation, expert knowledge, the only valid perspective and so on. Only in this way can a world perceived to be socially just for all be created.

## Towards making it happen

The powers of individuals – perceiving, thinking, imagining, talking, for example – include powers of association. It is a power expressed through communication, the ability to compare notes, explore differences and come to agreements about combining the powers of each in common projects. Each individual therefore has the potential to enter into association with any other individual; and, by implication, to walk away at will. It is this possibility of composing and decomposing associations that frightens established power most. Each new association has the potential to rot established order from the 'inside'. This, then, opens the chance for a new order built upon the co-dependent values of freedom and equality.

In the pursuit of social justice, each new association between individuals demands the negotiation of new rules of engagement to stage what needs to be prefigured for the accomplishment of a society that articulates *égaliberté* in all forms of social organisation. Research and education as processes integral to forming knowledge, understanding and critical insight upon which socially just decisions and courses of action depend is undertaken not just by specialised individuals but by the combination of the powers of seeing, listening, debating that all people can bring to bear in their demands for social justice and their visions of a better society.

In this context, for those individuals who see their major contributions to debates for a better society in their roles as researchers and educators, the key rules include to keep on asking questions, keep negotiating access to obtain a full range of views, keep problematising the frontiers between public and private, keep creating the conditions for debate about what is knowable and actionable, keep contributing to the debate with observations, ideas, insights. None of this is set in stone, it is an unending process driven, as Arendt (1998) puts it, by each new-born child. It is this constant drive for the public inclusivity for all that propels the never-ending negotiation of new rules for research and education through which new associations for mutual benefits can be the basis for making it happen.

# End of Part Two: Discussion on the implications for research education

The critical role of publics in realising futures for a better present

The chapters of the first part of the book addressed the issue of what went wrong with democracy and how that influenced education and research either to resist or to do the bidding of the corporate and political elites in the 'manufacture of consent' and the production of a 'phantom public' (Lippmann, 1927) manipulated by an 'invisible government' of experts (Lippmann, 1922; Bernays, 1928). The second part as a response sought the development of an effective public for a democracy of free *and* equal people under the principle of *égaliberté*, that is, the co-extensiveness of freedom and equality (Balibar, 1994), where disagreement leads to creative inclusion of differences (Rancière, 1999) rather than friend–enemy political relations (Schmitt, 1996; Strauss, 1988). There is then a different style of 'education' and 'research' that results from the responses to the issues raised in the first and second parts. If, as Hayek argued, the market is like a mind providing a collective rationality able 'spontaneously' to give the best solutions between competing demands, then research and education that is driven by that logic is judged solely by market considerations and practices. However, the market as mind is a reduction of the greater idea of the public as collective intelligence expressed through debate raised in the second part. We therefore have distinct possibilities for the development of education and research that serve the different conceptions of the public as either a 'phantom' whose consent and behaviour is in need of being manufactured or shaped according to market demands; or as an effective public driven by their combined intelligence through mutual education, research-based evidence and argumentation.

Part one essentially described two groups of researchers and educators. The first are simply technicians to the policy elites of the market place and politics. A second group can be designated as neoliberal and neoconservative fellow travellers. On the neoconservative wing of this group there are those like Bloom (1987) in the USA or the writers of the *Black Paper* (Cox and Dyson, 1975) in the UK, who underwrite forms of educational research that reinforce 'traditional', 'nationalistic' curricula along with respect for and obedience to authority, that is, to elites. On the neoliberal wing, dominated by market notions of 'efficiency' and effectiveness on the one hand and on the other the forms of knowledge, skills and ingenuity required to be market competitive. In particular there are those who in promoting, in contemporary terms, 'the knowledge society', essentially contribute to corporate agendas and elite purposes. This is even though – or perhaps because – these are undermined by popular media, post-truth discourses, and the manipulation of social media. Through the collection of Big Data, opinions and what counts as 'truth' can be shaped for targeted audiences in order to present both narratives of 'progress', with individual expertise, and talent as the driving forces of society and the economy; and as a supplement, friend–enemy narratives of identity and blame that are used to 'explain' why people have 'missed out' on the benefits of progress by blaming 'outsiders' such as 'liberal elites' who have brought in the outsiders. In this narrative, their very existence dilutes culture and racial purity and thus the sense of being at 'home'. They take what should rightfully belong to the 'native' population. The demand then is to 'take back control', by deporting outsiders and preventing or controlling their entrance by having strong frontiers. It is a simple story that can have many variations but always ends up with an 'us' versus 'them' who try to take away 'our' sovereignty, 'our' culture, 'our' jobs and wealth. Any evidence showing that this narrative is 'wrong' itself compounds the problem and reinforces the perception of expert liberal elites calling the experience-based knowledge of people 'wrong' and thus treating them either as fools, or stupid or ignorant.

Part two argued that countering corporate agendas and narratives that serve the interests of the elites involves a very different conception – and narrative – of the public, thus raising the possibility of alternative kinds of research and education. There are two forms: the first as a necessary step is a critique sustaining political actions such as resistance, protest and indeed revolution. The second involves creative acts of renewal based upon inclusivity of perspectives and their demands. This necessarily involves a different political aesthetic than that of the corporate forms of research and education by which knowledge, truth and evidence are debated and deployed to support arguments in the interests of all rather than just a privileged few. The critical or negative strategy involves 'speaking truth to power' by interrogating or deconstructing the ways in which 'facts' are produced, revealing contradictions, 'giving' voice to the marginalised and 'empowering' the vulnerable. In short, it engages with and reinforces an 'us–them' logic of struggle, protest and resistance resulting in either a populist right or a populist left politics (Mouffe, 2018). This in essence means that the idea of the public is inadequately conceptualised since it always excludes the 'them' from contributing to decisions about what counts as a social 'truth' or at its most general 'the good society'. To succeed it requires a revolution that replaces the 'them' with the 'us'. It can be conceived as a revolution in scientific terms (e.g., Kuhn, 1970) as well as in terms of radical political and social transformations (e.g., Polanyi, 2001). The most fundamental revolution would be to generate the conditions as argued in the chapters of part two for the emergence of a society of equals (Rosanvallon, 2013; Schostak, 2018) as the condition for the development of an inclusive and effective public. That means there are no enemies as such, only people who contribute their different views and demands that have to be taken into account. Research and education under these conditions thus demands the inclusion of more than a critical public as the criterion of truth discovery, knowledge, the formation of evidence and the creation of ever-inclusive narratives of the good society. It involves creative intelligence.

We then have at least four key contemporary forms: 1) corporate research and education with 2) their neoconservative and neoliberal fellow travellers; and against these 3) critical research and education that facilitates 4) research and education as the expression of a society of equals underpinned by the effective public through which knowledge is validated. This fourth kind of research and education in adopting the principle of the co-extensiveness of freedom with equality, starts with the individual in equal relation to others in the mutual quest for the freedom of each to draw out and develop their powers as social beings. Between the first two and the second two, there is a big gulf. However, both 'families' can subscribe to being 'evidence based' in seeking to provide evidence and facts about the actual effects of education and its bigger picture in terms of redistribution and reproduction. The neoliberal- and neoconservative-oriented education researchers focus their projects on the effectiveness of the delivery of policy while the counter researchers focus on its impacts on reinforcing social inequality, discrimination, marginalisation, exclusion, vulnerability, precarity, voicelessness – in short, the anti-democratic reproduction of privilege and wealth for the few while exploiting and discarding the rest.

In the first three forms of research and education, the assumption of evidence-based research is that by telling governments, corporations and the public what is actually happening, this in itself will change minds and affect policy. As the rise of the post-truth populist politics demonstrated through the successful campaigns of Trump and Brexit shows, evidence-based work has very little effect on creating narrative mantras, or slogans, or ways of facilitation. Clearly, evidence, facticity and indeed ways of capturing subjective response are essential to any alternative. However, that alternative – the fourth form that involves the constitution of the effective public – has to engage actively in mutual debate to create new narratives through which more inclusive, socially equal forms of organisation can be constructed. It is not enough to tell; indeed, telling is all too often counter-productive. Rather, talking and listening *with* others, being with them in their daily lives and observing what takes place seems to be a good place to start. What then becomes obvious is that people continually engage in relations with each other and the world about. They join in mutual projects, have arguments, make friends, have rivals. Instead of dissolving these relations to place individuals into categories deemed fit for the application of statistical techniques by which to explore significant correlations and probably causal relations, why not simply start with and preserve throughout analysis the forms of association individuals adopt with each other? There are two key powers to counter post-truth narratives then: the power to 'go and see' and the power to associate with others in engaging in mutually beneficial activities.

What came to be known as symbolic interactionism adopted this latter approach exemplified by Foote-Whyte in his *Street Corner Society*:

> Cornerville people appear as social work clients, as defendants in criminal cases, or as undifferentiated members of "the masses." There is one thing wrong with such a picture: no human beings are in it. Those who are concerned with Cornerville seek through a general survey to answer questions that require the most intimate knowledge of local life. The only way to gain such knowledge is to live in Cornerville and participate in the activities of its people. One who does that finds that the district reveals itself to him in an entirely different light. The buildings, streets, and alleys that formerly represented dilapidation and physical congestion recede to form a familiar background for the actors upon the Cornerville scene.
>
> (Foote-Whyte, 1943)

There is a useful comparison here with those journalists who seek to provide a picture of 'what is really going on'. For example, Rosen, a war journalist, distinguishes between those who stay in their comfort zone, the 'green zone' as he calls it, interviewing only official representatives for their 'news' and those who venture into the 'red zone', the zone where the action is:

> One reason for the failure of journalists to leave their green zones may be a combination of laziness and aversion to discomfort. But in Iraq, Afghanistan, other developing countries and areas of conflict in some countries, you have to leave your comfort zone. You might prefer an English speaking whiskey-drinking politician over six hours of bouncing along dirt roads in the heat and dust in order to sit on the floor and eat dirty food and drink dirty water and know you're going to get sick tomorrow, but **the road to truth involves a certain amount of diarrhoea**. [our emphasis]
>
> (Rosen, 2011)

The red and green zones echo the 'silo effect' – reinforced by a so-called social bubble heightened by social media technologies – where social actors keep themselves apart enclosed in their own mutually referencing communities, rendering evidence for the 'truth' concerning the structure and processes involved in situations difficult if not impossible. As Foote-Whyte (1943) put it: "It is only when the structure of the society and its patterns of action have been worked out that particular questions can be answered." Although Foote-Whyte focussed on his street corner society, the argument can be applied more broadly to the complexes of silos, bubbles and the varieties of sub-systems with their formal and informal organisations and associations that sustain them throughout society. Thus, it is a close analysis of these complexities that provides what may be called the 'problem profile' to be addressed by education and research in the development of a critical public as a condition for an effective democracy. However, going and seeing is not enough.

Working with others to make changes provides another dimension. Action research (c.f. Elliott, 1991) and the action learning of Revans (Boshyk and Dilworth, 2010) are popular examples. However, each can work perfectly well as just another way of micro-managing consent and behaviours in the policy interests of elites. The broader notion of 'work' developed by Dejours (1998; 2003) as a cooperative, democratic project by which each contributes their powers to obtain a greater mutual benefit provides a powerful framework. As explored in chapter 9, it keys into the legacies of the world-wide co-operative movement. More generally, through mutual decisions to associate with each other freely and equally, every self-forming group around a project – whether based around ideas of work, education, family, or any purpose whatever – can be described as a dynamically organising democratic unit where each is a member of a creative public contributing their powers of imagination, thinking, their views, ideas, beliefs, knowledge, skills, that through critical debate generates public intelligence for that unit. Through cooperation a plurality of democratic units can share insights. Competition necessarily inhibits this as each seeks to keep an advantage over the others in order to win dominance and thus reduce the freedom of others both to compete and to contribute insights as steps to a greater benefit than each alone can provide. As each individual and each grouping of individuals can provide a particular 'take' or 'perspective' on a given 'phenomenon', 'issue' or 'object', so by aggregating those 'takes' a fuller picture can be generated. Each 'take' provides evidence that promotes through discussion the education of views. The truth or validity of evidence is grounded – as in phenomenology or grounded theory – through the multiplicity of views that can be drawn together to test and contest the generalisability of accounts. What at first take is a high street in a city turns out on closer inspection, by seeing behind the front walls and talking with the people around, to be a film set. What at first sight is the story of a love affair or a fight, the biography of a hero or a villain, turns out to be scripted and acted. Behind the front is the narrative of an artistic project where people came together to write, direct and build the scenes. Similarly, behind the political narratives promoted by the Trump and Brexit campaigns there was a multiplicity of stories each having a partial imaginative grasp of the plurality. By keeping the views apart and framing them along a 'friend–enemy' axis, elites can take advantage of hierarchies to reinforce the partial views and manipulate the consent of targeted populations.

The close analysis of individuals in interaction, identifies the roles they play and how they are positioned as members of a *dramatis personae* in the narratives they tell of events whether felt by them to be familiar or strange, that are informed by histories shared by members of communities. Such narrativisation enables them to make sense of their experiences in order to project and predict possible outcomes and common futures. However, it is only by placing these narratives into debate that their contribution to an 'objective' can be evaluated as each individual provides what they count as evidence and this evidence is tested by other accounts.

Since no one can see and experience everything from the point of view of their own lived experiences, each difference of viewpoint adds to or challenges what different individuals and groups say about the rationality, apparent completion or justice of the explanations, interpretations, suppositions, descriptions and theories of what is 'real', 'true', 'good' about society, communities, organisations, peoples, nation states and the multiplicities of cultures, practices and forms of identity. It is this process of inclusion and challenge that counters the formation of any single structure of organised power from being able to repress alternative views in defining what is to count as reality. Thus the alternative narrative to elite narratives is that people can ground the creation of narratives in their own experience and through their own voices in conversation and debate with others. However, this can only be done if there are forms of organisation – units of democracy – that enable the powers of understanding, critique and creativity of each individual to engage freely and equally with those of others in the making of decisions and the undertaking of courses of action. It is this Spinozan-like focus that is fundamental to the mutual constitution of a public capable of associating with each other and in all their organisations engaging democratically to make decisions about the kind of society that is beneficial to all and not just those with the most political purchasing power and the biggest guns.

The struggle to create an effective public presumes a radical re-organisation of the hierarchical logics of corporate governance to be found everywhere impacting upon everyday life. It is this daunting prospect that makes it seem so unrealistic. But as discussed throughout the book, these ideas have long been 'lying around', mostly neglected not because they can't work, but because they can and thus if put into effect will threaten the privileges hierarchies provide for the few and their fellow travellers. Is it an impossible hope against contemporary power of elites?

How to begin?

Next, the final chapter writes against the odds in order to suggest how to undermine the work of elites and their fellow travellers – thus, making it happen.

# Chapter 12

# Making it happen

The feeling that everything is forever – capitalism, communism, the British weather – pervades everyday life, makes things predictable. You know what to expect when you get up in the morning – the same old same old. On this theme, Yurchak (2005: 1) starts his book with a quote from Andrei Makarevich, a song writer who when interviewed said: "It had never even occurred to me that in the Soviet Union anything could ever change. Let alone that it could disappear. No one expected it. Neither children, nor adults. There was a complete impression that everything was forever."

And so Yurchak titled his book: *Everything was Forever until it was No More*. So, perhaps everything can change – except maybe the British weather where the expectation is that it will change for the worse, so bring an umbrella, always.

The unexpected has a predictability that can be insured against. Except those times when they are so enormous, whatever system there was simply collapses. The speculators so desirous of a crisis, even they do not want such a complete collapse that their means of making money from it is taken away. Capitalism they believe has the eternal capacity to reinvent itself in every circumstance. While other systems fall, capitalism endures. That is their insurance. Still, they build bunkers and walls and store their wealth in tax havens, just in case.

Yet communism, and even western democracies in their days of revolution before they had become tamed, had the capacity to radically change society. The fear for elites is that they might do so again. They have their police. But what good are police when they too are hungry because the system has broken down? The dream of the robot under perfect control might yet save them from the hungry masses. This is the stuff of dystopian films and novels providing a background subversive narrative to everyone's – rich or poor – various humdrum realities of everyday routines, the disappointments, the daily troubles and the hopes that life could be better some day. Where the rich have their wealth to buy security and fund their dreams, what about the 'ordinary person' – the small people seen by the great leaders when they look down from plush executive offices – what of their hopes? Who speaks for them?

The rich have no problem making themselves heard, if they so wish. They speak for themselves and their money makes things happen in their interests. Take for example the Koch brothers. Their money is big enough to make things really happen on a grand scale. As billionaires they funded an organisation called *Americans for Prosperity* (AFP), which, according to Hertel-Fernandez et al. (2018), influenced a rightward move in the country's politics.

> AFP's laser-like focus on anti-union legislation is in part driven by the Kochs' libertarian embrace of free markets and limited government. But it also reflects strategic calculations. AFP has recognised that to make lasting change in US politics, the Koch network would need to permanently weaken the organisations that support liberal candidates and causes – and above all, the labor movement. Reflecting on why conservatives failed to build power in earlier decades, AFP's national president, Tim Phillips, explained that the Democrats "had the public employee unions ... which have only gotten stronger, have only gotten better-funded, have only gotten better organised". To succeed in electing conservative candidates and promoting right-leaning policy, then, AFP would need to hobble unions, especially those in the public-sector that were powerful state-level allies of Democrats.

When trade union member numbers fall, revenues fall and thus their overall capacity fund and staff campaigns falls. Against this nationally there are almost 3 million AFP citizen activists organised by 500 or more staff ready and able to engage in rallies and protests and make contacts with elected officials They were able to place staff at all governmental levels in the system, build upon existing partnerships, incubate talent, generate 'visibility' for electoral candidates who once elected will use their position to pass legislation, promote policies and encourage 'show downs' likely to weaken opposition, particularly by unions.

Impacts on local and national politics are systematically accomplished through collectives comprised of hundreds of millionaire and billionaire donors able to build organisations capable of changing the conditions under which politics takes place in a given electoral district. As a consequence:

> In presidential elections, Democrats lose around three percentage points after the passage of anti-union legislation, and turnout dips by around two points. So while there are many factors that might explain Donald Trump's surprise win in Wisconsin in 2016 by a mere 23,000 votes, a weaker labor movement less able to turn out Democratic voters might have been one important contributor to Trump's victory.

In the UK the most successful recent example of millionaire and billionaire funded organisations, including the set up of a new party to campaign to leave the EU, led to a win in a referendum to leave, a change in the leadership and policies of the main political parties, a 'snap election' which resulted in weakening the government; a dramatic fall in the value of the currency with subsequent impacts on the strength and prospects of the economy; potential threats to peace in Northern

Ireland due to issues of drawing a customs barrier between the north and the south; the increase in sentiment for Scotland to declare independence; and, of course, the opportunity for speculators to capitalise on the ups and downs of the markets.

The Rich, however, do not always get their way; the Koch's, for example, failed in their attempts to stop Trump becoming the Republican presidential nominee. However, what does that matter? Politics shifted their way. It is this disparity in power to shift politics in directions desired by wealth elites that has to be challenged and overcome if change for democracy and social justice is to happen.

## The path to change

Each unique path of individuals is always shaped by encounters and associations formed with others. Those paths can become very predictable whether comfortable, disturbing, friendly or hostile. In making it happen the voice is essential, the voice that knows it can be included feels empowered. The voice that knows it is not included rages. Michael Moore picks up on this rage writing about the appeal of Trump:

> From Green Bay to Pittsburgh, this, my friends, is the middle of England – broken, depressed, struggling, the smokestacks strewn across the countryside with the carcass of what we use to call the Middle Class. Angry, embittered working (and nonworking) people who were lied to by the trickle-down of Reagan and abandoned by Democrats who still try to talk a good line but are really just looking forward to rub one out with a lobbyist from Goldman Sachs who'll write them [a] nice big check before leaving the room. What happened in the UK with Brexit is going to happen here. Elmer Gantry shows up looking like Boris Johnson and just says whatever shit he can make up to convince the masses that this is their chance! To stick to ALL of them, all who wrecked their American Dream! And now The Outsider, Donald Trump, has arrived to clean house! You don't have to agree with him! You don't even have to like him! He is your personal Molotov cocktail to throw right into the centre of the bastards who did this to you! SEND A MESSAGE! TRUMP IS YOUR MESSENGER!
>
> (Moore, 2016)

Like it or not, as messenger Trump is then perceived as courageously speaking the 'truth' for those – whether working class or not – whose dreams feel wrecked (Nolte, 2015; Lee et al., 2016; Frank, 2016; Hague, 2016; Packer, 2016). From another point of view this speech becomes the dark and perverted echo as it were of the rhetorical figure of *parrhesia* – speaking truth courageously to power (c.f. Foucault, 2006). These two forms of 'truth speaking' to power contribute to the conditions for change when sufficient numbers find in the voices of truth speaking echoes of their own experiences, sentiments, values and perceptions of whether they and others fit or do not fit fairly into the world that gives to the rich and takes from the poor. If this is to be countered, and new paths constructed, just as the millionaires and billionaires have learnt the collective power of building networks and organisations to construct hegemonic power to reinforce inequality, so must those who want a democratic, socially just, more equal future. How?

If, as in the arguments put forward by Mouffe (2018), change is to happen from within liberal democracies by using whatever remains of their democratic-like institutions, then hegemony building strategies have to be developed. Some team has to be placed into strategic political positions in local and national governments. Examples of this can be seen in the 'movements' that focused around the symbolic leaderships of Bernie Sanders in the US and Jeremy Corbyn in the UK that sought to counter the success of the Trump and Brexit campaigns. A new interest, or perhaps more concerted interest, in left-wing politics had been stimulated from the 'ground up', notably among the young who joined 'Momentum' founded to support the leadership of Jeremy Corbyn in 2015, making it a major force in left-wing politics. Their handbook for activist training (Momentum, undated) provides some insights into their approach. The handbook contents were: personal stories; the response cycle; how to doorknock; policy talking points; and, how the Labour Party works. The advice under 'personal stories' included asking oneself 'why is this fight important'. Each member has "a sense of what is at stake, and why that means you must fight for a fundamental change in society." For each individual it suggests there are key experiences and background informing "the values, belief, and analysis we have today". Focusing on this provides a sense of one's own personal story that can be employed to explore what contributed to the personal move towards adopting a left political point of view. The personal political story then can be shared where relevant in order to persuade others as an element in the 'response cycle' for undertaking 'persuasive conversations', involving: acknowledging, asking, addressing and isolating. In the acknowledgement stage, no concerns are to be rejected "no matter how far-fetched or unethical". In a sense it is the hook to engage someone with a very different, even repugnant point of view, in a conversation until the person's specific objection, say to immigrants, can be isolated and "you can then introduce key policy points and statistics that clearly address the voter's concern". Even where the potential voter states a lack of interest in politics, the response is to notice something personal: "I notice you have children …. Did you know that …?" And finally, there is the moment to ask for some sign of commitment: "After addressing the person's concern, ask for support or gage what they are now thinking" for example, in terms of being able to count on their vote or that they will at least register to vote. All this learning about how to hold a persuasive conversation was then to be applied to knocking at doors. The first step was to make a good impression by looking positive, at ease and not afraid to make eye contact and emphasising being a member of the local community. Step two was to target the undecided voter or those whose support for other parties was weak. No time was to be wasted on the already decided. Step 3 focused on the key issues for the potential voter, a process of learning about the person to be persuaded, sharing one's own experiences relevant to their issue and tailoring messages about policy for them. In short, it was about building positive, personalised contacts as a ground for influencing their choice of political candidate. And finally there were the canvassing skills. Being confident and empathetic in tone, being aware of open or closed body language, relating personally by showing genuine curiosity, and maintaining eye contact. The process of course, had to be filled with general policy content that addressed the personal concerns of the potential voter. That meant the canvasser had to be well versed in policy talking points.

As well as training the canvasser, the activist handbook also provided information on how to get active in and contribute to the local Labour Party, how to become a branch officer and so on. By bringing Momentum members into the formal structures of the Labour Party, they could hope to influence its direction. Its success in doing this in a short period of time has been recognised as striking (Shabi, 2017). The techniques employed were, however, not particularly 'left wing' – they could be applied just as well by the Kochs' AFP. What differs are the political philosophies and the specific policies. Moreover, any of these could be re-imagined and applied in everyday life for purposes of engaging in conversation and persuasion, as indeed, the handbook suggested. Even more generally, the techniques can be taken out of the world of political campaigning and into the worlds of public relations or indeed, research and education and the more intimate worlds of building friendships to engage in projects of mutual interest. Nevertheless, there is a key difference with the approaches to curriculum development and critical educational debate in that the aim is not first about persuasion to a particular viewpoint but to openness to difference in order to develop understanding, knowledge and the use of evidence in critical debate in order to progress to creative solutions that are created without suppressing or ignoring disagreements. Here the process is not the canvassing of views to be sifted and shaped for particular political purposes but the creation of the public as the condition for democracy. There were at the time deep egalitarian commitments across key areas of the public sector in post-war British society. The war spirit of 'we're all in it together' motivated attempts to build the New Jerusalem under the Labour governments of 1945–51. Although watered down in later years, these social justice sentiments continued to the mid 1960s, at the time of the design of HCP that was funded by the Schools Council. In the language of the time, where 'man' should mean 'everyone', the broad spirit of inclusiveness and embeddedness in direct experience, evidence, imagination and the powers of reason is clear in one of the first Schools Council working papers on raising the school leaving age:

> The problem is to give every man some access to a complex cultural inheritance, some hold on his personal life and on his relationships with the various communities to which he belongs, some extension of his understanding of, and sensitivity towards, other human beings. The aim is to forward understanding, discrimination and judgement in the human field – it will involve

reliable factual knowledge, where this is appropriate, direct experience, imaginative experience, some appreciation of the dilemmas of the human condition, of the rough-hewn nature of many of our institutions and some rational thought about them.

(Schools Council, 1965. Source: Stenhouse, 1969)

The Schools Council came under political attack and no longer exists. Nor has there been anything that adequately takes its place. Indeed, curriculum development in Stenhouse's sense was progressively replaced by curriculum delivery shaped by testing.

If the structures and resources for the development of educational projects drawing on the egalitarian humanistic legacies of the HCP sort have been eroded, removed or diverted to promote market models, performance management and testing then how can they be revived and reinvented in contemporary circumstances? This question formed of a democratic demand returns attention to the purposeful political strategies of working to produce Mouffe (2018) style hegemonies and the significance of the Momentum strategy. As democratising projects, even if restricted to a particular political party, they potentially provide a platform, a theatre of action, as it were, for promoting, prefiguring and rebuilding democratic forms of organisation throughout society. The aim then is, if elected, it becomes government policy. In the theatre of action to construct this possibility, the *dramatis personae* is expanded from the actors required for party organisation and campaigns to include actors with a consciously wider agenda on other stages to produce a public, not a government.

Even if the development of political democratising strategies is a necessary step, they are not sufficient to transform all the forms of association that exist throughout society into the radical form articulated in the principle of *égaliberté*. These range from the momentary to the formalised corporations that cross national boundaries and those that in their range of connectivity are global and pervasive as with the Internet giants. What alternative possibilities are there?

## Prefigurative theatres

Fraser and Schostak (2005) as a project exercise imagined a 'smart city'. It was a sketch for project funding drawing on ideas and emerging technologies of the time. Its philosophical underpinnings were consistent with radically egalitarian forms of association:

> There are features of the Internet and its online communities which indicate the emergence of new cultural paradigms that are based on horizontal networks of association, peer-to-peer, point-to-point flows of information and communication that are neither time nor place dependent. The emergent feature of these networks is that they are self organising rather than hierarchically designed and controlled. It is at the stage when the infrastructure

impacts across communities and includes organisations other than schools (in the private, public and voluntary sectors) that the innovative aspects of the new technologies are most likely to be felt. A key research question is how they are to be integrated and managed and what will be the impact on schooling? This question will become all the more urgent as the kinds of infrastructure described below are embedded in national and international life with cultures forming on the basis of the kinds of connectivity that they sustain across time and place.

(Fraser and Schostak, 2005)

Peer-to-peer amplifies the individual's powers of association through the technologies of the Internet. That is to say, there is no mediating organisation where content is placed, organised, sifted, or in anyway moderated as in the case of Facebook where content is placed, stored and then accessible by others. Facebook is constructed as a central location where all material is stored. At this location there are software technologies to provide services of various kinds which enable the content to be managed, analysed and exploited for the purposes of the owners of social media applications, in particular to exploit it in some way to make money. It is essentially a centralised and hierarchical model of the web. Peer to peer is the web decentralised. There is no central holding and managing location. It was still early times for the technologies needed for peer-to-peer mobile relations. What was imagined was a digital city composed of peer-to-peer networks. At the extreme, in this virtual 'city' there is no necessary central organisation. Organisation modelled on markets, banks, health services and so forth could arise of course, just as now. However, it is in the fundamental unmediated peer-to-peer structure of free and equal association that a democratic ground could be constructed. In that sense, the collective intelligence, the ubiquitous eyes, ears and communications constituting the will of the public conceived in the discourses of the eighteenth-century revolutionaries can be manifested through the web. As with all technologies, there is the potential here either for freedom or for new forms of exploitation and control.

Contemporary developments in the de-centralised, distributed web of dynamic peer-to-peer relations include the digital currencies such as bitcoin that have no need of the financial system of banks to make payments or store wealth. Because payments can be made directly between peers using a digital currency not created by central banks, these exchanges are untraceable and thus cannot be managed by central authorities. They can be used for criminal as well as democratic purposes. A digital currency can be used to pay for work undertaken by people who would otherwise be unemployed. A co-operative venture for example could generate its own digital currency to facilitate the exchange of goods and services produced by its members. On that basis the only investment required is the capacity to work together in a peer-to-peer web environment. Given the global significance of the co-ooperative movement it would offer the possibility of a radically decentralised democratic alternative to hierarchically managed political and economic systems.

Each current co-operative and democratic venture through the principles of free and equal peer-to-peer relations prefigures the emergence of such a world. All such ventures are prefigurative theatres where people are brought together to stage in the present circumstances of the world's inequalities, the forms of association and organisation of the desired state of *égaliberté* in all matters; that is, prefiguring a world reformed for democracy in all spheres of life. The prefigurative imagination can be applied as a challenge to all the contemporary theatres of inequality that result in economic, social, cultural and political exploitation with all its forms of hierarchical management, surveillance, control, practices and instruments of violence. How to begin?

The steps required are those that go beyond protest and struggles between adversaries and begin building. It is more than the theatre of the oppressed (Boal, 1979). It takes the consciousness raising from the cultural theatre of plays, dance and song to the work-a-day occupations, the home, the street corners, the community. In these theatres of everyday living, as in the political campaign, the temptation is to begin with the already committed, open minded, and the undecided who can be tipped in the right way. The co-operative movement provides an already lived experience with all its successes and failures. Beyond this there is the 'hard to reach', the privatised domains that dominate every sphere of the lives of the mass of ordinary people. That is where the real work begins to counter the systematic hollowing out of democracy.

Even in the strictest of hierarchies the power of association presents a countervailing force. The demand by women, for example, for equal pay with men for doing equal jobs comes from creating an associational force based upon wider public opinion. However, as formulated this demand is founded on the principle of a meritocracy where some are more talented, more creative, more intelligent, more insightful, harder working and willing to take greater risks to succeed and thus deserve more money. It suspends the principle of co-dependency where all are necessary for the whole to work productively. As in any system of co-dependencies, remove one of its elements and it ceases to function. In that sense, each element is co-equally necessary. In human organisation all individuals have powers. Building co-dependencies means all equally benefit from the powers of others. The powers of the one who organises is not less nor more significant to the whole enterprise than the powers of the one who is organised. Without either, the organisation equally fails. Hierarchy pits the significance of the one at the top against the many below. However, without the many below, the top falls. The one at the top retains his or her power only if there is the means to take away or in some way reduce the countervailing power of the many below to organise as 'one' in the form of a union. The power to do so can only depend on rendering the mass powerless to organise by privileging obedience to elites over the sovereign use of one's powers in egalitarian peer-to-peer relations to reason, debate and freely formulate alternatives.

The prefiguring of obedience to hierarchical demands begins early. It is modelled in families, churches, schools, that is in all adult–child relations. The adult–

child model is a metaphor for hierarchies between classes, monarchs or tyrants and their subjects, bosses and employees, generals and their troops. Hence Kant's Enlightenment answer:

> But that the public should enlighten itself is more likely; indeed, if it is only allowed freedom, enlightenment is almost inevitable. For even among the entrenched guardians of the great masses a few will always think for themselves, a few who, after having themselves thrown off the yoke of immaturity, will spread the spirit of a rational appreciation for both their own worth and for each person's calling to think for himself. But it should be particularly noted that if a public that was first placed in this yoke by the guardians is suitably aroused by some of those who are altogether incapable of enlightenment, it may force the guardians themselves to remain under the yoke – so pernicious is it to instill prejudices, for they finally take revenge upon their originators, or on their descendants. Thus a public can only attain enlightenment slowly. Perhaps a revolution can overthrow autocratic despotism and profiteering or power grabbing oppression, but it can never truly reform a manner of thinking; instead, new prejudices, just like the old ones they replace, will serve as a leash for the great unthinking mass.
>
> Nothing is required for this enlightenment, however, except freedom; and the freedom in question is the least harmful of all, namely, the freedom to use reason publicly in all matters.
>
> (Kant, 1784)

This text still presents a demand that is far ahead of our times to deliver. Kant describes the task as a process of maturing – growing up – that can be reframed in the language of co-dependency. The powers of each, child and adult, co-produce the quality of family life. In a Spinozan logic, it is to the benefit of each to enhance the powers of the other to the fullest. Repression of powers removes the benefits they bring to the whole. In that sense the family prefigures a public whose democratic will demands no hindrance to the full development of the powers of each because this is the best way of securing the greatest benefit for all. The idea of the family as a prefigurative model for the public expands the prefigurative theatres for democratic publics into previously closed domains where structures of dominance prevail: the church, the school, the private sector of business organisation, the military, the government.

## Dramatis personae, narratives and curricula

Each prefigurative theatre has its *dramatis personae*, each character their biographies, each history of their relationship their narratives. The narratives trace an historical course that in the telling become available for reflection, opening up to challenge each telling and interpretation. What was left out? Was one perspective privileged over another? Did everyone get an equal say? Was a voice repressed? How was the story composed? What were the motives for it?

The constructed nature of histories, the organising power of narratives, their vital relation to social order are never quite realised until a crisis or a disaster robs you of them:

> If disaster comes, you will find that all the myths you once cherished are of no use to you. You will see what it is like to live in a society where morality has collapsed, causing all your assumptions and prejudices to crumble before your eyes.
>
> (Aronson, 2018)

At 93 this was one of the lessons that holocaust survivor Stanislaw Aronson wanted to pass on. And then in a reference to contemporary 'fake news', "do not underestimate the destructive power of lies." Having fled east to what is now western Ukraine, the family settled until rumours began to spread of mass deportations. An official denied the rumours as false. Anyone repeating them would be arrested. After two days the deportations began:

> My country and much of the continent was destroyed by lies. And now lies threaten not only the memory of those times, but also the achievements that have been made since. Today's generation doesn't have the luxury of being able to argue that it was never warned or did not understand the consequences of where lies will take you.

Lies, even the so called noble lies told for the 'public good' underpinning Plato's hierarchical social order of the Republic, are corrupting.

Education is the chance to debate the consequences of all stories told, to prefigure alternative stories, to combine one's powers freely, equally, in the development of creatively productive projects And in the process to learn from the experience in order to build on those experiences for co-operative projects throughout life. Such activities form the basis for a living, creative curriculum concerned to bring consequences to awareness. The curriculum then is composed through a complex of politics, education and work. Politics provides the narratives of the good political order, whether it is the Randian constitutive fiction of Atlas creating a world fit for billionaires or the promised land of freedom through equality of socialist utopias and narratives of struggles for freedom and equality (e.g., Hampton, 1984). Education opens debates on what is 'known', believed, valued, constructs arguments from evidence, critiques positions adopted and draws the resulting knowledge into living practice to create new more publicly relevant stories. Work is implicit in each, making explicit the conditions, costs and benefits of aggregating each participant's productive force as a contribution or a resistance to mutual projects.

Prefigurative theatres come into existence when the peer-to-peer power to associate adopts these three dimensions in all practices of exchange, aggregating powers and forming organisations. They become prefiguratively democratic when all relations are valued in terms of the principle of *égaliberté*. It is through this three-dimensional aspect of being in association that the *dramatis personae* emerges ranged as protagonists, co-operators, friends, enemies and so forth. How they account for their relationships with each other through their discourses, their exercise of powers, their practices of organisation produces the events, plots and sub-plots of a narrative that can be told from a multiplicity of viewpoints, that is, those of the *dramatis personae*. A course of systematic reflection upon all aspects provides materials for curriculum development from intuitions to well-founded generalisable knowledge. The fundamental question affecting general validity is: how to hear all voices? The curricular work involves discovering and including all voices, whether or not they have been marginalised, suppressed, denied their existence as equals. As a consequence new narratives of 'what happened, what is and what can be' are available to be written that are inclusive of the experience of all. In the process the double writing that hides its truth, whether produced against the grain of authoritarianism or to subvert the equal inclusivity of democratic freedom, is unravelled as new perspectives add additional dimensions to the events and objects under critical reflection. Finding differences, commonalities and unities across viewpoints, circumstances, contexts, hypocrisies can be unmasked and replaced by a new hegemony of public integrity. Brexit (Vitkovskaya, 2016) and Trump are illustrations of how a 'will of the people' can be exploited to overrule the full range of voices of the multitude, with demands that at best can only be heard as whispers.

To achieve public integrity, the good society for all, of necessity hierarchy is suspended so that research and the unfolding work of critically reflective education can identify and unpack the multiple accounts provided from the points of view of the full range of:

- the *dramatis personae*: their beliefs, values; what they count as knowledge, skills, know-how, what they take for granted as the way things work
- the ways in which they talk about and account for their experience and the reasons they give for their work practices
- how they define themselves, their roles, their sense of self
- the relationships (formal and informal) between the *dramatis personae*: emotional (love, hate etc.)
- power and its relation to gender, kinship, social class etc.
- the structures which maintain the *dramatis personae* in relationship (formal and informal): institutionally defined roles; socially defined roles; politically/legislatively defined roles
- the sequences of events that unfold in the production of something: events integral to the purpose; events which inhibit, distract from or obstruct the purpose; events which are accidental and irrelevant

- the nature of the stage upon which different events unfold: at work; at home; leisure places etc.
- the different contexts within which events take place: family, peer group, institutional, economic – market, social, political, religious, local-national-global
- the 'knowledge' produced and how, if at all, it is subjected to public scrutiny.

To sustain the work of narrative building for critical curricula requires the mutual production of life-supporting resources and the building of alliances establishing a frontier between the authoritarianism of hierarchy and the work of democracy in producing scripts of renewal that envision the good society.

## Towards renewal: The 5 Rs

In England there has been a long tradition that the 3 Rs is a sensible mantra for developing a basic curriculum for all – Reading (W)Riting and (A)Rithmetic (Goodson, 2015). Given that actually only one of the words begins with 'R' you can see that actually the specification might be seen more as an exhortation to illiteracy, but so much for tradition! As a counter to debased curricula there are the five Rs of educational research. They are presented here as a way of summarising the arguments that have been developed throughout this book. We do this summarisation tentatively because the issues are complex and a summary is always simplifying. Nevertheless, as a tentatively suggested mantra, it is offered as an antidote to some of the fashionable rhetorics that have accompanied the promotion of the neoliberal social, political and economic order. The problem we begin with may be stated as: 'How do we find our bearings in the blizzard of multiple voices as they experience sinking under the weight of ever-changing policy demands? How can we get a sense of where we have come from and where we might be going?' And then almost hidden, there is the motivation and underpinning rationale for thinking about renewal, the sixth R: the comprehensive and much needed overarching concept of resistance, an underwriting as it were, pushing back against the onslaughts of governmental and corporate power, to create much needed openings. In developing these 6 Rs there is the sense of feeling our way to answers in the exploration of democratic rights – the always uncompletable 7th R in which demands try to find resolution. Resistance, rights and resolution are always implicit in each act of the 5 Rs mantra.

### I REMEMBERING

One way to assess our position and direction is to analyse our historical context. Curriculum history as a field, for instance, can be set alongside the prefigurative narratives described above in order to assess the on-going continuities of curriculum (which are massive and preponderant) as well as the occasional episodes of change and transformation in relation to personal experience and potentials for change. Research projects can be developed that facilitate this process. The PROFKNOW proposal, for example, conducted for the European Union between 2003 and 2009 set out to try to understand the historical trajectory of the seven countries whose educational systems were being covered (PROFKNOW, 2003–2009). Similarly, in the Spencer Project in which historical patterns of school change were studied in the US and Canada, the studies were placed in their political context (Goodson, 2005).

## 2 REGRESS

One of the features of much of our politics in the second half of the twentieth century was belief in 'change' in an on-going 'progress narrative' establishing economic, political, educational, social and cultural rights. With the outset of the new economic order this has been reversed. The new age of austerity that was put in its place inaugurated the primacy of 'regress narrative' where younger generations face a future world that is more difficult and less affluent than is the case currently or was experienced by older generations.

The dawn of a 'regress narrative' transforms the political landscape and the positionality of 'change forces'. If things are getting worse change may not be progressive, as was once the case, but regressive. In fact in such a case the progressive position may be to 'conserve' the current situation rather than embrace changes towards a worse situation. In a regress narrative Goodson (2003) has argued at length that progressive social reforms face a classic 'crisis of positionality'. Prefigurative narrative construction for curricular development described above can move into the gaps created by crisis with narratives for democratic renewal.

## 3 RECONCEPTUALISATION

Living in a globalised world following the dominant ideology of neoliberalism requires a thorough re-conceptualisation not just of the meaning of politics but the nature of social inquiry – a task we have explored in the chapters of this book. As Graeber (2014; 2018) points out, much of the impetus of neoliberalism, beyond its pervasive dumbing down 'of the media' and knowledge nexus, is towards an attack on the social imagination in the production of 'bullshit jobs'. Any thought and inquiry which prefigures alternative worlds is discouraged and deconstructed. Our re-conceptualisation of social inquiry has to develop outside of and at the same time as attempts by neoliberal globalisation and neoconservative nationalism to disvalue imagination and critique, thus developing the potential for resistance and defending rights that are being subverted.

Whilst historical remembering is one strategy of redeveloping the social imagination there are many current possibilities. For whilst neoliberalism in an unholy alliance with neoconservatism seeks a uniform social and economic order, such universalising tendencies have been far from successful. Any social, educational and political inquiry that is seriously pursued will uncover considerable variety, tensions, contradictions and, indeed, hypocrisies in the social and political strategies of elites in response to global movements.

Any re-conceptualisation needs to move beyond the dominant narratives in education such as: 'school improvement', 'key competencies', 'change forces', 'restructuring initiatives', 'knowledge societies' and 'economic competitiveness' to explore the variegations and alternative conceptualisations which co-exist with these totalising impulses. Re-conceptualisation leads on to the analyses of re-contextualisation and from there to refraction.

## 4 REFRACTION

As an emerging concept 'refraction' draws on a range of existing traditions and approaches in the social sciences with several key areas for exploration and investigation. As noted in chapter 2 Kristol (1995: 359) employed the idea of 'refraction' in relation to popularism and the will of the people. Their anger and their demands can be refracted, bent, splintered but ultimately cannot be denied. Hence they are available to be used as a populist ploy and used by neoconservatives. Research, however, cannot ignore such refraction but identify the democratic nucleus, as Mouffe (2018) calls it, in the refractions in the voices heard across a multitude. In research, work and education refraction can be identified as a 'bending', an 'inflection' of views when there is a change in direction arising from individuals' and groups' own beliefs, practices and trajectories that are at odds with dominant waves of reform and policies imposed on their lives by elites.

Refraction, therefore, can be studied in two ways: firstly as a type of 'bending' or mediation that occurs in various ways and for numerous reasons; secondly as a splitting, fragmenting that occurs due to the changes of ideas, experiences and values. Each refracted split has as its nucleus a demand having the power to establish political frontiers that align people one side or another thus setting them against each other. Refraction then can be the name given to those crucial elements of analysis that in highlighting 'changes of direction' and 'splits' finds in them articulations of a 'demand' that is the basis for new alignments across political frontiers. This in turn enables critical analysis to educe alternative and prefigurative antecedents, forms and models of practice in the interaction between ideology and material structures on the one hand, and on the other, individual as well as collective practice and action as a ground for evolving prefigurative democratic strategies in the creation of a mutually educative public.

Such an approach, we suggest, has three strengths. Firstly, from this perspective, we suggest that research in the field that is contextualised and analysed in relation to historical periodisation and the broader movements, cycles and waves of reform brings to attention the political frontiers that have been historically contested and how they have been contested. This provides a legacy of discourses, knowledge, arguments and strategies available for contemporary re-imagining for present purposes. Secondly, in researching current practice within a broader social-historical context, we can better understand and illuminate the effects of ideology and power by seeing how these are exerted through policies and how they are resisted, refracted and contested in people's lives. Resistance, refraction and contestation provides insight into the political demands and rights that are the nucleus around which orientations change and fragment. Thirdly, in these discovered nuclei of demand, the potential for their refraction into, for example, authoritarian or democratic demands can be explored as a basis for prefigurative democratic strategies

Together these approaches to the exploration of people's political demands overcome any sense of determinism implicit in approaches that analyse power and ideology as totalising and actors as merely passive and subject to its effects. The suggested approach does this by attempting to account for and examine alternative discourses, movements, practice and forms of organisation by exploring the conditions under which they occur. Moreover, in attempting to address the apparent dichotomy of structure and agency, qualitative accounts of people across multiple perspectives in order to explore how, and to what extent, their own trajectories, life histories and work identities influence their practice, mediate policies and in negating the effects of ideology and power give insight into the emergence of a political nucleus and its potential for a popular demand and the construction of a 'public will'. In this process, approaches that elucidate prefigurative practice, politics, discourse and language through narrative inquiry, and the ways in which actors make meaning of their own lives and professional practice, not only offer us detailed pictures of subjective realities but also allow us to highlight alternative practices and oppositional discourses that are often overlooked, or brushed aside, in official discourse.

## 5 RENEWAL

The process outlined above is a staged trajectory for the renewal of our social future. Far from being an act of golden age nostalgia, acts of remembering highlight the many reversals of common rights that have accumulated since the neoliberal movement began around 1980. Historical memory then can be an important repository of alternative imagined futures as well as pasts. In a regress narrative the past may be thought to be better than the future – but crucially not without reconceptualisation.

Refraction shows how in fact the combined neoliberal and neoconservative insurgency is actually mediated and repositioned in a given society. Such an approach can be deployed across a variety of contemporary societies – in particular, for example, post-colonial societies that have learnt how to resist and preposition hegemonic initiatives. As Jane Jacobs argues in her prophetic last book, *Dark Age Ahead* (Jacobs, 2004), there is a paradox here. The societies least able to refract and renew are those at the centre of the new economic order such as England and the USA. She says: "ironically societies that were great cultural winners in the past are in special peril of failing to adapt successfully in the face of new realities" (Jacobs, 2004: 175).

Hence renewal, we have argued, can be sought in the 'periphery', not the hegemonic centre currently occupied by wealthy elites predominantly informed by neoliberal and neoconservative discourses. The so-called 'periphery' is the multitude and its potential as a public capable of articulating a general will of the public. This can, we have argued, be exploited for right-wing populist purposes as well as for left-wing purposes. We have further argued that it is in the creation of political frontiers – between right and left – that the potential for the multitude to become a critical and creative public is at stake. It is in siding with one side or the other that splits occur in the multitude and give rise to the potential, so clearly seen by Kristol (1995; 2011), for manipulating the 'public' as a split entity for one side as opposed to the other. This was evident in the use of the 'will of the people' by the Tory government under Theresa May to push for a 'hard Brexit', that is, for a complete split from Europe. It was equally used by the left under the leadership of Jeremy Corbyn to push for a socialist Brexit. What was ignored was the democratic demand to be heard, not for political party purposes but for social and economic justice. In the demand to be heard is not a single 'will of the people' but a multiplicity of voices with contradictory demands. These multiple demands, often in disagreement with each other, become the critical basis upon which renewal depends. How, as Rancière (1999) puts it, can forms of organisation be created that are faithful to the disagreements? This we argue is the work of the three-dimensional activity of research-education-work to prefigure democratic solutions. It is summed up by the 5 Rs approach where the researcher and educationist through their work explore the resistances, articulate the demand, and prefigure the forms of democratic organisation in every form of association, exchange and interaction. Renewal for a socially just democratic future depends on discovering the potential in each relationship in everyday activity for prefiguring co-productive forms of association and developing co-operative forms of organisation. If this is the start, where and when will it come to a democratic conclusion?

# Conclusion: No end

Really, what we're looking for is a game changer. What we've found are the conditions under which all games are possible: the powers through which individuals form associations and judge their powers to be more or less the same when it comes down to being stripped naked – after all, what is Trump without his wealth, his Towers and their golden elevators and his body guards? Just another ageing man with a combover. It is the contemporary arrangement of powers that placed him in his Presidency. There is nothing essentially natural about this. Trump alone is not smart enough nor strong enough to do it all himself. There have to be others, combining their powers in a project that enabled him to stand where he stands. In principle, then, powers can always be recombined to produce alternatives. If that is true, then literally, it is a game changer.

We all know that. The hard bit is that it's a very long game with many players, billions in fact. And some have a head start in being able to buy the allegiance of many millions of those billions. As millionaires know, the only way to become a millionaire is to get others to work for you in ways that take away the rights of workers to the products of their work. It all adds up. So, they protect their rights to own the work of others by having guards, judicial systems and politicians who will do their bidding in enforcing the rights of appropriation through contracts, copyrights and patents. Wages are simply the contracted exchange made for giving up ownership of the work accomplished. What in this relation does the worker possess beyond the powers of his or her body out for hire at a price principally decided by the employer? It's all legal. Each bid is made in a game that becomes increasingly biased in their favour.

If all this is known, then why doesn't the simple fact of knowing change things? Knowing is not enough, it seems. People have to care too and believe that change is possible. All you have to do is look around to see the symbols and machineries of power ranged against any protest to know that knowing is not enough. And they know that we know that they know – and that after the protest, they know, and we too, little will change. But that's not entirely true, is it? We know too that there have been revolutions. We know that rights have been hard fought and won. And that's the problem, the hard bit. Quiet enjoyment, going out with friends, having a family, watching them grow, helping them to have a good and decent life – this is what has to be given up, or put in jeopardy by entering the hard fight. We hope we don't have to do it. Others might do it for us. That's up to them.

That's not fair of course. Think of it another way. It is precisely the demand for quiet enjoyment that is at stake. And it is a real demand to have a decent enjoyable life. It begins there in that demand. It is there in that demand that I can explore and enjoy my powers that enable me to come to know the world and learn also with others how as 'we' our powers can be added up to attain things that could not have been brought about otherwise. Isn't that a way forward? A basis for renewal?

Look around again: instead of the massive powers of the rich in their bunkers, their palaces, their places of presidency, being impregnable, what we have seen in the Brexit and Trump events is a kind of flailing of the elites in the tides of the events that they hope benefit them but which surpass them. And we see the ordinary person abandoned or cut adrift in the currents let loose by decisions made elsewhere. This sense of abandonment, being cut adrift is a continuation of the picture painted by tyrants: "A tyrant always relies on a dissociated group of separate, isolated individuals, reduced to enslavement by their own passions and, in a way, crushed by a general will that is already the final and transcendental cause of their own decisions" (Lucchese, 2009: 161). But look again, there is potential to change the aesthetics beloved of the rich and powerful that sees them as the Atlas figure (Rand, 1957) whose shrug sends shudders around the world. A little refraction goes a long way! See instead a tidal wave of demands. Or look again, but more closely: the tidal wave itself is composed of multiplicities of bodies in interaction, where some form associations that are fleeting, others more lasting, yet others organised to accomplish some mutually desired goal. Rather than something liquid (Bauman, 2000) there is something solid here. The building blocks of any human endeavour are to be found in the power to associate one with another. What then, if the renewal so desired, is to be found in ourselves and in helping people build what they need to be built? Isn't that, in the end, what research and education are for?

Brought together, instead of separated into different domains, work, education and research combine the powers of thought, learning by sharing understandings, critical reflection through debate between a multiplicity of viewpoints, and mutually constructive action in the world to produce what we need. Everywhere, in that case, is a site of prefigurative struggle and action to bring a socially just world into being. In this the experience of educators and researchers in all fields of life play – potentially – a critical and strategic role. They touch on people's lives everywhere.

It is in entertaining such a thought that Atlas suddenly feels tiny and shivers. An expert is called. What, when the event happens, you know, the dystopian future when all collapses due to global warming or in some accident someone pushes the button to send those stocks of missiles on their way, or a terrible unstoppable plague breaks out … what can we do to stop the hordes from storming our bunkers and taking our stores of food? We won't even be able to trust our private police to defend us ... will there be robot technology to save us? Remember, that's what the moneyed asked Rushkoff (2018).

It's a puzzle really. How do we continue to build a world where we keep giving them the wealth we create that gives them the power over us? Perhaps all those people we work with as educators and researchers don't know how to stop doing this. We could tell them of course, we educators and researchers, we could tell everyone. We could do the research and build the curricula that put it all together as communities become the classrooms, as it were, of social experiment, Dewey-like, only better, more deeply conceived to make learning-working-and-researching a continuously prefigurative creative space for living together. Imagine it, just like those 28 Rochdale pioneers back in 1844 not realising their little shop would create the world-wide cooperative movement – it's just about a class size really – that continues the practices, the principles, the forms of organisation that support a couple of billion people today. Perhaps if we think about it, do some research and learn together, we could, a bit like those 28 pioneers, create the wealth in our communities that we share equally among ourselves. That ought to be enough to renew the world. There's no end to what we could do.

# References

Agamben, G. (1998) *Homo Sacer: Sovereign Power and Bare Life*. Stanford, CA: Stanford University Press

Agamben, G. (2005) *State of Exception*. Chicago: University of Chicago Press

Agamben, G. (2009). What is an Apparatus? In G. Agamben, *What is an Apparatus? And Other Essays*. Translated by D. Kishik and S. Pedatella. Stanford: Stanford University Press

Ahmed, N. M. (2012) Capitalism, Covert Action and State-Terrorism: Towards a Political Economy of the Dual State. In: E. Wilson (Ed.), *The Dual State: Parapolitics, Carl Schmitt and the National Security Complex*. London: Ashgate

Albright, M. (2018) *Fascism: A Warning*. New York: Harper Collins

Amadae, S. M. (2015) *Prisoners of Reason. Game Theory and Neoliberal Political Economy*. Cambridge, New York: Cambridge University Press

Amnesty International (2014) *The Human Cost of Fortress Europe: Human Rights Violations Against Migrants and Refugees at Europe's Borders*. London: Amnesty International;http://www.sos-europe-amnesty.eu/content/assets/docs/The_Human_Cost_of_Fortress_Europe_July_2014.pdf. Accessed 21/08/2015

Amnesty International (2017) *Dangerously Disproportionate: The Ever-Expanding National Security State in Europe*. London: Amnesty International; https://www.amnesty.org/download/Documents/EUR0153422017ENGLISH.PDF. Accessed 20/09/2018

Anderson, B. (1983) *Imagined Communities. Reflections on the Origin and Spread of Nationalism*. London and New York: Verso

Arendt, A. (1998) *The Human Condition*, with an introduction by M. Canovan. Chicago: University of Chicago Press. First published in 1958

Arlidge, J. (2009) I'm doing 'God's work'. Meet Mr Goldman Sachs, *The Times*November 8; https://www.thetimes.co.uk/article/im-doing-gods-work-meet-mr-goldman-sachs-zflqc78gqs8. Accessed 02/08/2018

Aronson, S. (2018) I survived the Warsaw ghetto. Here are the lessons I'd like to pass on, *The Guardian*September 5; https://www.theguardian.com/commentisfree/2018/sep/05/survived-warsaw-ghetto-wartime-lessons-extremism-europe. Accessed 28/09/2018

Audier, S. (2012) Penser le "neo-libéralisme". In *Le colloque Lippmann. Aux origins du "néo-libéralisme"*. Nouvelle edition augmentée, Serge Audier. Lormont: Éditions Le Bord de l'Eau

Austin, J. L. with Leander, A. (2019) Visibility: Practices of Seeing and Overlooking. In C. Bueger, A. Drieschova and D. Hopf (Eds), *Mapping International Practices*. Cambridge: Cambridge University Press

Ayers, B. and Ayers, R. (2011) Education Under Fire: Introduction, *Monthly Review* 63(3), 1–4

Balibar, É. (1994) "Rights of Man" and "Rights of the Citizen": The Modern Dialectic of Equality and Freedom. In Balibar, É. *Masses, Classes, Ideas: Studies on Politics and Philosophy Before and After Marx.* New York: Routledge. Originally published as "La proposition de l'égaliberté". In *Les Conférences du Perroquet,* n° 22. Paris, Novembre 1989

Balibar, É. (1998) *Spinoza and Politics.* Translated by P. Snowdon. London, New York: Verso

Balls, S. and Youdell, D. (2007) Hidden Privatisation in Public Education, Preliminary Report, Education International 5th World Congress, July, Brussels; http://pages.ei-ie.org/quadrennialreport/2007/upload/content_trsl_images/630/Hidden_privatisation-EN.pdf. Accessed 16/04/2019

Barber, M. (2007) *Instruction to Deliver.* London: Politico

Barbrook, R. and Cameron, A. (1995) The Californian ideology, archived at Imaginary Futures; http://www.imaginaryfutures.net/2007/04/17/the-californian-ideology-2/. Accessed 02/08/2018. First published in *Mute* magazine 1(3); http://www.metamute.org/editorial/articles/californian-ideology

Barlow, K. (2008) *The Labour Movement in Britain from Thatcher to Blair,* with a foreword by J. Mortimer. Frankfurt am Main, New York, Oxford: Peter Lang. First published in 1997

Bauman, Z. (2000) *Liquid Modernity.* Cambridge, Oxford: Polity Press in association with Blackwell Publishers Ltd

Beder, S. (2008) The Corporate Assault on Democracy, *The International Journal of Inclusive Democracy* 4(1); https://www.academia.edu/5960080/The_Corporate_Assault_on_Democracy. Accessed 14/04/2019

Bell, D. (1973) *The Coming of Post-Industrial Society.* New York: Basic Books

Benkler, Y., Faris, R., Roberts, H. and Zuckerman, E. (2017) Study: Breitbartled rightwing media ecosystem altered broader media agenda, *Columbia Journalism Review*August 16; https://www.cjr.org/analysis/breitbart-media-trump-harvard-study.php. Accessed 19/06/2018

Benn, M. (2012) *School Wars: The Battle for Britain's Education.* London, New York: Verso

Bennett, D. (2010) Commentary: The inequality delusion, *Bloomsberg Business Week*21 October; https://www.bloomberg.com/news/articles/2010-10-21/commentary-the-inequality-delusion. Accessed 14/04/2019

BERA (2018) *Ethical Guidelines for Educational Research,* 4th Edition. London: British Educational Research Association

Berman, A. (2012) The 0.000063% election: How US politics became the politics of the "super rich", *Al Jazeera, In Depth.* February 25;http://www.aljazeera.com/indepth/opinion/2012/02/20122217200429526.html. Accessed 29/07/2012

Berman, M. (1982) *All That Is Solid Melts Into The Air: The Experience Of Modernity.* New York: Penguin Books

Bernays, E. L. (1928) *Propaganda.* New York: Horace Liveright

Bernays, E. L. (1947) The Engineering of Consent, *The Annals of the American Academy of Political and Social Science,* Vol. 250, March

Bhatt, K. (2015) Dangerous history: What the story of black economic cooperation means for us today, *yes! Magazine*October 7; https://www.yesmagazine.org/commonomics/dangerous-history-what-the-story-of-black-economic-development-means-for-us-today-20151007. Accessed 21/09/2018

# References

Billig, M. (1995) *Banal Nationalism*. London, Thousand Oaks: Sage

Birdwhistel, R. L. (1973) *Kinesics and Context: Essays on Body-Motion Communication*. Harmondsworth: Penguin

Blacker, D. (2013) *The Falling Rate of Learning and the Neoliberal Endgame*. Winchester: Zero Books

Bleiker, R. (2000) *Popular Dissent, Human Agency and Global Politics*. Cambridge: Cambridge University Press

Bloodworth, J. (2016) *The Myth of Meritocracy: Why Working-Class Kids Get Working-Class Jobs*. London: Biteback Publishing Ltd

Bloom, A. (1987) *The Closing of the American Mind*, with a foreword by S. Bellow. New York: Simon & Schuster

Boal, A. (1979) *Theatre of the Oppressed*. London: Pluto. New Edition 2008

Boétie, de la, É. (1552) *The Politics of Obedience: The Discourse of Voluntary Servitude*. http://etiennedelaboetie.net/wp-content/uploads/sites/1010/2010/02/the-politics-of-obedience_the-discourse-of-voluntary-servitude.pdf. Accessed 16/04/2019

Boltanski, L. and Chiapello, E. (2002)The New Spirit of Capitalism, Paper presented to the Conference of Europeanists, March 14–16, Chicago

Boltanski, L. and Thévenot, L. (2006) *On Justification: Economies of Worth*. Translated by Catherine Porter. Princeton: Princeton University Press

Booth, W. C. (1974) *A Rhetoric of Irony*. Chicago and London: University of Chicago Press

Boshyk, Y. and Dilworth, R. L. (Eds) (2010) *Action Learning: History and Evolution*. Basingstoke, New York: Palgrave Macmillan

Bouton, T. (2007) *Taming Democracy: "The People," the Founders, and the Troubled Ending of the American Revolution*. Oxford, New York: Oxford University Press

Bowater, D. (2011) Youth unemployment reaches 1986 levels, *The Telegraph*November 16; https://www.telegraph.co.uk/finance/jobs/8891863/Youth-unemployment-reaches-1986-levels.html. Accessed 28/07/2018

Bowman, A., Ertürk, I., Froud, J., Sukhdev, J., Law, J., Leaver, A., Moran, M. and Williams, K. (2014) *The end of the experiment? From competition to the foundational economy*. Manchester: Manchester University Press

Brace, C. L. (1872) *The Dangerous Classes of New York: Twenty Years' Work Among Them*. New York: Wynkoop & Hallenbeck

Bruner, J. S. (1965) Man: A Course of Study. Occasional Paper No. 3. The Social Studies Curriculum Program. Educational Services Incorporated. Cambridge, Mass. http://www.macosonline.org/research/Bruner_MACOS%20-Occasional%20Paper%203.pdf. Accessed 31/07/2012

Buchanan, J. M. and Tullock, G. (1962) *The Calculus of Consent: Logical Foundations of Constitutional Democracy*. Ann Arbor: University of Michigan Press

Bullough, O. (2018) *Moneyland: Why Thieves & Crooks Now Rule the World & How to Take it Back*. London: Profile Books

Bump, P. (2017) Donald Trump's inaugural crowds don't quite measure up to Barack Obama's, *The Washington Post*January 20; https://www.washingtonpost.com/news/the-fix/wp/2017/01/20/donald-trumps-inaugural-crowds-dont-quite-measure-up-to-barack-obamas/?utm_term=.68407e46d2e8. Accessed 21/09/2018

Burke, P., (1993) *History and Social Theory*. New York: Cornell University Press

Bush, G. W. (2002) President delivers State of the Union Address, *The White House*; https://georgewbush-whitehouse.archives.gov/news/releases/2002/01/20020129-11.html. Accessed 28/06/2018

Cadwalladr, C. (2017) Revealed: How US billionaire helped to back Brexit, *The Guardian* February 26; https://www.theguardian.com/politics/2017/feb/26/us-billionaire-mercer-helped-back-brexit. Accessed 28/06/2018

Cadwalladr, C. (2017a) The Great British Brexit robbery: How our democracy was hijacked, *The Observer*, May 7; https://www.theguardian.com/technology/2017/may/07/the-great-british-brexit-robbery-hijacked-democracy. Accessed 04/11/2017

Cadwalladr, C. (2017b) Trump, Assange, Bannon, Farage… bound together in an unholy alliance, *The Guardian*, October 29; https://www.theguardian.com/commentisfree/2017/oct/28/trump-assange-bannon-farage-bound-together-in-unholy-alliance. Accessed 05/11/2017

Cadwalladr, C. (2017c) Robert Mercer: The big data billionaire waging war on mainstream media, *The Guardian*, February 26; https://www.theguardian.com/politics/2017/feb/26/robert-mercer-breitbart-war-on-media-steve-bannon-donald-trump-nigel-farage. Accessed 29/06/2018

Cadwalladr, C. (2018) Threats, bullying, vindictiveness: How Arron Banks repels charges against him, *The Guardian* November 3; https://www.theguardian.com/global/commentisfree/2018/nov/03/threats-bullying-and-vindictiveness-how-arron-banks-repels-charges-against-him. Accessed 15/04/2019

Cameron, D. (2011) David Cameron on immigration: full text of the speech, *The Guardian* April 14; https://www.theguardian.com/politics/2011/apr/14/david-cameron-immigration-speech-full-text. Accessed 16/04/2019

Campbell, J. (1968) *The Hero with a Thousand Faces*. Princeton University Press

Capdevilla, R. and Callaghan, E. M. (2008) 'It's not Racist. It's Common Sense': A Critical Analysis of Political Discourse Around Asylum and Immigration in the UK, *Journal of Community & Applied Social Psychology*, 18, 1–16

Cicourel, A. V. (1964) Method and Measurement in Sociology, New York: Free Press; London: Collier-Macmillan

Chabris, C. and Simons, D. (2010) *The Invisible Gorilla: And Other Ways our Intuition Deceives us*. London: Harper Collins

Clay, H. (1832) *In Defence of the American System, Against the British Colonial system*. Washington: Gales and Seaton; https://ia902701.us.archive.org/15/items/speechhenryclay00clay/speechhenryclay00clay.pdf. Accessed 21/07/2018

Coghlan, A. and MacKenzie, D. (2011) Revealed – the capitalist network that runs the world, *New Scientist* October 19; https://www.newscientist.com/article/mg21228354-500-revealed-the-capitalist-network-that-runs-the-world/. Accessed 29/07/2018

Cohen, M. R. (1944) *A Preface to Logic*. New York: Dover

Cohen, N. (2017) Russia's free pass to undermine British democracy, *The Guardian* October 21; https://www.theguardian.com/commentisfree/2017/oct/21/russia-free-pass-undermine-british-democracy-vladimir-putin. Accessed 15/04/2019

Comaroff, J. and Comaroff, L. (1999) Occult Economies and the Violence of Abstraction: Notes from the South African Postcolony, *American Ethnologist*, 26(2), 279–303

Comaroff, J. (2007) Terror and Territory: Guantanamo and the Space of Contradiction, *Public Culture*, 19(2), 381–405

Cooper, D. (1971) *The Death of the Family*. Harmondsworth: Pelican

Cox, C. B. and Dyson, A. E. (1975) *Black Paper*. London: Dent

Credit Suisse Report (2017) *Global Wealth Report*. Zurich: CREDIT SUISSE AG Research Institute

Crépon, S., Dézé, A. and Mayer, N. (2015) *Les faux-semblants du Front National: Sociologie d'un parti politique*. Paris: Presses de Sciences Po

Cronin, D. (2013) *Corporate Europe: How Big Sets Policies on Food, Climate and War*. London: Pluto Press

Crouch, C. (2004) *Post-Democracy*. Cambridge, Malden: Polity Press

Crouch, C. (2011) *The Strange Non-Death of Neoliberalism*. Cambridge: Polity

Cuban, L. (1984) *How Teachers Taught: Constancy and Change in American Classrooms, 1890–1980*. New York: Longman

Curtis, A. (1992) *Pandora's Box: A Fable From the Age of Science*. BBC documentary, six episodes

Curtis, A. (2002) *The Century of the Self*. BBC documentary, four episodes

Curtis, A. (2011) *All Watched Over by Machines of Loving Grace*. BBC documentary, three episodes

Curtis, A. (2016) *HyperNormalisation*. BBC documentary, October 16

Daily Mail Comment (2016) Why the free Press must shine a light on this unelected court, *The Daily Mail*April 15; https://www.dailymail.co.uk/debate/article-3996182/DAILY-MAIL-COMMENT-free-Press-shine-light-unelected-court.html. Accessed 15/04/2019

Das, S. (2011) *Extreme Money: Masters of the Universe and the Cult of Risk*. Pearson Education, Financial Times Press

Davidson, J. D. and Rees-Mogg, W. (1997) *The Sovereign Individual: How to Survive and Strive During the Collapse of the Welfare State* (subtitle later changed to: *Mastering the Transition to the Information Age* for 1999 Touchstone Edition). New York: Simon & Schuster

Davis, O. (2018) The anti-police of Mai '68 fifty years on, *Modern and Contemporary France*, 26, 2, 107–114

Deacon, M. (2016) EU referendum: Who needs experts when we've got Michael Gove?, *The Telegraph*June 6; https://www.telegraph.co.uk/news/2016/06/06/eu-referendum-who-needs-experts-when-weve-got-michael-gove/. Accessed 13/07/2016

Deacon, M. (2016) EU referendum: Who needs experts when we've got Michael Gove?, *The Telegraph*June 6; https://www.telegraph.co.uk/news/2016/06/06/eu-referendum-who-needs-experts-when-weve-got-michael-gove/. Accessed 13/07/2016

Dejours, C. (1998) *Souffrance en France: La banalisation de l'injustice social*, Edition augmenté d'une preface et d'une postface 2009. Paris: Éditions du Seuil

Dejours, C. (2003) *L'évaluation du travail à l'épreuve du reel: Critique des fondements de l'évaluation*. Une conference-débat organisée par le groupe Sciences en questions, Paris, INRA, 20 Mars 2003. Paris: INRA Editions

Delingpole, J. (2016) Toffs hate Brexit: It's the peasants' revolt, *Breitbart*March 10; http://www.breitbart.com/london/2016/03/10/toffs-hate-brexit-its-the-peasants-revolt/. Accessed 28/06/2018

Denzin, N. (1991) *Images of Postmodern Society: Social Theory and Contemporary Cinema*. London: Sage

Deranty, J-P. (2008) Work and the Precarisation of Existence, *European Journal of Social Theory* 11(4), 443–463

Dewey, J. (1916) *Democracy and Education: An Introduction to the Philosophy of Education*. New York: Macmillan

Dewey, J. (1927) *The Public and its Problems*. Athens: Swallow Press, Ohio University Press

Dewey, J. (1938) *Experience and Education*. New York: Collier

Diamond, J., and Almasy, S. (2017) Trump's immigration ban sends shockwaves, *CNN Politics*, January 30; https://edition.cnn.com/2017/01/28/politics/donald-trump-executive-order-immigration-reaction/index.html. Accessed 15/04/2019

Dijk, van, T. A. (1992) Discourse and the Denial of Racism, *Discourse and Society* 3, 87–118

Dijk, van, T. A. (2008) News, Discourse and Ideology. In T. Hanitzsch and K. Wahl-Jorgensen (Eds), *Handbook of Journalism Studies*, 191–204. Hillsdale, NJ: Erlbaum

Dorling, D. (2015) *Injustice: Why Social Inequality Still Persists* (Revised Edition). Bristol: Polity Press

Drutman, L. (2011) The political one percent of the one percent, *Sunlight Foundation*, December 13; http://sunlightfoundation.com/blog/2011/12/13/the-political-one-percent-of-the-one-percent/. Accessed 14/04/2019

Drutman, L. (2015) *The Business of America is Lobbying: How Corporations Became Politicised and Politics Became More Corporate*. Oxford, New York: Oxford University Press

Ducheyne, S. (2017) *Reassessing the Radical Enlightenment*. London, New York: Routledge

Durkee, A. (2016) Here's a breakdown of how African-Americans voted in the 2016 election, *MIC*November 14; https://mic.com/articles/159402/here-s-a-break-down-of-how-african-americans-voted-in-the-2016-election#.gPNbGtSnx. Accessed 17/09/2017

Durkheim, E. (1982) *The Rules of Sociological Method*. Edited with an introduction by S. Lukes, translated by W.D. Halls. New York, London, Toronto, Sydney: The Free Press

Earl, J., Moran, C. and Ward-Perkins, Z. (2017) *The Econocracy: The Perils of Leaving Economics to the Experts*. Manchester: Manchester University Press

edmundberger (2013) A counter-history of the Californian ideology, *Deterritorial Investigations*April 30; https://deterritorialinvestigations.wordpress.com/2013/04/30/a-counter-history-of-the-california-ideology/. Accessed 09/08/2018

Eisenhower, D. D. (1961) Farewell Address, *American Rhetoric*; http://www.americanrhetoric.com/speeches/dwightdeisenhowerfarewell.html. Accessed 06/02/2012

Eisenstadt, S. N. (Ed.) (2002) *Multiple Modernities*. Transaction Publishers. Originally published by *Daedalus*, Winter 2000 2000. Abingdon, New York: Routledge Edition 2017

Elliott, J. (1991) *Action Research for Educational Change*. Milton Keynes: Open University Press

Elliott, L. (2016) Brexit is a rejection of globalisation, *The Guardian*June 26; https://www.theguardian.com/business/2016/jun/26/brexit-is-the-rejection-of-globalisation. Accessed 28/06/2018

Etzion, D. and Davis, G. F. (2008) Revolving Doors? A Network Analysis of Corporate Officers and U.S. Government Officials, *Journal of Management Inquiry*, 17(3), 157–161

Falafil (2006) Quel paradigme du don ? En clé d'intérêt ou en clé de don ?. Réponse à Frédéric Lordon, *Revue du MAUSS* 1(27), 127–137

Farhi, P. (2016) How Breitbart has become a dominant voice in conservative media, *The Washington Post*January 27; https://www.washingtonpost.com/lifestyle/style/how-breitbart-has-become-a-dominant-voice-in-conservative-media/2016/01/27/a705cb88-befe-11e5-9443-7074c3645405_story.html?utm_term=.e54f3d640163. Accessed 03/10/2018

Faulkner, N. with Dathi. S. (2017) *Creeping Fascism: Brexit, Trump and the Rise of the Far Right*. London: Public Reading Rooms

Feyerabend, P. (1975) *Against Method*. London: NLB

Fielding, M. (Guest Editor) (2005) Reclaiming the Radical Tradition in State Education, *Forum* 47(2&3), 43–232

Fielding, M. (2009) Public Space and Educational Leadership: Reclaiming and Renewing Our Radical Traditions, *Educational Management Administration Leadership* 37, 497–521

Fielding, M. and Moss, P. (2011) *Radical Democratic Education and the Common School.* London: Routledge.

Foley, S. (2011) What price the new democracy? Goldman Sachs conquers Europe, *The Independent*November 18; http://www.independent.co.uk/news/business/analysis-and-features/what-price-the-new-democracy-goldman-sachs-conquers-europe-6264091.html. Accessed 29/07/2012

Foote-Whyte, W. (1943) *Street Corner Society: The Social Structure of an Italian Slum.* University of Chicago Press

Foucault, M. (2006) *Discourse and Truth: The Problematization of Parrhesia,* 6 lectures given by M. Foucault at the University of California at Berkeley, October–November 1983, edited by J. Pearson in 1985. Archived: http://foucault.info//system/files/pdf/DiscourseAndTruth_MichelFoucault_1983_0.pdf. Accessed 27/07/2016

Frank, T. (2016) Millions of ordinary Americans support Donald Trump. Here's why, *The Guardian*March 8; https://www.theguardian.com/commentisfree/2016/mar/07/donald-trump-why-americans-support. Accessed 27/07/2016

Frank, T. (2018) Forget Trump – populism is the cure, not the disease, *The Guardian*May 23; https://www.theguardian.com/books/2018/may/23/thomas-frank-trump-populism-books. Accessed 03/10/2018

Frankfurt, H. G. (2005) *On Bullshit.* Princeton and Oxford: Princeton University Press

Fraser, K. and Schostak, J. F. (2005) edCity – a New Learning Environment, *British Computer Society,* https://ewic.bcs.org/content/ConWebDoc/7692

Freedland, J. (2017) The new age of Ayn Rand: How she won over Trump and Silicon Valley, *The Guardian*April 10; https://www.theguardian.com/books/2017/apr/10/new-age-ayn-rand-conquered-trump-white-house-silicon-valley. Accessed 22/07/2018

Frégier, H.-A. (1840) *Des Classes Dangereuses de la Population dans les Grandes Villes.* Paris, London: Chez J.-B Baillière

Friedman, M. (1962, 1982) *Capitalism and Freedom* (Preface, 1982 Edition). London: University of Chicago Press

Freeland, C. (2013) *Plutocracy: The Rise of the New Global Super Rich and the Fall of Everyone Else.* New York: Penguin Group. First published in 2012 by Penguin Press

Freire, P. (1972) *Pedagogy of the Oppressed.* Middlesex: Penguin.

Fromm, E. (1942) *The Fear of Freedom.* Abingdon: Routledge & Kegan Paul. Published inRoutledge Classics, 2000

Fukuyama, F. (1992) *The End of History and the Last Man.* New York: Free Press. 2nd Paperback Edition with a new afterword published by Simon & Schuster in 2006

Fullan, M. (1999) *Change Forces: The Sequel.* London: Falmer Press

Fullan, M. (2000) The Return of Large-scale Reform, *The Journal of Educational Change,* 1(1), 5–28

Galbraith, J. K. (2016*) Welcome to the Poisoned Chalice: The Destruction of Greece and the Future of Europe.* New Haven and London: Yale University Press

Garfinkel, H. (1967) *Studies in Ethnomethodology.* Prentice-Hall

Gibson-Graham, J. K. (1996) *The End of Capitalism (As We Knew It): A Feminist Critique of Political Economy.* Oxford: Blackwell

Giddens, A. (1991) *Modernity and Self-Identity: Self and Society in the Late Modern Age.* Stanford, CA: Stanford University Press

Giddens, A. (1998) *The Third Way: The Renewal of Social Democracy*. Cambridge, Malden: Polity Press

Giroux, H. A. (1989) *Schooling for Democracy: Critical Pedagogy in the Modern Age*. London: Routledge

Giroux, H. A. (2004) Public Pedagogy and the Politics of Neo-liberalism: Making the Political more Pedagogical, *Policy Futures in Education*, 2(3&4), 494–503

Giroux, H.A. (2005). Cultural Studies in Dark Times: Public Pedagogy and the Challenge of Neoliberalism, *Fast Capitalism*; http://www.uta.huma/agger/fastcapitalism/1_2/giroux.htm

Giroux, H. A. (2014) *Zombie Politics and Culture in the Age of Casino Capitalism*, 2nd Edition. New York: Peter Lang Publishing Inc.

Giroux, H. A. (2018) *American Nightmare: Facing the Challenge of Fascism*. San Francisco: City Lights Books

Glaser, B. G. and Strauss, A. L. (1967) *The Discovery of Grounded Theory: Strategies for Qualitative Research*. Aldine: Atherton

Goffman, E. (1970) *Strategic Interaction*. Oxford: Basil Blackwell

Goodson, I. (1994) *Studying Curriculum: Cases and Methods*. Buckingham: Open University Press

Goodson, I. (1997) The Educational Researcher as Public Intellectual, The Lawrence Stenhouse Lecture, BERA Conference, University of York

Goodson, I.F. (2003) *Professional Knowledge, Professional Lives: Studies in Education and Change*. Maidenhead and Philadelphia: Open University Press

Goodson, I.F. (2005) *Learning, Curriculum and Life Politics: The Selected Works of Ivor F. Goodson*. Abingdon: Taylor and FrancisGoodson, I. F. (2014) *Curriculum, Personal Narrative and the Social Future*. London and New York: Routledge

Goodson, I. F. (2015) The five Rs of educational research, *Power & Education* 7(1), 34–38

Goodwyn, L. (1978) *The Populist Movement: A Short History of the Agrarian Revolt in America*. Oxford, London, New York: Oxford University Press

Gore, A. (2007) *The Assault on Reason*. Penguin Press

Graeber, D. (2014) *Debt: The First 5,000 Years*. Brooklyn, London: Melville House. First published in 2011

Graeber, D. (2018) *Bullshit Jobs: A Theory*. New York: Simon & Schuster

Graham, D. A. (2017) Why Trump Invokes 'Common Sense', *The Atlantic* August 4; https://www.theatlantic.com/politics/archive/2017/08/trump-common-sense/535872/. Accessed 17/09/2018

Grinspun, R. and Kreklewich, K. (1994) Consolidating Neoliberal Reforms – "Free Trade" as a Conditioning Framework, *Studies in Political Economy* 43, 33–61

Habermas, J. (1984) *Theory of Communicative Action*, Vol. 1. London: Heinemann

Hague, W. (2016) Donald Trump is speaking harsh truths, and the world needs to listen, *The Telegraph* April 7; http://www.telegraph.co.uk/news/2016/04/06/donald-trump-is-speaking-harsh-truths-and-the-world-needs-to-lis/. Accessed 27/07/2016

Halpern, D. (2015) *Inside the Nudge Unit: How Small Changes can Make a Big Difference*, with a foreword by R. H. Thaler. London: W. H. Allen

Hamilton, D. (1980) Adam Smith and the Moral Economy of the Classroom System, *Journal of Curriculum Studies*, 12(4), 281–298

Hammersley, M. (Ed.) (2007) *Educational Research and Evidence-based Practice*. Los Angeles, London: Sage

Hampton, C. (1984) *A Radical Reader. The struggle for change in England, 1381–1914*, Harmondsworth, New York: Penguin Books

Hardt, M. and Negri, A. (2009) *Commonwealth*. Cambridge, MA: The Belknap Press of Harvard University Press

Hargreaves, A. (1994) *Changing Teachers, Changing Times: Teachers' Work and Culture in the Postmodern Age*. New York: Teachers' College Press

Harrison, D. and Kjellberg, H. (2014) *Theories of Markets: An Inter-disciplinary Review*. Paper read at the 30th IMP conference, Bordeaux, September 4–6; http://www.imp group.org/uploads/papers/8208.pdf. Accessed 15/06/2016

Harvey, D. (2003) *The New Imperialism*. Oxford: Clarendon Press

Harvey, D. (2005) *A Brief History of Neoliberalism*. Oxford: Oxford University Press

Harvey, D. (2014) *Seventeen Contradictions and the End of Capitalism*. London: Profile Books

Haseler, S. (2000) *The Super-Rich: The Unjust New World of Global Capitalism*. London: Macmillan Press; New York: St Martin's Press

Hayek, F.A. (1944) *The Road to Serfdom*. Chicago: University of Chicago Press

Hawkes, S. (2012) Banker bashing bad for Britain, *The Sun*, February 1; http://www. thesun.co.uk/sol/homepage/news/4100615/Banker-bashing-bad-for-Britain.html. Accessed 30/07/2012

Haymes, S., Vidal de Haymes, M. and Miller, R. (2015) *The Routledge Handbook of Poverty in the United States*. Abingdon and New York: Routledge

Hellerstein, E. and Legum, J. (2016) The phony debate about political correctness, *Think Progress* January 14; https://thinkprogress.org/the-phony-debate-about-political-correctness-f81da03b3bdb/. Accessed 16/09/2018

Henley, J. (2015) Meet Srdja Popovic, the secret architect of global revolution, *The Guardian* March 8; https://www.theguardian.com/world/2015/mar/08/srdja-popovic-revolution-serbian-activist-protest. Accessed 17/09/2018

Herman, E. S. and Chomsky, N. (1988) *Manufacturing Consent: The Political Economy of the Mass Media*. New York: Pantheon Books

Hernstein, R. J. and Murray, C. (1994) *The Bell Curve: Intelligence and Class Structure in American Life*. New York, London: Free Press

Hertel-Fernandez, A., Tervo, C. and Skocpol, T. (2018) How the Koch brothers built the most powerful rightwing group you've never heard of, *The Guardian* September 26; https:// www.theguardian.com/us-news/2018/sep/26/koch-brothers-americans-for-prosperity-rightwing-political-group. Accessed 16/04/2019

Hilgers, M. (2011) The Three Anthropological Approaches to Neoliberalism, *International Social Science Journal* 61(202). UNESCO, Oxford: Blackwell

Hobsbawm, E. (1994) *Age of Extremes: The Short Twentieth Century, 1914–1991*. London: Penguin

Holyoake, G. J. (1858) *Self-help by the People*. London: John Watts

Howard, M. (2005) Text of Howard immigration speech, BBC News April 10; http:// news.bbc.co.uk/2/hi/uk_news/politics/vote_2005/frontpage/4430453.stm. Accessed 01/08/2018

Hunsicker, L. M. (1925) *A Study of the Relationship between Rate and Ability*. PhD thesis, Faculty of Philosophy, Columbia University

Huntington, S. P. (1996) *The Clash of Civilizations and the Remaking of World Order*. Simon & Schuster

Husserl, E. (1960) *Cartesian Meditations: An Introduction to Phenomenology*. Translated by D. Cairns. The Hague, Boston, London: Martinus Nijhoff Publishers

Husserl, E. (1970 *The Crisis of European Sciences and Transcendental Phenomenology: An Introduction to Phenomenological Philosophy*. Translated with an introduction by D. Carr. Evanston: Northwestern University Press

Israel, J. (2001) *Radical Enlightenment: Philosophy and the Making of Modernity*. Oxford: Oxford University Press

Jackson, B. (2012) Freedom, the Common Good, and the Rule of Law: Lippmann and Hayek on Economic Planning, *Journal of the History of Ideas*, 73(1), 47–68

JacksonB. (2012a) Property-Owning Democracy: A Short History. In M. O'Neill and T. Williamson (Eds), *Property-Owning Democracy: Rawls and Beyond*. Malden, Oxford: Wiley-Blackwell

Jacobs, J. (1961) *The Death and Life of Great American Cities*. London: Vintage, Penguin Random House

Jacobs, J. (2004) *Dark Age Ahead*. London and New York: Vintage/Random House

Jessop, B. (2011) Rethinking the Diversity of Capitalism: Varieties of Capitalism, Variegated Capitalism, and the World Market. In G. Wood and C. Lane (Eds), *Capitalist Diversity and Diversity within Capitalism*. London: Routledge

Johnson, B. (2013) We should be humbly thanking the super-rich, not bashing them, *The Telegraph*November 17; https://www.telegraph.co.uk/politics/0/should-humbly-thanking-super-rich-not-bashing/. Accessed 15/04/2019

Johnson, J. (2003) *Born Rich*, documentary; https://www.youtube.com/watch?v=km_JmxnzTvc. Accessed 19/07/2018

Johnson, J. (2006) *The One Percent*, documentary; https://www.youtube.com/watch?v=eiInW0DYw_A. Accessed 19/07/2018

Johnson, S. (2016) Liam Fox: Brexit campaign is peasants' revolt against elite, *The Telegraph*March 04; https://www.telegraph.co.uk/news/newstopics/eureferendum/12183215/Liam-Fox-Brexit-campaign-is-peasants-revolt-against-elite.html. Accessed 28/06/2018

Jones, S. D. (2012) *Masters of the Universe: Hayek, Friedman, and the Birth of Neoliberal Politics*. Princeton and Oxford: Princeton University Press

*Journal of Curriculum Studies* (2016) Rethinking John Dewey's *Democracy and Education* on its Centennial, *Journal of Curriculum Studies* 48(1), 1–150

*Journal of Historical Sociology* (1988 to present) Oxford & Malden, MA: Blackwell Publishing

Judt, T. (2010) *Ill Fares the Land*. London: Allen Lane

Kahn, P. W. (2011) *Political Theology: Four New Chapters on the Concept of Sovereignty*. New York: Columbia Press

Kakutani, M. (2018) The death of truth: How we gave up on facts and ended up with Trump, *The Guardian*July 14; https://www.theguardian.com/books/2018/jul/14/the-death-of-truth-how-we-gave-up-on-facts-and-ended-up-with-trump

Kamin, L. J. (1974) *The Science and Politics of I.Q.* Maryland, Potomac: Lawrence Erlbaum Associates

Kant, I. (1784) An answer to the question: What is Enlightenment?http://theliterarylink.com/kant.html

Katsiaficas, G. (2018) *The Global Imagination of 1968: Revolution and Counterrevolution*. Oakland: PM Press

Keane, J. (2016) The 18th-century Enlightenment and the problem of public misery, *The Conversation*; https://theconversation.com/the-18th-century-enlightenment-and-the-problem-of-public-misery-57541. Earlier version published in *Spiked Review*, March 2016; http://www.spiked-online.com/spiked-review/article/paine-and-misery/18198#.V2EZ6Vd0vwx

Keen, S. (2011) *Debunking Economics – Revised and Expanded Edition: The Naked Emperor Dethroned?* London and New York: Zed Books

Kent, D. (2018) 'I follow a different person every day': using strangers to explore the city, *The Guardian* September 21; https://www.theguardian.com/cities/2018/sep/21/i-follow-a-different-person-every-day-using-strangers-to-explore-the-city. Accessed 21/09/2018

Khanna, S. (2013) "A microcosm of women's democracy": The co-operative movement and women's rights, *New Statesman* March 15; https://www.newstatesman.com/old-statesman/2013/03/microcosm-womens-democracy-co-operative-movement-and-womens-rights. Accessed 21/09/2018

Khomami, N. (2017) #MeToo: How a hashtag became a rallying cry against sexual harassment, *The Guardian* October 20; https://www.theguardian.com/world/2017/oct/20/women-worldwide-use-hashtag-metoo-against-sexual-harassment. Accessed 22/09/2018

Kirby, P. (2016) Leading People 2016: The educational backgrounds of the UK professional elite, *The Sutton Trust*; https://www.suttontrust.com/wp-content/uploads/2016/02/Leading-People_Feb16.pdf. Accessed 02/09/2018

Kirk, A. and Dunford, D. (2016) EU referendum: Leave supporters trust ordinary "common sense" more than academics and experts, *The Telegraph* June 22; https://www.telegraph.co.uk/news/2016/06/16/eu-referendum-leave-supporters-trust-ordinary-common-sense-than/. Accessed 13/07/2018

Klein, N. (2007) *The Shock Doctrine: The Rise of Disaster Capitalism*. Metropolitan Books; published by Penguin2008

Kohl, H. (1967) *36 Children*. New York, London: Penguin

Kotkin, S. (2015) Public talk at NYPL titled "Stalin: Paradoxes of Power", S. Kotkin and S. Zizek, March 31; http://www.nypl.org/events/programs/2015/03/31/stephen-kotkin-slavoj-zizek; and: https://www.youtube.com/watch?v=Z9voDV_ZsB8

Kozol, J. (1967) *Death at an Early Age*. New York, London: Penguin

Kristol, I. (1995) *Neoconservatism: The Autobiography of an Idea*. Chicago: Elephant Paperbacks, Ivan R. Dee

Kristol, I. (2011) *The Neoconservative Persuasion. Selected Essays 1942–2009*, Himmelfarb, G. (Ed.), foreword by Kristol, W.New York: Basic Books

Kuhn, T. (1970) *The Structure of Scientific Revolutions*, 2nd Edition. Vols. I and II. Foundations of the Unity of Science, Chicago: University of Chicago Press

Kusch, F. (2008) Battleground Chicago. The Police and the 1968 Democratic National Convention, Chicago: University of Chicago Press

Kwarteng, K., Patel, P., Raab, D., Skidmore, C. and Truss, E. (2012) *Britannia Unchained: Global Lessons for Growth and Prosperity*. Basingstoke, New York: Palgrave Macmillan UK. Kindle Edition

Labaree, D. F. (2010) How Dewey Lost: The Victory of David Snedden and Social Efficiency in the Reform of American Education. In D. Tröhler, T. Sclag and F. Osterwalder (Eds), *Pragmatism and Modernities*. Rotterdam, Boston, Taipei: Sense Publishers

Laclau, E. (2005) *Populist Reason*. London: Verso

Lafuente, J. L. (2012) The MONDRAGON Cooperative Experience: Humanity at work, *Management Innovation Exchange*; http://www.managementexchange.com/story/mondragon-cooperative-experience-humanity-work. Accessed 23/09/2018

Lanier, J. (2013) *Who Owns the Future?*London: Allen Lane. Updated in 2014 by Penguin Books

*Laws and Objects* (1844) *Laws and Objects of the Rochdale Society of Equitable Pioneers*, archived at the Rochdale Pioneers Museum; https://www.rochdalepioneersmuseum.coop/wp-content/uploads/2014/08/REPS-Laws-and-Objects-1844.pdf. Accessed 16/04/2019

Lawson, N. (2016) Brexit will complete Margaret Thatcher's economic revolution, *The Telegraph*September 23; https://www.telegraph.co.uk/news/2016/09/23/brexit-will-complete-margaret-thatchers-economic-revolution/. Accessed 18/06/2018

Leclercq, J. (2017) *Extrême gauche et anarchisme en Mai 68. Avant, pendant, après: 50 ans d'histoire*. Paris: L'Harmattan

Lee, M. J., Murray, S., Diamond, J., Gray, N. and Kopan, T. (2016) Why I'm voting for Trump CNN talks to more than 150 people in 31 cities to explore what's driving the Trump phenomenon, *CNN politics*January 28; http://edition.cnn.com/2016/01/27/politics/donald-trump-voters-2016-election/. Accessed 27/07/2016

Lefort, C. (1988). *Democracy and Political Theory*. Oxford: Polity Press

Leith, S. (2017) Trump's rhetoric: A triumph of inarticulacy, *The Guardian*January 13; https://www.theguardian.com/us-news/2017/jan/13/donald-trumps-rhetoric-how-being-inarticulate-is-seen-as-authentic. Accessed 16/04/2019

Lenz, M. (2012) Intentionality without Objectivity? – Spinoza's Theory of Intentionality. In A. Salice (Ed.), *Intentionality: Historical and Systematic Perspectives*, with an introduction by J. Searle, (Basic Philosophical Concepts). München: Philosophia-Verlag. Chapter archived at: https://www.academia.edu/1566267/Spinoza_on_Intentionality

Letelier, O. (1976) Economic 'Freedom's' Awful Toll; The 'Chicago Boys' in Chile, *Review of Radical Political Economics*, 8, 44–52

Levenson Inquiry (undated) Levensen Inquiry: Culture, practice and ethics of the press; http://www.levesoninquiry.org.uk/. Accessed 01/08/2012

Levitsky, S. and Ziblatt, D. (2018) *How Democracies Die*. New York: Penguin Random House

Lewin, K. (1946) Action Research and Minority Problems, *Journal of Social Issues* 2(4), 34–46

Lewis, M. (2015) *Flash Boys: A Wall Street Revolt*, with a new afterword. New York: W. W. Norton & Company

Lieberman, A. (Ed.) (1995) *The Work of Restructuring Schools*. New York: Teachers College Press

Lippmann, W. (1922) *Public Opinion*. Harcourt Brace and Company

Lippmann, W. (1927) *The Phantom Public*. New York: Macmillan; New Brunswick, New Jersey: 13 Transaction Publishers

Longworth, R. C. (2016) Disaffected rust belt voters embraced Trump. They had no other hope, *The Guardian*November 21; https://www.theguardian.com/commentisfree/2016/nov/21/disaffected-rust-belt-voters-embraced-donald-trump-midwestern-obama. Accessed 15/04/2019

Lowe, R. (1867) *Primary and Classical Education: An Address – Delivered before the Philosophical Institutions of Edinburgh on Friday November 1, 1867*. Edinburgh: Edmonton and Douglas

Lucchese, Del, F. (2009) *Conflict, Power, and Multitude in Machiavelli and Spinoza: Tumult and Indignation*. London: Continuum

Lyotard, J. (Ed.) (1984) *The Postmodern Condition: A Report on Knowledge*. Minneapolis: University of Minnesota Press

Lyotard, J-L. (2011) *Discourse, Figure*. Translated by A. Hudek and M. Lydon, with an introduction by J. Mowitt. Minneapolis, London: University of Minnesota Press

MacInnes, P. (2019) Adam Curtis and vice director Adam McKay on how Dick Cheney masterminded a rightwing revolution, *The Guardian* January 18; https://www.theguardian.com/film/2019/jan/18/adam-curtis-and-vice-director-adam-mckay-on-how-dick-cheney-masterminded-a-rightwing-revolution. Accessed 18/01/2019

Mack, M. (2010) *Spinoza and the Specters of Modernity: The Hidden Enlightenment of Diversity from Spinoza to Freud*. New York, London: Continuum

Mack, A. and Rock, I. (1998) *Inattentional Blindness*. Cambridge MA, London: MIT Press

MacLean, N. (2017) *Democracy in Chains: The Deep History of the Radical Right's Stealth Plan for America*. Brunswick, London: Scribe Publications Pty Ltd

Mailer, N. (1968) Miami and the Siege of Chicago. An Informal History of the Republican and Democratic Conventions of 1968, New York: Random House; reissued 2018

Marcuse, H. (1964) *One-Dimensional Man: Studies in the Ideology of Advanced Industrial Society*, with an introduction by D. Kellner. London and New York: Routledge

Marsh, J. (2011) *Class Dismissed: Why We Cannot Teach or Learn Our Way Out of Inequality*. New York: Monthly Review Press

Marwick, A. E. (2013) *Status Update: Celebrity, Publicity, and Branding in the Social Media Age*. New Haven and London: Yale University Press

Mason, P. (2013) *Why it's Still Kicking Off Everywhere: The New Global Revolutions*, revised and updated 2nd Edition. London, New York: Verso

Mauss, M. (1973) Techniques of the Body, *Economy and Society* 2(1), 70–88

Mayer, J. (2010) Covert operations: The billionaire brothers who are waging a war against Obama, *The New Yorker*, August 30; https://www.newyorker.com/magazine/2010/08/30/covert-operations. Accessed 30/07/2018

Mayer, J. (2016) *Dark Money: The Hidden History of the Billionaires Behind the Rise of the Radical Right*. Brunswick, London: Scribe

Mayhew, K. C. and Edwards, A. C. (1936) *The Dewey School: The Laboratory School of the University of Chicago 1896–1903*, with an introduction by J. Dewey. New York and London: Appleton-Century Company Incorporated

McCormack, W. (2017) The populist ploy, *The New Republic* February 17; https://newrepublic.com/article/140265/populist-ploy-irving-kristol-predicted-trump-uprising-liberal-elites. Accessed 04/07/2018

McCormick, J. P. (2006) Contain the Wealthy and Patrol the Magistrates: Restoring Elite Accountability to Popular Government, *American Political Science Review*, 100(3), 147–163

McCormick, J. P. (2011) Post-Enlightenment Sources of Political Authority: Biblical Atheism, Political Theology and the Schmitt-Strauss Exchange, *History of European Ideas*, 37, 175–180

McCormick, J. P. (2011a) *Machiavellian Democracy*. Cambridge: Cambridge University Press

McCormick, J. P. (2015) Tribunes and Tyrants: Machiavelli's Legal and Extra-Legal Modes of Controlling Elites, *An International Journal of Jurisprudence and Philosophy of Law*, 28(2), 252–266

McCulloch, G. (1995) Essay Review of Changing Teachers, Changing Times, by A. Hargreaves, *British Journal of Sociology of Education*, 16(1), 113–117

McGill, A. (2016) The Trump Bloc, *The Atlantic* September 14; https://www.theatlantic.com/politics/archive/2016/09/dissecting-donald-trumps-support/499739/. Accessed 17/09/2018

Meek, J. (2014) *Private Island: Why Britain Now Belongs to Someone Else*. London: Verso

Meyer, J. and Rowan, B. (1978) The Structure of Educational Organizations. In J. Meyer and W. Marshall et al. (Eds), *Environments and Organizations: Theoretical and Empirical Perspectives*, 78–109. San Francisco: Jossey-Bass

Millar, J. (2017) 'They're THWARTING the will of the people' Fury at last-ditch REMAINER PLOT to stop Brexit, *Sunday Express* January 5; http://www.express.co.uk/news/uk/754241/brexit-remainer-plot-hillary-benn-select-committee. Accessed 21/04/2017

Miller, B. and Lapham, M. (2012) *The Self-Made Myth And the Truth about How Government Helps Individuals and Businesses Succeed*. San Francisco: Berrett-Koehler Publishers, Inc.

Mills, C. (1959) *The Sociological Imagination*. London: Oxford University Press

Mills, C.Wright (2000) *The Power Elite*. New Edition, with a new afterword by A. Wolfe. Oxford, New York: Oxford University Press. First published in 1956

Momentum (undated) *Momentum Activist Handbook*. London: Momentum; https://momentum.nationbuilder.com/activist_training; and https://d3n8a8pro7vhmx.cloudfront.net/momentum/pages/2255/attachments/original/1508413441/Momenuntum_Activist_Handbook_Low_res.pdf?1508413441. Accessed 27/09/2018

Monbiot, G. (2016) Billionaires bought Brexit – they are controlling our venal political system, *The Guardian*, July 13; https://www.theguardian.com/commentisfree/2016/jul/13/billionaires-bought-brexit-controlling-britains-political-system. Accessed 13/07/2016

Mondon, A. and Winter, A. (2018) Understanding the mainstreaming of the far right, *Opendemocracy*, August 26; https://www.opendemocracy.net/can-europe-make-it/aurelien-mondon-aaron-winter/understanding-mainstreaming-of-far-right. Accessed 17/09/2018

*Monthly Review* (2011) Education Under Fire, *Monthly Review* 63(3), 1–142 http://archive.monthlyreview.org/index.php/mr/issue/view/MR-063-03-2011-07/showToc; Accessed 23/08/2015

Moore, M. (2016) 5 reasons why Trump will win, *The Huffington Post* July 23; http://www.huffingtonpost.com/michael-moore/5-reasons-why-trump-will-_b_11156794.html

Mouffe, C. (2018) *For a Left Populism*. London, Brooklyn: Verso

Mouffe, C. (2018a) Populists are on the rise but this can be a moment for progressives too, *The Guardian* September 10; https://www.theguardian.com/commentisfree/2018/sep/10/populists-rise-progressives-radical-right. Accessed 10/09/2018

Mounk, Y. (2018) *The People Vs. Democracy: Why our Freedom is in Danger & How to Save It*. Cambridge, London: Harvard University Press

Murray, C. (1999) The underclass revisited, *American Enterprise for Public Policy Research*; http://aei.org/wp-content/uploads/2014/07/-underclass-revisited_141758407046.pdf. Accessed 15/04/2019

Murray, C. (2005) The advantages of social apartheid. U.S. experience shows Britain what to do with its underclass – get it off the streets, *Sunday Times* April 3; https://www.thetimes.co.uk/article/the-advantages-of-social-apartheid-3tmcb3pcvw7. Accessed 16/04/2019

Negri, A. (1991) *The Savage Anomaly: The Power of Spinoza's Metaphysics and Politics*. Minneapolis, Oxford: University of Minnesota Press

Negri, A. (2008) The Labour of the Multitude and the Fabric of Biopolitics, *Globalisation Working Papers* Issue 08/3, Institute on Globalization and the Human Condition, McMaster University; https://globalization.mcmaster.ca/research/publications/working-papers/2008/ighc-wps_08-3_negri.pdf. Accessed 30/08/2018

Neiwert, D. (2017) *Alt-America: The Rise of the Radical Right in the Age of Trump*. London, New York: Verso

Nixon, J. (2014) *Hannah Arendt and the Politics of Friendship*. London and New York: Bloomsbury

Nolte, J. (2015) The great truth-teller of 2015: Donald J. Trump, *Breitbart*December 24; http://www.breitbart.com/big-government/2015/12/24/the-great-truth-teller-of-2015-donald-j-trump/. Accessed 27/07/2016

Norton, A. (2004) *Leo Strauss and the Politics of American Empire*. New Haven and London: Yale University Press

O'Connell, M. (2018) Why Silicon Valley billionaires are prepping for the apocalypse in New Zealand, *The Guardian*, February 15; https://www.theguardian.com/news/2018/feb/15/why-silicon-valley-billionaires-are-prepping-for-the-apocalypse-in-new-zealand. Accessed 04/03/2018

Owen, R. (1816) *A New View of Society Or, Essays on the Principle of the Formation of the Human Character, and the Application of the Principle to Practice*. Political Economy Reference Archive; http://www.marxists.org/reference/subject/economics/owen/index.htm. Accessed 02/07/2012

Oxfam (2010) The global economic crisis and developing countries; http://www.oxfam.org/en/research/global-economic-crisis-and-developing-countries. Accessed 31/12/2014

Oxfam (2014) Even it up. Time to end extreme inequality, Oxford: Oxfam; http://policy-practice.oxfam.org.uk/publications/even-it-up-time-to-end-extreme-inequality-333012. Accessed 31/12/2014

Oxfam (2017) Just 8 men own same wealth as half the world, January 16; https://www.oxfam.org/en/pressroom/pressreleases/2017-01-16/just-8-men-own-same-wealth-half-world. Full report: *An Eonomy for the 99%*; https://d1tn3vj7xz9fdh.cloudfront.net/s3fs-public/file_attachments/bp-economy-for-99-percent-160117-en.pdf. Accessed 13/08/2018

Packer, G. (2016) Head of the class. How Donald Trump is winning over the white working class, *The New Yorker*May 16; http://www.newyorker.com/magazine/2016/05/16/how-donald-trump-appeals-to-the-white-working-class. Accessed 27/07/2016

Paine, T. (1791) Rights of Man: Being and Answer to Mr Burke's attack on the French Revolution, London: J. S. Jordan. In: T. Paine, *Collected Writings: Common Sense / The American Crisis / The Rights of Man / The Age of Reason / A Letter Addressed to the Abbe Raynal*. Coyote Canyon Press. Kindle Edition

Peterson, W. H. (2004) The Meaning of Market Democracy, *The Free Market* 24(12); https://mises.org/library/meaning-market-democracy. Accessed 02/09/2018

Pettifor, A. (2014) *Just money: How society can break the despotic power of finance*. Commonwealth Publishing; https://vdocuments.site/documents/just-money-ann-pettifor.html. Accessed 16/04/2019

Phelps, E. S. (2010) Capitalism vs. Corporatism, *Critical Review*, 21(4), 401–414

Phelps, E. S. (2013) *Mass Flourishing: How Grassroots Innovation Created Jobs, Challenge, and Change*. Princeton: Princeton University Press

Phipps, C. (2016) 'Enemies of the people': British newspapers react to judges' Brexit ruling, *The Guardian* November 4; https://www.theguardian.com/politics/2016/nov/04/enemies-of-the-people-british-newspapers-react-judges-brexit-ruling. Accessed 21/06/2018

Piketty, T. (2014) *Capital in the Twenty-First Century*. Cambridge, Mass: The Belknap Press of Harvard University Press

Pittman, A. (2018) 'It's all fake': in Trump's heartland, talk of White House chaos rings hollow, *The Guardian* September 9; https://www.theguardian.com/us-news/2018/sep/09/trump-supporters-mississippi-white-house-op-ed-woodward. Accessed 09/09/2018

Pleasance, C. (2018) Bizarre moment Donald Trump HUGS a US flag as he is applauded after his speech railing against illegal migration and blaming Democrats for family separations at the border, *The Daily Mail* June 20; https://www.dailymail.co.uk/news/article-5864255/Donald-Trump-HUGS-flag-applauded-illegal-immigration-speech.html. Accessed 14/04/2019

Plowden (Lady) and Committee (1967) *Children and their Primary Schools*. London: HMSO

Polanyi, K. (2001) *The Great Transformation: The Political and Economic Origins of Our Time*, with a foreword by J. E. Stigliz and introduction by F. Block. Boston: Beacon Press. First published in 1944

Popovic, S., Milivojevic, A. and Djinovic, S. (2006) *Nonviolent Struggle 50 Crucial Points: A Strategic Approach to Everyday Tactics*. Belgrade: Centre for Applied NonViolent Action and Strategies (CANVAS) 2007 Edition

Postel, D. (2003) Noble lies and perpetual war: Leo Strauss, the neo-cons, and Iraq, *openDemocracy* October 16; http://www.mafhoum.com/press6/165C39.htm. Accessed 19/04/2019

Postman, N. and Weingarten, C. (1969) *Teaching as a Subversive Activity*. New York: Dell

PROFKNOW (2003–2009) 'Professional knowledge in education and health' (PROFKNOW): Restructuring work and life between state and citizens in Europe, University of Brighton, UK; University of Gothenburg, Sweden; National and Kopodistorian University of Athens, Greece; University of Joensuu, Finland; University of Barcelona, Spain; University of the Azores, Portugal; St. Patrick's College, Dublin, City University, Ireland; University of Stockholm, Sweden – £1 million; https://www.gu.se/digitalAssets/1321/1321776_profknow-final-activity-report.pdf. Accessed 16/04/2019

Quiggin, J. (2010) *Zombie Economics: How Dead Ideas Still Walk Among Us*. Princeton: Princeton University Press

Quigley, C. (2013) Creating a cooperative culture: Lessons from Mondragón, *PACA* November 3; https://philadelphia.coop/mondragon2013/. Accessed 23/09/2018

Ranicière, J. (1999) *Disagreement*. Minneapolis: University of Minnesota Press

Rancière, J., Panagia, D. and Bowlby, R. (2001) Ten Theses on Politics, *Theory and Event* 5(3), Johns Hopkins University Press

Rancière, J. (2004) *The Politics of Aesthetics*, with an afterword by S. Zizek, translated with an introduction by G. Rockhill. London, New York: Continuum

Rancière, J. (2005) *La Haine de la Démocratie*. Paris: La Fabrique éditions

Rancière, J. (2011) *Althusser's Lesson*. Translated by E. Battista, London, New York: Continuum

Rancière, J. (2014) *Moments Politiques: Interventions 1977–2009*. Translated by M. Foster. New York, Oakland: Seven Stories Press. First published by Lux Éditeur, Montréal in 2009

Rand, A. (1957) *Atlas Shrugged* (35th anniversary ed., 1992). New York: Dutton

Rapoza, K. (2011) World's rich richer than ever: Wealth growth beats GDP avgs, *Forbes*; http://blogs.forbes.com/kenrapoza/2011/06/24/worlds-rich-richer-than-ever-wealth-growth-beats-gdp-avgs/

Reagan, R. (1983) Ronald Reagan, "Evil Empire Speech" (8 March 1983), Voices of Democracy, The U.S. Oratory Project; http://voicesofdemocracy.umd.edu/reagan-evil-empire-speech-text/. Accessed 28/06/2018

Rees-Mogg, J. (2018) Full text of Jacob Rees-Mogg's Brexit speech, *BrexitCentral*; https://brexitcentral.com/read-full-text-jacob-rees-mogg-brexit-speech/. Accessed 15/08/2018

Reid, P. (2010) Goldman Sachs' revolving door, *CBS News* April 7; http://www.cbsnews.com/8301-31727_162-20001981-10391695.html. Accessed 19/05/2012

Reilly, S. and Heath, B. (2017) Steve Bannon's own words show sharp break on security issues, *USA Today* January 31; http://www.usatoday.com/story/news/2017/01/31/bannon-odds-islam-china-decades-us-foreign-policy-doctrine/97292068/. Accessed 06/02/2017

Revesz, R. (2017) Donald Trump's presidential counsellor Kellyanne Conway says Sean Spicer gave 'alternative facts' at first press briefing, *The Independent* January 22; https://www.independent.co.uk/news/world/americas/kellyanne-conway-sean-spicer-alternative-facts-lies-press-briefing-donald-trump-administration-a7540441.html. Accessed 21/09/2018

Reynolds, D. and Stringfield, S. (1996) Failure free schooling is ready for take off, *Times Education Supplement*, January 19. 10

Roberts, L. and Schostak, J. (2012) Democracy Matters in Race Matters: Obama, Desire, Hope and the Manufacture of Disappointment, *Discourse* 33(3) June 2012

Roberts, Y. (2012) The price of inequality by Joseph Stigliz – review, *The Guardian*, Friday 13; http://www.guardian.co.uk/books/2012/jul/13/price-inequality-joseph-stiglitz-review. Accessed 30/07/2012

Rogers-Cooper, J. (2011) Crowds and Spinoza's Concept of the Political, *Mediations: Journal of the Marxist Literary Group*, 25(2) Marx or Spinoza; http://www.mediationsjournal.org/articles/crowds-and-spinozas-concept-of-the-political. Accessed 15/04/2019

Rosanvallon, P. (2012) *Counter-Democracy: Politics in an Age of Distrust*. Translated by A. Goldhammer, with a foreword by G. Stedman Jones. Cambridge: Cambridge University Press

Rosanvallon, P. (2013) *The Society of Equals*. Translated by A. Goldhammer. Cambridge, MA, London: Harvard University Press. First published in 2011 by Éditions du Seuil

Rosen, N. (2011) Western media fraud in the Middle East, *Al Jazeera, Opinion* May 18; http://www.aljazeera.com/indepth/opinion/2011/05/201151882929682601.html. Accessed 04/06/2012

Rosenfeld, S. (2011) *Common Sense: A Political History*. Cambridge, London: Harvard University Press

Ruddick, S. (2010) The Politics of Affect: Spinoza in the Work of Negri and Deleuze, *Theory, Culture and Society*, 27(4), 21–45

Runciman, D. (2018) *How Democracy Ends*. London: Profile Books

Rushkoff, D. (2018) How tech's richest plan to save themselves after the apocalypse, *The Guardian* July 24; https://www.theguardian.com/technology/2018/jul/23/tech-industry-wealth-futurism-transhumanism-singularity. Accessed 24/07/2018

Rushton, J. P. and Jensen, A. R. (2005) Thirty Years of Research on Black-White Differences in Cognitive Ability, *Psychology, Public Policy, & the Law* 11, 235–294

Sachs, J. (2000) Interview, conducted 15/06/2000, see section headed The Meaning of "Shock Therapy"; http://www.pbs.org/wgbh/commandingheights/shared/minitext/int_jeffreysachs.html#17. Accessed 01/07/2018

Samuel, R. and Thompson, P. (1990) *The Myths We Live By*. London and New York: Routledge

Samuels, W. J. (1977) The Political Economy of Adam Smith, *Ethics*, 87(3), 189–207

Sandlin, J., O'Malley, M. and Burdick, J. (2011) Mapping the Complexity of Public Pedagogy: 1894–2010, *Review of Educational Research* 81(3) 338–375

Savoie, D. J. (2010) *Power: Where is it?* Queens: McGill University Press

Schatzman, M. (1973) *Soul Murder: Persecution in the Family*. London: Allen Lane

Schmitt, C. (1996) *The Concept of the Political*. Translation, introduction and notes by G. Schwab with L. Strauss's notes on Schmitt's essay, translated by J. Harvey Lomax, foreword by T. B. Strong. Chicago and London: University of Chicago Press

Schmitt, C. (2005) *Political Theology: Four Chapters on the Concept of Sovereignty*. Translated with an introduction by G. Schwab and foreword by T. B. Strong. Chicago and London: Chicago University Press. First published as *Politische Theologie: Vier Kapitel zur Lehre von der Souveranitat*. Berlin: Dunker & Humblot, 1922

Schmitter, P. C. (1974) Still the Century of Corporatism?, *The Review of Politics* 36(1), The New Corporatism: Social and Political Structures in the Iberian World, 85–131

School of Barbiana, (1969) *Letter to a Teacher*. Translated by Nora Rossi and Tom Cole. Harmondsworth, Middlesex: Penguin

Schostak, J. F. (1983) *Maladjusted Schooling: Deviance, Social Control and Individuality in Secondary Schooling*. London, Philadelphia: Falmer. Routledge Library Editions 2012 (hardback), 2014 (paperback)

Schostak, J. F. (1986). *Schooling the Violent Imagination*. London, New York: Routledge and Kegan Paul.

Schostak, J. F. (1989) Developing More Democratic Modes of Teacher–Pupil Relationships: 'The Early Years Listening and Talking Project', *Journal of the Educational Research Network of Northern Ireland* 2, 2–24; archived at: https://www.academia.edu/2442181/Two_papers_Democratic_modes_of_teacher-pupil_relationships_and_practical_policy_making_in_early_years_education_or_making_democracy_real_

Schostak, J. F. (1990) Practical Policy Making in a Primary School, *Journal of the Educational Research Network of Northern Ireland*, 3, 2–24; archived at: https://www.academia.edu/2442181/Two_papers_Democratic_modes_of_teacher-pupil_relationships_and_practical_policy_making_in_early_years_education_or_making_democracy_real_

Schostak, J. F. (1993) *Dirty Marks: The Education of Self, Media and Popular Culture*. London: Pluto Press

Schostak, J. F. (1999) Action Research and the Point Instant of Change, *Educational Action Research Journal*, 7(3), 399–417

Schostak, J. F. (2002) *Understanding, Designing and Conducting Qualitative Research in Education: Framing the Project*. Buckingham, Philadelphia: Open University Press

Schostak, J. F. (2006) *Interviewing and Representation in Qualitative Research Projects*. Open University Press

Schostak, J. F. (2010) Qualitative Research: Participant Observation. In E. Baker, B. McGaw and P. Peterson (Eds), *International Encyclopedia of Education*, 3rd Edition. Elsevier

Schostak, J. F. and Schostak, J. R. (2008) *Radical Research: Designing, Developing and Writing Research to make a Difference*. London: Routledge

Schostak, J. F. and Schostak, J. R. (2013) *Writing Research Critically and Radically – the Power to Make a Difference*. London, New York: Routledge

Schostak, J. F. (2018) Towards a Society of Equals: Dewey, Lippmann, the Co-operative Movement and Radical Democracy Undermining Neo-liberal Forms of Schooling, *Power & Education*, 10(2), 139–165

Schram, S. F. (2015) *The Return of Ordinary Capitalism: Neoliberalism, Precarity, Occupy*. Oxford, New York: Oxford University Press

Schreber, D. P. (1955, 1988) *Memoirs of my Nervous Illness*. Translated by I. Macalpine and R. Hunter. London: Dawson. 2nd Revised Edition Cambridge, MA: Harvard Belknap

Schutz, A. (2001) John Dewey's Conundrum: Can Democratic Schools Empower?, *Teachers College Record* 103(2), 267–302

Schutz, A. (1964) 'The stranger: an essay in social psychology', in: Collected papers. Vol. II. Studies in social theory, The Hague: Martinus Nijhoff

Scott, P. D. (1996) *Deep Politics and the Death of JFK*. California: University of California Press

Sculthorpe, T. (2016) The revolving door between Google and European governments has spun at least EIGHTY times in the past decade, new research reveals, *The Daily Mail* June 5; http://www.dailymail.co.uk/news/article-3626126/The-revolving-door-Google-European-governments-spun-EIGHTY-times-past-decade-new-reseach-reveals.html. Accessed 15/07/2016

Shabi, R. (2017) Momentum's grassroots democracy can make Labour an unstoppable force, *The Guardian* June 14; https://www.theguardian.com/commentisfree/2017/jun/14/momentum-grassroots-democracy-labour-unstoppable. Accessed 27/09/2018

Sharpe, G. (1973) *The Politics of Nonviolent Action*. Extending Horizons Books. Available at: https://www.aeinstein.org/bookstores/english-bookstore/

Sharpe, G. (2010) *From Dictatorship to Democracy: A Conceptual Framework for Liberation*, 4th U.S. Edition. The Albert Einstein Institution. Originally published in Bangkok in 1993 by the Committee for the Restoration of Democracy in Burma in association with Khit Pyaing (*The New Era Journal*); http://www.aeinstein.org/organizations/org/FDTD.pdf

Shor, I. (1980) *Critical Teaching and Everyday Life*. Boston: South End Press

Siddiqui, S. (2017) LeBron James joins NFL in hitting back at Trump: 'The people run this country', *The Guardian* September 25; https://www.theguardian.com/sport/2017/sep/25/nascar-owners-threaten-anthem-protesters-as-presidents-cup-and-nba-prepare-to-start. Accessed 15/05/2019

Simon, B. (1960) *The Two Nations and the Educational Structure 1780–1870*. First published as *Studies in the History of Education, 1780–1870*. London: Lawrence and Wishart

Skinner, B. F. (1976) *Walden II*. New York: Macmillan; London: Collier Macmillan

Smith, A. (1759) *The Theory of Moral Sentiments*. With an introduction by H. W. Schneider, 2018. Digireads.com publishing, eBook ISBN ISBN: 13: 978-1-4209-0901-2

Smith, A. (1762) *Glasgow Edition of the Works and Correspondence: Lectures on Jurisprudence*, Vol. 5. Liberty Fund

Smith, A. (1776, 1961) *An Inquiry into the Nature and Causes of the Wealth of Nations* (Representative selections). Edited with an introduction by B. Mazlish. Indianapolis: Bobbs-Merrill

Smith, A. (1795) *Essays on Philosophical Subjects*. London: T. Cadell and W. Davies

Spinoza, B.de (1993) *Ethics and Treatise on the Correction of the Intellect*. Translated by A. Boyle and revised by G. H. R. Parkinson, with an introduction and notes by G.H.R. Parkinson. London: J. M. Dent, Everyman

Spinoza, B.de (2004) *A Theologico-Political Treatise and a Political Treatise*. Dover Philosophical Classics

Standing, G. (2011) *The Precariat: The New Dangerous Class*. London, New York: Bloomsbury

Stein, B. (2006) In class warfare, guess which class is winning, *The New York Times*November 26

Stenhouse, L. (1969) *Handling Controversial Issues in the Classroom*. Reprinted from Education Canada; archived at University of East Anglia, Norwich, UK; https://www.uea.ac.uk/documents/4059364/4994243/Stenhouse-1969-Handling+controversial+issues+in+the+classroom.pdf/8087d2cd-c2c1-4299-8fd8-936af528da03. Accessed 16/04/2019

Stenhouse, L. (1975) *An Introduction to Curriculum Research and Development*. London: Heinemann

Stewart, H. (2012) £13tn hoard hidden from taxman by global elite, *The Guardian*July 21; https://www.theguardian.com/business/2012/jul/21/global-elite-tax-offshore-economy. Accessed 01/08/2012

Stiglitz, J. E. (2012) *The Price of Inequality*. London, New York: Penguin

Stocker, P. (2017) *English Uprising: Brexit and the Mainstreaming of the Far Right*. London: Melville House

Strauss, L. (1952) *Persecution and the Art of Writing*. London, Chicago: The University of Chicago Press

Strauss, L. (1988) *What is Political Philosophy? And Other Studies*. Chicago and London: The University of Chicago Press. Originally published in 1959 by The Free Press

Streeck, W. (2014) *Buying Time: The Delayed Crisis of Democratic Capitalism*. London, New York: Verso

Streeck, W. (2016) *How Will Capitalism End? Essays on a Failing System*. London, Brooklyn: Verso

Stullich, S., Morgan, I. and Schak, O. (2016) *State and Local Expenditures on Corrections and Education: A Brief from the U.S. Department of Education, Policy and Program Studies Service*. July; https://www2.ed.gov/rschstat/eval/other/expenditures-corrections-education/brief.pdf. Accessed 02/09/2018

Sunstein, C. R. and Thaler, R. H. (2009) *Nudge: Improving Decisions about Health, Wealth and Happiness*. London, New York: Penguin Books Ltd. First published in 2008 by Yale University Press

Swaine, J. (2017) Donald Trump's team defends 'alternative facts' after widespread protests, *The Guardian*January 23; https://www.theguardian.com/us-news/2017/jan/22/donald-trump-kellyanne-conway-inauguration-alternative-facts. Accessed 21/04/2017

Taplin, J. (2017) *Move Fast and Break Things: How Facebook, Google, and Amazon Have Cornered Culture and What It Means For All Of Us*. London: Pan Macmillan

Tarnoff, B. (2016) Donald Trump, Peter Thiel and the death of democracy, *The Guardian* July 21; https://www.theguardian.com/technology/2016/jul/21/peter-thiel-republican-convention-speech. Accessed 14/08/2018

Taylor, F. W. (1919) *The Principles of Scientific Management*. New York, London: Harper and Brothers

Taylor, J. (1991) Are you politically correct?, *New York Magazine* January 21, 30–40; https://books.google.co.uk/books?id=PukCAAAAMBAJ&printsec=frontcover&dq=New+York+Magazine+-+21+Jan+1991&hl=en&sa=X#v=onepage&q=New%20York%20Magazine%20-%2021%20Jan%201991&f=false. Accessed 16/09/2018

Telegraph Obituary (2013) Professor James Buchanan, *The Telegraph* January 09; https://www.telegraph.co.uk/news/obituaries/finance-obituaries/9791656/Professor-James-Buchanan.html. Accessed 26/07/2018

Thatcher, M. (1985) TV Interview for *A Week in Politics*, Channel 4, Margaret Thatcher Foundation; https://www.margaretthatcher.org/document/105955. Accessed 25/07/2018

Thatcher, M. (1986) Speech at Lord Mayor's Banquet, Margaret Thatcher Foundation; https://www.margaretthatcher.org/document/106512. Accessed 28/07/2018

Thatcher, M. (1987) Interview for *Woman's Own* ("No such thing as society"), Margaret Thatcher Foundation; https://www.margaretthatcher.org/document/106689

Thiel, P. (2009) The education of a libertarian, *Cato Unbound* April 13; https://www.cato-unbound.org/2009/04/13/peter-thiel/education-libertarian. Accessed 22/07/2018

Thoreau, H. D. (2018) *Walden; or, Life in the Woods*, Project Gutenberg eBook; http://www.gutenberg.org/ebooks/205

Thorndike, E. L. (1914) Units and Scales for Measuring Educational Products, First Annual Conference on Educational Measurements. September. *Bulletin of the Extension Division*. Indiana University 12(10), 128–141

Thorndike, E. L. (1922) *The Psychology of Arithmetic*. New York: Macmillan Co.

Thorndike, E. L. (1940) *Human Nature and The Social Order*. New York: Macmillan Co.

Thorndike, E. L. and Gates, A. I. (1929) *Elementary Principles of Education*. New York: Macmillan Co.

Tocqueville, de, A. (1863) *Democracy in America*, Vol. 1. Translated by H. Reeve and edited with notes by F. Bowen. 3rd Edition. Cambridge: Silver and Francis; https://books.google.fr/books?id=xZfiBEzcPTEC&printsec=frontcover&hl=fr&source=gbs_ge_summary_r&cad=0#v=onepage&q&f=false. Accessed 15/04/2019

Touré (2018) Sorry to bother you: Is this the most shocking anti-capitalist film ever? *The Guardian* August 19; https://www.theguardian.com/film/2018/aug/19/sorry-to-bother-you-is-this-the-most-anti-capitalist-film-ever. Accessed 15/04/2019

Tragesser, R. S. (1977) *Phenomenology and Logic*. Ithaca and London: Cornell University Press

Travis, A. (2013) Immigration bill: Theresa May defends plans to create 'hostile environment', *The Guardian* October 10; https://www.theguardian.com/politics/2013/oct/10/immigration-bill-theresa-may-hostile-environment. Accessed 01/08/2018

Travis, A. (2017) England and Wales have highest imprisonment rate in Western Europe, *The Guardian*March 14; https://www.theguardian.com/society/2017/mar/14/england-and-wales-has-highest-imprisonment-rate-in-western-europe. Accessed 02/09/2018

Treanor, J. (2012) Serious Fraud Office to investigate Libor manipulation, *The Guardian*-July 6; http://www.guardian.co.uk/business/2012/jul/06/serious-fraud-office-libor-investigation. Accessed 01/08/2012

Trump, D. J, with Schwartz, T. (1987) *Trump: The Art of the Deal.* New York: Ballantine Books

Trump, D. (2016) Transcript of Donald Trump's Immigration Speech, *The New York Times*September 1; https://www.nytimes.com/2016/09/02/us/politics/transcript-trump-immigration-speech.html. Accessed 01/08/2018

Tucker, I. (2018) 'I thought: what do I have to offer?' The woman digitalising the Democrats, *The Observer*July 29; https://www.theguardian.com/technology/2018/jul/29/digitalising-democratic-party-jessica-alter-tech-for-campaigns. Accessed 29/07/2018

Tyack, D. and Hansot, E. (1992) *Learning Together: A History of Coeducation in American Public Schools.* New York: Russell Sage

Tyack, D. and Tobin, W. (1994), The 'Grammar' of Schooling: Why has it been so Hard to Change?, *American Educational Research Journal*, 31(3), 453–479, Fall

Tye, L. (1998) *The Father of Spin: Edward L. Bernays and the Birth of Public Relations.* New York: Crown Publishers. Also published in 2002 by Picador.

Tyrrell, I. (1991) American Exceptionalism in an Age of International History, *The American Historical Review*, 96(4), 1031–1055

Urken, A. B. (1991) The Condorcet-Jefferson Connection and the Origins of Social Choice Theory, *Public Choice* 72, 213–236

Varoufakis, Y. (2015) Yanis Varoufakis: No Time for Games in Europe, *The New York Times*, February 16; https://www.nytimes.com/2015/02/17/opinion/yanis-varoufakis-no-time-for-games-in-europe.html?_r=1. Accessed 05/03/2017

Varoufakis, Y. (2015a) *The Global Minotaur: America, Europe and the Future of the Global Economy.* London: Zed Books Ltd

Vitali, S., Glattfelder, J. B. and Battiston, S. (2011) The Network of Global Corporate Control, *PLoS ONE* 6(10) 1–36; http://journals.plos.org/plosone/article?id=10.1371/journal.pone.0025995. Accessed 06/09/2015

Vitkovskaya, J. (2016) 'The decision must be accepted': Read British prime minister's full speech to Parliament on Brexit vote, *The Washington Post*, June 27; https://www.washingtonpost.com/news/worldviews/wp/2016/06/27/the-decision-must-be-accepted-read-david-camerons-speech-to-parliament-on-the-e-u-referendum/. Accessed 02/07/2016

Wallerstein, I. (2004) *World-Systems analysis: An Introduction.* Durham and London: Duke University Press

Walt, S. M. (2011) The Myth of American Exceptionalism, *Foreign Policy*October 11;https://foreignpolicy.com/2011/10/11/the-myth-of-american-exceptionalism/. Accessed 28/07/2012

Walters, J. (2018) 'Are they going to shoot me?': Statue of Liberty climber on her anti-Trump protest, *The Guardian*July 7; https://www.theguardian.com/us-news/2018/jul/07/statue-of-liberty-protester-patricia-okoumou-interview. Accessed 03/10/2018

Walzer, M. (1985) *Spheres of Justice: A Defence of Pluralism and Equality.* Oxford: Blackwell

Waterfield, R. (trans.) (1994) *Plato: Republic*. Oxford World's Classics, Oxford University Press

Weber, M. (2001) *The Protestant Ethic and the Spirit of Capitalism*. London and New York: Routledge. First published in 1930 by Allen and Unwin

Weber, P. (2016) Stephen Colbert resurrects his Colbert Report 'The Word' segment to define 'Trumpiness', *The Week*July 19; http://theweek.com/speedreads/636881/stephen-colbert-resurrects-colbert-report-word-segment-define-trumpiness. Accessed 20/04/2017

Weigel, M. (2016) Political correctness: How the right invented a phantom enemy, *The Guardian*November 30; https://www.theguardian.com/us-news/2016/nov/30/political-correctness-how-the-right-invented-phantom-enemy-donald-trump. Accessed 01/08/2018

West, C. (2017) Pity the sad legacy of Barack Obama, *The Guardian*January 9; https://www.theguardian.com/commentisfree/2017/jan/09/barack-obama-legacy-presidency. Accessed 28/07/2018

West, D. M. (2014) *Billionaires: Reflections on the Upper Crust*. Washington: The Brookings Institution

Westbury, I. (1973) Conventional Classrooms, 'Open' Classrooms and the Technology of Teaching, *Journal of Curriculum Studies* 5(2), 99–121

White, M. (2009) An open letter to students, *Adbusters*November 25; https://www.adbusters.org/blogs/blackspot-blog/open-letter-students.html. Accessed 18/09/2018

Wilkinson, R. and Pickett, K. (2009) *The Spirit Level: Why Equality is Better for Everyone*. London: Allen Lane

William James Studies (2016) Pragmatism, Phenomenology and Cognitive Science, *William James Studies* 12(1), 1–94; http://williamjamesstudies.org/wp-content/uploads/2016/05/Pragmatism-Phenomenology-and-Cognitive-Science_WJS_Vol-12_No-1_Spring-2016.pdf. Accessed 10/09/2018

Williams, R. (1989) as quoted in *The Times Higher Educational Supplement*, December 29, 21

Williamson, J. (1993) Democracy and the "Washington Consensus", *World Development*, 21(8), 1329–1336; http://www.visionaryvalues.com/wiki/images/Williamson_DemocracyandWashingtonConsensus.pdf. Accessed 01/07/2018

Williamson, J. (2004) *The Washington Consensus as Policy Prescription for Development*. A lecture in the series "Practitioners of Development" delivered at the World Bank on January 13, Institute for International Economics; https://piie.com/publications/papers/williamson0204.pdf. Accessed 01/07/2017

Wing, N. (2010) Mike Huckabee: WikiLeaks Source Should Be Executed (VIDEO), *HuffPost Politics*November 30, updated December 6, 2017; https://www.huffpost.com/entry/mike-huckabee-wikileaks-execution_n_789964. Accessed 14/04/2019

Wohlstetter, A. (1958) The delicate balance of terror, *Rand Corporation*; https://www.rand.org/pubs/papers/P1472.html. Accessed 15/04/2019

Wolff, M. (2016) Ringside with Steve Bannon at Trump Tower as the president-elect's strategist plots "An entirely new political movement" (Exclusive), *The Hollywood Reporter*November 18; https://www.hollywoodreporter.com/news/steve-bannon-trump-tower-interview-trumps-strategist-plots-new-political-movement-948747. Accessed 03/10/2018

Wolin, S. (2008) *Democracy Incorporated: Managed Democracy and the Spector of Inverted Totalitarianism*, with a new preface by the author. Princeton and Oxford: Princeton University Press

Woodin, T. (Ed.) (2014) *Co-operation, Learning and Co-operative Values: Contemporary Issues in Education*. Abingdon, New York: Routledge

Young, M. and Schuller, T. (Eds), (1988) *The Rhythms of Society*. London, New York: Routledge

Yurchak, A. (2005) *Everything was Forever, until it was No More*. Princeton and Oxford: Princeton University Press

Zimmer, B. (2010) Truthiness, *The New York Times Magazine*, October 13; http://www.nytimes.com/2010/10/17/magazine/17FOB-onlanguage-t.html. Accessed 20/04/2017

Zizek, S. (1991) *Looking Awry: An Introduction to Jacques Lacan through Popular Culture*. Cambridge, MA; London: MIT Press

Zizek, S. (2013) The simple courage of decision: A leftist tribute to Thatcher, *New Statesman* April 17; http://www.newstatesman.com/politics/politics/2013/04/simple-courage-decision-leftist-tribute-thatcher. Accessed 22/08/2014

# Index

Abrahams, P. 15
accumulation by dispossession 16–17, 18, 85
action research 144
Agamben, G. 9, 119–20
Ahmed, N. M. 9
Almasy, S. 48
Albright, M. 123
Alt-Right 114, 148
Amadae, S. M. 90
America First 39
American Dream 8, 39, 59, 171
American Revolution 2, 44, 140, 142
Americans for Prosperity (AFP), 170, 173
Amnesty International 130
analysis 90–4
Anderson, B. 89, 100
Annaliste School 15
*April 6 Movement* 116
Arab Spring 74, 77, 115, 116, 122
Arendt, H. 23, 84, 162
Arlidge, J.
Aronson, S. 178
Assange, J. 8
*Atlas Shrugged* 10, 11, 38
Atlas, 55, 141, 178, 186; trope 39
Audier, S. 24
austerity 6, 90; experiment 44
Austin, J. L. 89
axis of evil 24
Ayers, B. 83, 144
Ayers, R. 83, 144

Balibar, E. 23, 63, 78, 81, 125, 150
Balls, S. 84
Banks, A. 9, 66
Bannon, S. 1, 25, 48, 79
Barber, A. 45, 80

Barbrook, R. 51, 79
Barlow, K. 43
Bateson, G. 51
Baudelaire, C. 133
Bauman, Z. 186
Bayle, P. 84
Beatles, The 51
Beauvoir, S. de 114
Beder, S. 13
Bell, D. 15
Benkler, Y. 189
Bennett, D. 13
Berman, A. 9
Berman, M. 83
Bernays, E. 6, 7, 9, 11, 46, 58, 61, 80, 163
Bhatt, K. 135
Big Data 55, 59, 60, 109, 128, 164; big numbers 72
Billig, M. 8
Birdwhistel, R. L. 51
Black Papers 6, 163
Blacker, D. 18, 44
Blair, T. 42, 72, 80
Blankfein, L. 50
Bleiker, R. 78
Bloodworth, J. 138
Bloom, A. 6, 37, 91, 92, 113
Boal, A. 176
Boetie, la, E. 56, 141
Boltanski, L. 12
Booth, W. C. 25
Boshyk, Y. 167
Bouazizi, M. 116
Bouton, T. 45, 60, 72, 80
Bowater, D. 44
Bowman, A. 84
Brace, C.L. 46
bracketing 101

Brexit 9, 13, 18, 24, 25, 34, 47, 55, 59, 71, 79, 100, 159, 165, 167, 184
Brietbart 1, 2, 48
Britannia Unchained 40
British Education Research Association (BERA) 159
Bruner, J. 6, 153
Buchanon, J. M. 42, 45, 46, 90, 127
Buffett, W. 13, 29, 57
Bullough, O. 72
bullshit 35, 46, 100, 181
Burke. P. 15
Burt, C. 92
Bush, G. 24

Cadwalladr, C. 9, 25, 34, 48, 66, 140
Calhoun, J. C. 42
Californian ideology 50, 79
Callaghan, E. M. 115
Cambridge Analytics 9
Cameron, A. 51, 79
Cameron, D. 43, 46, 47
Campbell, J. 94–5
Capdevilla, R. 115
cases 68–9; see also generalisation
Castaneda, C. 51
Ceaucescu, N. 141
Centre for Applied Nonviolent Strategies (CANVAS) 117
Chabris, C. 89
change 14–15
Chomsky, N. 6
Chiapello, E. 12
Chicago Boys 27
choice architecture 45–8, 49
choice theory 45; public 42; rational 28; social 127–8
Cicourel, A. V. 101
class 13
Clay, H. 39
Clinton, B. 80
Clinton, H. 48, 114
Coghlan, A. 44
Cohen, N. 34
Cohen, M. R. 90, 94
Colbert, S. 34
Comaroff, J 9; and L.11
common sense 24, 47–8, 115
*conatus* 69, 87
Condorcet, N. 127
Cooper, D. 51

cooperative movement 19, 31, 85, 134–6, 143, 176, 184; digital currency 175; schools 143
Corbyn, J. 106, 172, 184
corporatism 57–8, 62, 160–1
countervailing forms of organisation 5, 17, 73, 119, 120, 138, 141, 144, 159, 176
courage 100, 132, 171
Cox, C. B. 6, 163
Credit Suisse Report 13
Crépon, S. 115
Cridland, J. 11
crisis 10, 26, 70; financial 9, 44, 120–1, 142; of power 50
Cronin, D. 44, 60–1
Crouch, C. 99, 142
Cuban, L. 15
curriculum 5–6, 10, 15, 47, 72, 116, 134, 151, 155, 157, 173–4, 178–9; basic 180; hidden 120, 144, 146; prefigurative 147–8
Curtis, A. 7, 27–9, 41, 43, 46, 52–3, 94

Das, S. 11, 50
data 25, 41, 47, 48, 54, 55, 60, 75, 91, 102, 140, 155, 156, 157, 158, 159; see Big Data
Davidson, J. D. 39, 54, 55, 59, 72, 79, 130
Davis, G. F. 9
Davis, O. 113
Deacon, M. 34
debate 5, 19, 23, 34, 36, 49, 61, 64, 67, 68, 76, 80, 82, 85, 92, 93, 94, 96, 100, 101, 102, 107, 109, 114–15, 121, 123, 125, 126–35, 139–40, 147–8, 154–5, 156, 159, 161–2, 163, 164, 165, 167–8, 173, 176, 178, 186
Dejours, C. 85, 134, 167
democracy 7, 23; and capitalism 40, 71; counter-democracy 130; and education 8; equality 56; free market 9; hollowing out of 18; inclusive 23; managed 80; post 45; of powers 84; property owning 42, 127–8; protest 74; radical 64–5, 72–3; representative 17; self government 30; and sovereignty 79–80; taming of 7, 72, 80; voice 62
Delingpole, J. 25
Denzin, N. 15
Derrida, J. 114
Descartes, R. 67, 84; doubt 101, 102
desires culture 7

Dewey, J. 8, 80, 86–7, 91, 136, 143, 159–61, 187
Diamond, B. 12
Diamond, J. 48
Dijk, van, T. A. 47, 115
Dilworth, R. L. 167
Dinovic, S. 117
*dispositif* 9, 36, 120
Dorling, D. 54, 138
double writing 38, 40, 46, 179
dramatis personae 51, 71, 132, 133, 167, 174, 177–80
Drutman, L. 9, 44
D'Souza, D. 113
Ducheyne, S. 80, 84
Dunford, D. 34
Durkee, A. 114
Durkheim, E. 91–2
Dyson, A. E. 6, 163

Earl, J. 11, 28, 71, 141
econocracy 28
edmundberger 51, 79
education 23–4, 80, 87; educe 69, 72, 76, 93, 96, 101, 102, 121, 182; democratic 16, 17, 19, 143; educated picture 69; and equality of development of powers 76, 77–9; progressive 153; and work 85, 138–9
Education Act 1870 44
Edwards, A. C. 80
*égaliberté* 23, 63, 78, 81, 125, 127, 150, 161, 163, 174, 176, 179
egalitarian 42, 53, 176
*eidetic variation* 102
Eisenhower, D. D. 9
Eisenstadt, S. N. 84
elites 7, 9, 18, 25, 47, 68, 77, 92, 123, 163, 168; enlightenment 37; global power 95; liberal 24, 25, 33, 46, 106, 107, 164; power 141; and schools 76
Elliott, J. 159, 167
Elliott, L. 25
enemy within 25
Enlightenment 2, 25, 29, 33, 37, 78, 148, 177; multiple 84; radical 101
equality 8, 11, 13, 23, 62; of intelligence 77; and logic of reason and power 79–84
Erhard, L. 26
ethics guidelines 156–9
Etzion, D. 9

evidence 2, 3, 7, 9, 27, 34, 69, 91, 93, 100, 139, 140, 147, 148, 153, 155, 160, 163, 164–7, 173, 178; evidence based narratives 140; evidence based policy 145–6
Evil Empire 24
exception 9; exceptionalism 32
expanded reproduction 16–17
experts 34
expertise 34
extimate 67

facts 3, 23, 33–5, 89, 113, 131, 159, 164, 165; social 91–2
fake news 99, 100, 178
Falafil 87
Faulkner, N. 123
fantasy 35, 39, 46, 69, 93, 94, 95; narrative 25
Farage, N. 25
Farhi, P. 1
feminism 52, 115, 120; sexist 48, 92; women 6, 39, 40, 48, 54, 55, 60, 74, 78, 112, 114, 115, 135, 140, 176
Feyerabend, P. 66
fictions 66
figure 67–8
figurative 124; power 63
figuring the real 67; see also prefigurative
Fielding, M. 5, 19, 86, 136, 143
financial crash 29, 44, 74, 120–1; instruments 29; weapons of mass destruction 29
Foley, S. 9
Foote-Whyte, W. 166
Foucault, M. 100, 171
Fox, L. 25
*France Insoumise* 106
Frank, T. 104, 171
Frankfurt, 35
Fraser, K. 174–5
Frégier, H-A. 46
Freedland, J. 38
freedom 3, 8, 24–5, 35–6, 40, 42, 49, 52, 59, 63, 69, 76–7, 85, 86, 100, 105–10, 114, 115, 124; to associate 143, 151; and equality 2, 3, 5, 8–9, 11, 18, 24, 63, 81, 106, 110, 125, 135, 140, 142, 153, 161, 163, 178; and Kant 177; principle of 23
Freeland, C. 61
Freire, P. 6, 150

French Revolution 32, 88, 109, 111, 129
Freud, S. 7
Friedman, M. 8, 10, 26–7, 31, 41, 43, 71, 79, 120
friend-enemy 24, 31, 35, 48, 57, 74,163, 164, 167
Fromm, E. 100, 124
Fukuyama, F. 8
Fullan, M. 14

Galbraith, J. K. 122
game theory 41, 90
Garfinkel, H. 101
Gates, A. I. 90
generalisation 23, 48, 57, 67, 69, 90, 92, 102, 113, 119, 141, 158, 161, 167, 179, 184
Ghonim, W. 117
Gibson, W. 39
Gibson-Graham, J. K. 84
Giddens, A. 15, 80
Gipps, C. 159
Giroux, H. 6, 11, 12, 15, 19, 29, 95, 123
Glaser, B. G. 101
glasnost 26, 132
Global Wealth Report 13
Goffman, E. 131, 151
Goldman Sachs 9, 50
Goodson, I. 15, 19, 76, 180, 181
Goodwyn, L. 105–6
Gore, A. 7
gorilla 89
Gove, M. 34
Graeber, D. 181
Graham, D. A. 115
Greenspan, A. 10, 38
Grinspun, R. 95

Habermas, J. 101
Hague, W. 171
Halpern, D. 45, 93
happiness machines 7
Hamilton, D. 82
Hamilton, W. 82
Hammersley, M. 93
Hampton, C. 178
Hansot, E. 15
Hardt, M. 65, 152
Hargreaves, A. 15
Harrison, D. 84
Harvey, D. 4, 11, 12, 16, 17, 85, 86, 142
Haseler, S. 44

Hayek, F. A. 8, 10, 24, 26, 31, 42, 52, 58, 71, 79, 113, 163
Hawkes, S. 11
Haymes, S. 18
Heath, B. 1
Hellerstein, E. 114
Henley, J. 116
Herman, E. S. 6
Hernstein, R. J. 92
Hertel-Fernandez, A. 170
hierarchy 79–84
Hilgers, M. 11
historical periods 14
Hobbesbawn, E. 16
Holyoake, G. J. 31, 135
Hoover, H. C. 7
Hoskins, Sir J. 43
hostile environment 47, 130, 134, 157
Howard, M. 47
Huckabee, M. 8
Humanities Curriculum Project (HCP) 6, 144, 147–8, 153, 155, 157, 158–9, 173
Hunsicker, L. M. 90
Huntington, S. P. 57, 92, 113
Husserl, E. 65, 69, 101
hypernormalisation 29

ideas lying around 24–30, 31, 35, 71
imaginary order 65–6
imagined communities 89, 100
immigrants 33, 55, 114, 123, 130, 148
inattentional blindness 89–90
*Indignados* 74
inequality 11, 73
insolence of nobles 73
intelligence 26; community of 86; creative 165; equality of 73; public 94–6, 167
intentionality 69
invisible government 9, 61, 163; hand of market 10
IQ 26, 92
irony 25–6
Israel, J. 80, 84

Jackson, A. 104
Jackson, B. 24, 42,104
Jacobs, J. 109, 110,183–4
James, W. 101
Jefferson, T. 104
Jenson, A. R. 92
Jessop, B. 84
Johnson, B. 59

Johnson, J. 38
Johnson, S. 25
Jones, S. D. 61
Joseph, Sir K. 28, 29, 43
Journal of Curriculum Studies 80
just society 76, 138

Kahn, p. W. 79
Kakutani, M. 35
Kamin, L. J. 92
Kant, I. 25, 177
Katsiaficas, G. 112, 113
Keane, J. 84
Keen, S. 71, 142
Kent, D. 133
Khanna, S. 135
Khomami, N. 140
Kirby, P. 18
Kirk, A. 34
Kjellberg, H. 84
Klein, N. 10, 142
knowledge 65–8, 76, 101; *eidetic variation* 102; essence or invariant structures of 65; cross checking 100–2; phenomenological 101
Koch brothers 45, 46, 170, 173; Charles 94
Kohn, H. 6
Kotkin, S. 77
Kozol, J. 6
Kreklewich, K. 95
Kristol, I. 30–1, 32, 33–4, 37, 46, 57, 67, 79, 92, 123, 182, 184
Kuhn, T. 24, 66, 89, 113, 159, 164
Kusch,
Kwarteng, K.

Labaree, D. F. 80
laboratory school 86, 112, 136, 143
Lacan, J. 56, 65, 67, 78, 114, 126, 131
Laclau, E. 115, 118
Lafuente, J. L. 152
laissez-faire 26–7
Lanier, J. 47
Lapham, M. 38, 54
Lawson, N. 40
Leander, A. 89
leadership 34; heroic 62; leaderlessness 120
leave campaign 34
Leave.EU 66
Lee, M. J. 171
Lefort, C. 79, 107

Legum, J. 114
Lehman Brothers 7, 71, 120
Leith, S. 115
Lenz, M. 69–70
Letelier, O. 27
Levitsky, S. 72
Lewin, K. 144
Lewis, C. S. 96
Lewis, M. 47
liberal elite ; establishment 1–2
lie 35, 46; simplifying stories 66
libertarian 40
LIBOR (London Interbank Offered Rate) 11
Lieberman, A. 14
Lippmann, W. 6, 24, 34, 42, 46, 58, 66, 80, 89, 95, 164
London Interbank Offered Rate 11
Longworth, R. C. 24
Lovelock, J. 52
Lowe, R. 5, 44, 64, 83, 143
Lucchese, Del, F. 61, 64, 65, 67, 76, 79, 101, 186
Lyotard, J-L. 15, 67–8

MacDonald, B. 155–6, 159
Machiavelli, N. 61, 62, 73–4, 129, 130
MacInnes, P. 94–5
Mack, A. 89
Mack, M. 61, 80, 84, 89
MacKenzie, D. 44
MacLean, N. 45, 46, 72, 80
Mahfou, A. 116
Mailer, N. 113
Major, J. 42
Man a Course of Study 6, 153, 155
manufacture of consent 6, 10, 34, 46, 58; engineering of 7, 58
Marcuse, H. 63
Marsh, J. 18, 44
Marwick, A. E. 138
Mason, P. 74, 112, 120
masters 56–61, 126; discourses of 78; as father 78; as père-version 78; of the universe 11, 50, 61, 62, 141
methematics 3, 28–9, 91, 92, 93, 94, 95, 101,127, 155
Mauss, M. 87, 110–11
May, T. 38, 47, 134, 184
Mayer, J. 44, 45, 112, 113
Mayhew, K. C. 80, 136, 143
Mazur, P. 7
McCulloch, G. 16

McCormack, W. 33, 46
McCormick, J. P. 62, 73–4, 129
McGill, A. 114
McKay, A. 95
#MeToo 140
Meek, J. 17
Mélenchon, J-L. 106
Mercer family 9, 25, 48, 66
method 6, 41, 54, 70, 77, 90, 91, 93, 95, 101, 105, 136, 160,
Meyer, J. 15
Millar, J. 34
Miller, B. 38, 54
Mills, C. W. 15, 38
Milosevic, S. 117
mirror groups 71
Mises, von L. 24, 72, 79
modernity 78, 82; architectures 80; Cartesian 85; multiple 84; Spinozan 85
Momentum 172–3
Monbiot, G. 25
Mondon, A. 115
Mondragon 146
monetarist revolution 27–8, 43; experiment 44
Mont Pelerin Society 24
Monthly Review 83
Moore, M. 171
Morgan, J.P. 9, 11
Morris, R. 44, 60
Moss, P. 5, 19, 136, 143
Mouffe, C. 52, 63, 71, 103–6, 115, 123, 164, 172, 174, 182
Mounk, Y. 103–4
Mubarak, H. 116–7, 118, 119
multitude 23, 56, 64–5, 76, 86, 100, 152, 153, 161, 179, 182, 184
Murray, C. 72, 92
myth 11, 12

narratives 13, 19, 25, 29, 30, 51, 74, 83–4, 85–6, 138, 140–2, 144, 164–8, 169, 177–80, 181, 182; anti-democratic 138; of regress 181; democratic renewal; of decline 40; of entrepreneurs 53–4; inquiry 183 181; picture 74; and populism 33, 165; and popular culture 39; of sovereign individual 54; and work 85–6
National Football League (NFL) 32
National Rifle Association (NRF) 114
Nazism 123
Neda 115

Negri, A. 64–5, 81, 152
Neiwert, D. 18, 114
neoconservative 9, 31, 33, 34, 37–8, 40, 44, 46, 47, 52, 72, 82, 92, 95, 107, 123, 153, 163, 165, 181, 182, 183, 184; fellow travellers 95, 164–5, 168
Neo-Liberal principles 10–11
neoliberal economics 11, 12, 79, 90, 121, 142, 165; experiment 44; market 47; neoliberalism 38, 43; stealth strategies 49; tropes 38
new social movements 74, 109, 130
Nixon, J. 8
Nixon, R. 99
Noble Lie 11, 31, 37, 41, 138
Nolte, J. 171
normalisation 28
Norton, A. 10, 142
nudge 45–6, 49, 72, 93
Nuit Debout 120

Obama, B. 45, 46, 74, 132
obedience 56, 63, 78, 79, 138, 163, 176
objectivity 3, 23, 36, 128, 161,
Occupy 74, 103, 115, 120, 121, 122
O'Connell, M. 40, 54
Okoumou 137, 147
Olin foundation 113
*Otpor* 116–7, 122
Owen, R. 31, 82, 85, 134
Oxfam 56, 61, 121

Packer, G. 171
Paine, T. 2
paradigm 24, 27, 41, 50, 66, 89, 91, 127,155, 159, 174
paramount reality 101
*parrhesia* 171
peer-to-peer 174, 175–6, 179
Pen, Le M. 115
people, the 23, 72, 103; and truth 100–2
perestroika 26, 132
Peterson, W. H. 72
Pettifor, A. 122,
Phelps, E. S. 58–9
Phipps, C. 18
Pickett, K. 18
Piketty, T. 18, 60
Pittman, A. 100
Plato 11, 13, 37, 138, 148; *Republic* 11, 31
Pleasance, C. 8
Plowden Report 6

## Index

*Podemos* 106, 122
Poe, E. A. 133
Polanyi, K. 24, 164
police 57, 141–2
policing 113–15
politics, aesthetics of 89; agonistic 52; deep 9; of friendship 84; prefigurative 19; zombie 29
political, *the* 9, 64, 71,106, 152; frontier 107, 109, 113–15; post 103; and research and education 75
politically correct (PC) 48, 74, 114
Popovic, S. 117, 119
Popper, K. 24
populism 33–5, 46, 79; experiment 44, 46; left 115, 123; populist turn 103–5, 165
Postel, D. 31, 32
Postman, N. 6, 153
power 17, 63–8; collective 64; countervailing 73; figurative 63; market 59; place of 78, 79, 80, 107; private 25; public 25; of research 63–4
powers 59; of all 76; of the body 62; democracy 76; education of 77–9; flourishing of 59; of individuals 91; of oligarchs 62; of people 140; and potential 69; taming 64
precariat 46
prefigurative 19, 63, 124,132–3, 134–6, 139, 187; action 142–7, 148–9; curriculum 147–8; future 123–4
principles and procedures for evaluation 156–9; theatres 174–7
PROFKNOW 181
propaganda 7; rules of engagement 150–1; society of 7; struggle 139
protest 3, 12, 32, 50, 77, 79, 88, 103, 107, 112, 113, 115–20, 121–3, 124, 125, 137–8, 147, 164, 170, 176, 185
protestant ethic 31
public 2, 8; consent 9; effective 3, 7, 4, 23; 'eyes' 35, 100, 107, 109–10, 140–2, 151, 158–9, 175, 178; intelligence 94–6, 167; phantom 23, 80, 89, 95; and private 25–6; space 4, 121, 125, 133, 134; and what counts 90–4; sector 121
public relations 7

qualitative 9, 155, 183
Quiggin, J. 29, 71, 142
Quigley, C. 146

racism 47–8, 55, 92, 115; anti- 52
radical inclusivity 49
Rancière, J. 57, 59, 64, 66, 71, 72–3, 90, 126, 130, 134, 140, 141, 152, 164, 184,
Rand, A. 10, 11, 38, 50, 52, 53, 79, 125, 141, 178, 186
Rapoza, K. 121
rational expectations 42, 43
rational procedure 91
Reagan, R. 17, 24, 41, 42, 52, 71, 153
reason 25, 78; iron cage of 82, 101; technical 78
Rees-Mogg, W. 39, 54, 55, 59, 72, 79
Rees-Mogg, J. 40
Reid, P. 9
Reilly, S. 1
Reform Act 1868, 5
refraction 14, 182–3, 186,
Research Assessment Framework (REF) 95
researcher 68–73; and power 73–5
Revans, R. 167
Revesz, R. 131
revolution 77
Reynolds, D. 93, 108
Rhode, J. 52
Rhodes-Boyson, Sir 51
Rivera, C. 121
Roberts, L. 5, 8, 13, 77, 107, 116
Roberts, Y. 12
Rochdale Pioneers 31, 134–5, 187
Rock, L. 89
Rogers-Cooper, J. 64–5
Roosevelt, F. D. 6
Rosanvallon, P. 88, 109, 110, 111, 128–30, 136, 140, 142, 149, 164
Rosen, N. 166
Rosenfeld, S. 115
Rougier, L. 24
Rowan, D. 15
Rubin, R. 38
Ruddick, S. 64, 69
Runciman, D. 72
Rushkoff, D. 50–1, 72, 187
Rushton, J. P. 92
Russian election interference 34

Sachs, J. 26–7
Said, K. 116
Samuel, R. 95
Samuels, W. J. 141
Sanders, B. 172

Sanders, N. 106
Sandlin, J. 6
Savoie, D. 17
Schatzman, M. 93
Schmitt, C. 9, 31, 79, 163
Schmitter, P. C. 57–8, 160
schools 8, 30–1; classroom 82; education 8; high reliability 93; marketisation 84; and Republicanism 30–1; social reproduction 8
School of Barbiana 6, 150, 154
schooling 23–4, 76, 79, 80; and equality 80; and modernity 78
Schools Council 173–4
Schostak, J. 5, 6, 8, 13, 17, 19, 23, 47, 71, 77, 95, 103, 107, 116, 120, 121, 139, 141, 144, 156, 164, 174–5
Schostak, J. R. 8, 13, 19, 23, 71, 103, 120, 121, 139, 141, 144, 156
Schram, S. F. 121
Schreber, D. P. 93
Schuller, T. 14, 15
Schutz, A. 80, 86,
Schutz, Alfred 101, 133
Scott, P. D. 9
scrutiny 139–140
Sculthorpe, T. 61
self help 135
self improvement 30–1
self made 39, 43, 44
self organising network 52, 54, 174
September 11, 2001 24
Shabi, R. 173
Sharpe, G. 116–7, 119, 122
shock therapy 26
Siddiqui, S. 24, 32
Silicon Valley billionaires 38, 54
Simon, B. 5, 12
Simon, W. 113
Simons, D. 89
Simons, H. 159
Shor, I. 6
situationists 133
Skinner, B. F. 93
Smith, A. 10, 62, 82, 141
Snowden, E. 140
social injustice 13
social mobility 18
Sovereign Individual 39–40, 55–6, 60, 62
sovereign decision 79; and teacher 79
Sovereignty 9, 39–40, 79; and democracy 79–80; equality of 81; radical 81

Spinoza, B. de 61–2, 64–7, 69, 76, 79, 81–2, 84–7, 101–2, 108, 125, 126, 140, 152, 168, 177; doubt 101
Standing, G. 45, 46
statistics 43, 90–1, 94, 127–8, 165, 172
Statue of Liberty 137–8, 146
stealth architectures 47, 49
Stein, B. 13, 57
Stenhouse, L. 6, 144–5, 147–8, 153, 157
Stewart, H. 9
Stigliz, J. E. 12, 138
Stocker, P. 18
Stow, D. 82
stranger 109, 127, 133, 154
Strauss, L. 31–2, 35, 163; reading between the lines 35; double writing 40, 46; and Spinoza 76
Strauss, A. L. 101
Streeck, W. 71
Strinfield, S. 93, 108
Stullich, S. 72
subjectivity 23, 64, 79, 120, 130, 152
Summers, L. 38
Sunstein, C. R. 45
Swaine, J. 35
symbolic interactionism 166
Syriza 74, 122
system 11, 12

Tahrir Square 116, 117, 118, 122, 132
Taplin, J. 54
Tarnoff, B.
Taylor, F. W. 89
Taylor, J. 114
Thaler, R. H. 45
Thatcher, M. 6, 12, 17, 25, 27–8, 39, 42, 43, 46, 52, 71, 72, 153; of the Left 44, 74, 106
Thatcherism 40
The 5 Rs 180–4
The Golden Years 16
The Journal of Historical Sociology 15
Thernstrom, S. 114
Thévenot, L. 12
Thiel, P. 40, 54–5, 72
third way 80
Thompson, P. 95
Thoreau, H. D. 93
Thorndike, E. L. 90, 92
time 14–16
Tobin, W. 15
Tocqueville, A. de 56

totalitarianism 24
Touré 59
Tragesser, R. S. 70
Travis, A. 47, 72
Treanor, J. 9
triangulation 70, 152; cross-checking 100–1; *eidetic variation* 102
tribunes 73
Trump, D. 1, 2, 3, 8, 9, 18, 24, 25, 32–3, 34, 35, 38, 39, 44, 46, 48–9, 55, 100, 171, 179, 185, 186; craziness 99; supporters 35, 114–5; as voice 171; wall 48
Trump campaign 13, 34–5, 40, 47–8, 55, 71, 74, 79, 93, 159, 165, 167, 172, 179
Trumpiness 35
truth 2, 23, 25, 29, 30–5, 100–2, 132, 148, 159–61, 166, 171; learning of 100–2; *parrhesia* 171; place of 90–4; post 100, 164–5; truthful hyperbole 35, 46
truthiness 34, 100
Tucker, I. 49
Tullock, G. 42, 45, 46, 90, 127
Tyack, D. 15
Tye, L. 6, 7, 46
tyrant 67, 73–4, 77, 141, 177
Tyrrell, L. 9

UKIP 66
UK UnCut 53, 122
underclass 72, 78
Urken, A. B. 90, 127

validity 3, 23, 36, 70, 161, 167, 179
Varoufakis, Y. 120, 131
Vitali, S.
Vitkovskaya, J. 179
voice 115, 171, 179
voluntary servitude 56–61

wall, 134; Berlin 26, 132; Mexico 48
Wallerstein, E. 84

Walt, S. M. 9
Walters, J. 137
Walzer, M. 12
Washington consensus 27
Waterfield, R. 13
Watts, A. 51
Weber, M. 82, 101
Weber, P. 35, 100
Weigle, M. 48, 114
Weiner, J. 114
Weingarten, C. 6, 153
West, C. 44
West, D. M. 44, 60
Westbury, I. 15
White, M. 121
WHO 13
Wikileaks 8
Wilkinson, R. 18
will of the people 33, 34, 58, 72, 103–4, 128, 129, 131, 161, 179, 182, 184
Williams, R. 95
Williamson, J. 27
Wilson, M. 143
Wing, N. 8
Winter, A. 115
Wohlstetter, A. 41
Wolf, C. 121
Wolff, M. 1
Wolin, S. 60, 80
Woodin, T. 85, 143
work 85–6, 134–6, 138–9

Yogi, M. M. 51
Youdell, D. 84
Young, M. 14, 15
Yurchak, A. 26, 28–9, 169

Ziblatt, D. 72
Zimmer, B. 34, 100
Zizek, S. 44, 74, 77, 106, 141
zombie economics 29, 142; politics 29